WEST SYRIAN LITURGICA

For the past three centuries, studies on the West Syrian liturgy have been mainly concerned with the texts or tracing the history of the rites. West Syrian liturgical theology has received little attention. This is the first book to explain the important orientations of the West Syrian liturgical tradition.

What is the role of liturgy in the life and witness of the Church? What does the Church aim to accomplish in and through the liturgy? How is the celebration related to the fundamental principles of the Christian faith? These are some of the questions that this book attempts to answer. An historical sketch of West Syrian liturgy and summary of the structure of the celebrations, namely the Daily Office, Anaphora and other sacraments, sets the context for the deeper explorations into the West Syrian liturgy. Explaining the meaning of the arrangement of the liturgy in various liturgical units, Fr Varghese draws on the West Syrian liturgical commentaries and homilies on liturgical celebrations. Other oriental orthodox liturgical traditions and East Syrian sources are also examined, and key theological principles and ecclesiological and eschatological dimensions are explored. A bibliography of the West Syrian liturgy and a glossary of Syriac terms is provided.

LITURGY, WORSHIP AND SOCIETY

SERIES EDITORS

Dave Leal, Brasenose College, Oxford, UK
Bryan Spinks, Yale Divinity School, USA
Paul Bradshaw, University of Notre Dame, UK and USA
Gregory W. Woolfenden, Ripon College, Cuddesdon, Oxford, UK
Phillip Tovey, Diocese of Oxford and Oxford Brookes University, UK

This new series comes at a time of great change in liturgy and much debate concerning traditional and new forms of worship, the suitability and use of places of worship, and wider issues concerning the interaction of liturgy, worship and contemporary society. Offering a thorough grounding in the historical and theological foundations of liturgy, books in the series explore and challenge many key issues of worship and liturgical theology which are currently in hot debate – issues set to make a significant impact on the place of the church in contemporary society. Presenting an ecumenical range of books, comparing and contrasting liturgical practices and concerns within various traditions and faiths, this series will appeal to those in university and theological colleges; adult education colleges; those on other ministry or lay ministry training courses; and practitioners and those involved in worship in churches across a broad ecumenical range.

Other titles in the series include

Death Liturgy and Ritual
Volume I: A Pastoral and Liturgical Theology
Volume II: A Commentary on Liturgical Texts
Paul P.J. Sheppy

Daily Liturgical Prayer
Origins and Theology
Gregory W. Woolfenden

Rituals and Theologies of Christian Baptism:
Beyond the Jordan
Bryan D. Spinks

Inculturation of Christian Worship
Exploring the Eucharist
Phillip Tovey

West Syrian Liturgical Theology

BABY VARGHESE

ASHGATE

Published by
Ashgate Publishing Limited
Gower House
Croft Road
Aldershot
Hants GU11 3HR
England

Ashgate Publishing Company
Suite 420
101 Cherry Street
Burlington, VT 05401-4405
USA

Ashgate website: http://www.ashgate.com

British Library Cataloguing-in-Publication Data

Varghese, Baby
  West Syrian liturgical theology. – (Liturgy, worship and society)
  1. Syrian Orthodox Church – Liturgy 2. Syrian Orthodox Church – Liturgy – History
  I. Title
  264'.0163

Library of Congress Cataloging-in-Publication Data

Varghese, Baby
  West Syrian liturgical theology / Baby Varghese.
    p. cm. – (Liturgy, worship and society series)
  Includes bibliographical references.
  ISBN 0-7546-0618-X (alk paper) – ISBN 0-7546-0619-8 (pbk. : alk. paper)
  1. Syrian Church – Liturgy. 2. Liturgies. 3. Syrian Church – Doctrines. I. Title. II. Series.

  BX177.V37 2004
  264'.0163–dc22

2003059507

ISBN 0 7546 0618 X cased   ISBN 0 7546 0619 8 paperback

Printed on acid-free paper

Typeset in Times New Roman by J.L. & G.A. Wheatley Design, Aldershot

Printed in Great Britain by MPG Books Ltd, Bodmin, Cornwall

Contents

Preface

It is a privilege to speak of one's own religious tradition, a tradition in which one was born and brought up. It is often difficult for an Eastern Christian, especially for a priest, to be critical of his own spiritual and liturgical heritage, for obvious reasons.

This book is a *coup d'essai*, or a first attempt to sketch the important orientations of the West Syrian liturgical tradition. As a first attempt, my account has gaps. In relation to secondary literature, several important works or latest editions of books were not available to me, as I live in South India. However, most of the published materials relating to the West Syrian tradition were consulted. In the bibliography, I have omitted several titles that are aimed at beginners. Those interested in further reading can use the nearly complete bibliography compiled by Sebastian Brock and J.M. Sauget.

In the case of secondary literature, I have given special preference to Eastern Orthodox writers. As a member of an ancient Eastern Church, I am convinced that the factors that divide the Chalcedonian and the non-Chalcedonian (or Eastern and Oriental) Orthodox Churches are 'not theological'.[1] In fact both share the same doctrinal, liturgical and spiritual traditions. Similarly, both the Orthodox families have several elements in common with the Ancient East Syrian Church. The common *lex orandi* needs to be rediscovered as a first important step towards the unity of the Eastern Churches. Then the Eastern tradition can enter into fruitful dialogue with the Churches of the West.

In spite of the divisions, theological differences and diverse liturgical practices, the Churches of the West are becoming increasingly aware of the common elements in the *lex orandi*. Thanks to the liturgical movement, they have at least been able to identify their common interests in the field of liturgics. One of the most conspicuous results of the liturgical movement is the emergence of an 'ecumenical liturgical theology', taking the liturgical experience of others into account. The Churches of the East have not yet become active participants – with the exception, perhaps, of the late Fr A. Schmemann – in this dialogue.[2]

The liturgists have often simply identified the East with the Byzantine tradition. But the 'Churches East of Byzantium' have remained rather faithful to the *lex orandi* of the early Eastern tradition. The history and expression of the *lex orandi* 'East of

---

[1] See 'The Dialogue between the Orthodox Church and the Oriental Orthodox Churches' (= Joint Commission of the Theological Dialogue between the Orthodox Church and the Oriental Orthodox Churches: 20–24 June 1989, Anba Bishoi Monastery, Egypt), *Sourozh* 42 (Nov. 1990), 38–43. Text also in *SVTQ* 34/1 (1990), 78ff.

[2] The 'Conferences Saint Serge – Paris' (since the 1950s), organized by the St Sergius Orthodox Theological Institute, have been dedicated to liturgical studies from an ecumenical perspective. However, they have not attracted the attention of non-French-speaking circles.

Byzantium' provide several examples of inculturation, adaptations or even 'prudent conservatism' for survival in a hostile religio-political situation. Each of the non-Byzantine Eastern Churches – Coptic, Ethiopian, Syrian, Armenian and East Syrian – needs to be studied separately, giving attention to the celebration and articulation of the *lex orandi*. Then a synthesis should be attempted, taking its Byzantine expression into account. This is an ecumenical necessity. Linguistic limitations and the limited availability of source materials do not permit me to undertake such an ambitious project. However, I hope one day to undertake a synthesis of the East Syrian and West Syrian liturgical theologies. I hope that the present work will serve as a 'starting-point' for me as well as for others who are interested in such a task.

Abbreviations

AS I–III	*Anaphorae Syriace*, Vol.I–III (Rome, 1939–)
CSCO	*Corpus Scriptorum Christianorum Orientalium* (Louvain)
DS	*Dictionnaire de Spiritualité* (Paris, 1932)
DTC	*Dictionnaire de Théologie Catholique* (Paris, 1907)
ECQ	*Eastern Churches Quarterly* (Ramsgate)
EL	*Ephemerides Liturgicae* (Rome)
EO	*Echos d'Orient* (Paris)
GLS	*Grove Liturgical Studies*
GOFS	*Göttinger Orientforschungen*, Reihe 1, Syriaca (Göttingen)
Harp	*The Harp*: a Review of Syriac and Oriental Studies (Kottayam)
JTS	*Journal of Theological Studies* (Oxford)
LEW	Brightman, *Liturgies Eastern and Western* (Oxford, 1896)
LMD	*La Maison Dieu* (Paris)
OC	*Oriens Christianus* (Wiesbaden)
OCA	*Orientalia Christiana Analecta* (Rome)
OCP	*Orientalia Christiana Periodica* (Rome)
ODB	*The Oxford Dictionary of Byzantium*, 3 vols (Oxford, 1991)
OS	*L'Orient Syrien* (Vernon)
OTS	The Orthodox Theological Seminary, Kottayam (Manuscripts of)
Pampakuda	A Collection of Syriac Manuscripts and a place from which Syriac texts were published (Kerala, S. India)
Pd'O	*Parole de l'Orient*, Kaslik, Lebanon, 1970–
PG	J.P. Migne, *Patrologia Graeca*, Paris, 1857–66
PO	*Patrologia Orientalis*, Paris, 1907–
ROC	*Revue de l'Orient Chrétien* (Paris, 1896–1946)
SC	*Sources chrétiennes* (Paris)
SL	*Studia Liturgica* (Nieuwendam)
SVSP	St Vladimir Seminary Press (New York)
SVTQ	*St Vladimir Theological Quarterly* (New York)

Introduction

West Syrian liturgy belongs to the Antiochene family of liturgies, of which the East Syrian ('Nestorian'), Byzantine, Armenian and the Maronite liturgies are the other members.[1] The West Syrians and the East Syrians have remained rather faithful to the early Syriac tradition.

The West Syrian tradition had its origin and development in and around the city of Antioch, and the centre of the East Syrian tradition was Edessa. Following the Council of Chalcedon (451), the majority of the monks and clergy of Alexandria and Antioch were opposed to the 'Dyophysite Christology', and were called 'Monophysites' or 'non-Chalcedonians'. The non-Chalcedonians of Antioch were known as 'Jacobites' (after Jacob Baradeus, the sixth-century organizer of the Church) or as 'Syrian Orthodox' in modern times. (They always used the title 'orthodox' to refer to themselves.)

There are five Churches that follow the West Syrian liturgy: (1) the Syrian Orthodox Church; (2) the Malankara Orthodox Church (both the autocephalous and that attached to the Syrian Orthodox Church of Antioch; (3) the Syrian Catholic Church of Antioch; (4) the Syro-Malankara Church (Kerala); and (5) the Independent Church of Malabar. To this list, we can add the Marthoma Syrian Church (Reformed Syrians, as they called themselves in the beginning) and the Saint Thomas Evangelical Church.[2]

In this book we shall quote from the liturgical texts used by the Syrian and the Malankara Orthodox Churches. However, in the case of the Festal Breviary (*Penkitho*) we shall use the Catholic edition from Mosul as well.

A Brief History of West Syrian Liturgy

A detailed description of the history of West Syrian liturgy is beyond the scope of this work. However, for those who are not familiar with the Syriac tradition we shall give a brief outline.

The West Syrians inherited the Antiochene anaphora in its fifth-century form. The Antiochene Church had adopted the Jerusalemite anaphora of Saint James, probably in the first half of the fifth century. Evidence suggests that the Chalcedonians and the non-Chalcedonians continued to use the anaphora of St James even after their definite

---

[1] See, I.H. Dalmais, 'The Eastern Liturgical Families', in A.G. Martimort (ed.), *The Church at Prayer*, Vol.I (Collegeville, 1987), pp. 27–43.

[2] The Marthoma Syrian Church is a reformed body of the Syrian Christians of Kerala, who organized themselves as a separate Church in the middle of the nineteenth century. The Saint Thomas Evangelical Church is a break-away group of the Marthomites since 1961.

separation. Following the expulsion by the Emperors Justin I (518–527) and Justinian (527–568), the non-Chalcedonians took refuge in the Syriac-speaking areas of Mesopotamia and organized their own liturgical tradition, incorporating a large number of hymns, especially those of the poet theologians such as Ephrem (+373) and Jacob of Serugh (+521). The West Syrian liturgy in its present form is a Mesopotamian version of the Antiochene tradition. Thus we can find several common elements in the East and the West Syrian liturgies.[3]

The translation of the anaphora of Saint James was the most significant development in the history of the West Syrian liturgy. Recent studies have pointed out three stages in the development of the Syriac Saint James.[4]

1   The Old Syriac version(s) made in the sixth century (attested in a few fragments), which also served as the basis for the Armenian and Ethiopian versions of St James.
2   The so-called 'New and Correct Recension' attributed to Jacob of Edessa (+708). A few manuscripts claim that Jacob had corrected the Old Syriac version on the basis of the existing Greek texts.
3   The *Textus Receptus*.

In the thirteenth century Gregory Bar Hebraeus (1226–86) abridged the *Textus Receptus* and this shorter version is used by the Churches of the West Syrian tradition in India. The history of Syriac St James shows how the West Syrians felt free to revise, add or abridge the Jerusalemite anaphora, which they believed to be of apostolic origin. Following the structure and themes of St James, the West Syrians composed about eighty anaphoras.[5] Today about a dozen of them are in use.

One of the most original West Syrian liturgical creations is the prayer form known as the *sedro*, a long exposition or meditation on a theme. John I, Patriarch of Antioch (+648), is believed to be the author of this type of long prayers, which gradually replaced the litanies of Antiochene origin. In the next centuries, an introduction, known as *prooimiun*, was added to the *sedro*.[6]

Liturgical Diversity

The Syrian Orthodox Church almost never insisted on liturgical uniformity. In fact almost every monastery and diocese had its own liturgical books reflecting diverse

---

3 B. Varghese, 'Some Common Elements in the East and the West Syrian Liturgies', *The Harp* 13 (2000), 65–76.

4 See B. Varghese, *The Syriac Version of St James. A Brief History for Students*, GLS 49, Cambridge, 2001.

5 Patriarch Ignatius Barsoum gives a list of 79 anaphoras: *The History of Syriac Literature and Sciences* (Pueblo, 2000), pp. 20–21. In his introduction to the edition of the anaphoras, A. Raes gives a list of 80. *AS* I.1, xxxix–xlii (details of the manuscripts). See also I.E. Rahmani, *Les liturgies orientales et occidentales* (Beyrouth, 1929), pp. 295–313.

6 J. Mateos, 'Trois recueils anciens de Prooemia syriens', *OCP* 33 (1967), 457–82.

liturgical practices. This diversity was regarded as a sign of 'spiritual vigour' and 'wealth of devotions'. Dionysius Bar Salibi's opinion on the question is representative:

> The fact that people of every country pray differently, and have something which singles them out from the rest, goes to their credit, first because it indicates the wealth of their devotions and spiritual vigor, and secondly because it is a sign of the incomprehensibility of God, who wishes to be glorified in different ways in different countries and towns.[7]

The Monastic movement played a vital role in shaping the liturgical and the spiritual traditions of the Syrian Orthodox Church. The monasteries often enjoyed considerable freedom in the case of liturgical matters. The socio-political conditions of the Syrians as a minority made it rather difficult to bring the dioceses and the monasteries under a centralized authority, as in the Byzantine or Latin traditions. Even the East Syrian Patriarchate of Seleucia-Ctesiphon (later of Baghdad) had the final word in liturgical matters. But in the Syrian Orthodox Church the situation was different. People lived in close relationship with ascetics who always maintained simple faith and traditions of folk wisdom. This has left traces of influences in the liturgical texts and in the commentaries. Liturgical diversity seems to have been rooted in the monastic background.

Diversity existed in the case of almost every liturgical celebration, including the Eucharist. A detailed enumeration of this striking characteristic, though interesting, is beyond the scope of the present work. However, we shall give a couple of examples. In his *History of Syriac Literature and Sciences*, Patriarch Mar Ignatius Ephrem I Barsoum quotes from the *Beth Gazo* (*Treasure of Hymns*) of the principal feasts, compiled by Metropolitan Shem'un of Ain Wardo (1490), which very well illustrates the diversity of liturgical practices:

> To begin with, we have the Order of the Nativity according to the tradition of the Church of the Forty Martyrs in Mardin; the Order of the Epiphany revised by Jacob of Edessa . . . Then, the Order of the Presentation of Our Lord in the Temple according to the tradition of Mardin; the Order of Forgiveness for the Lent; a second Order according to the tradition of Mardin; the Order of the Consecration of Branches . . . from a copy of (the Pontifical of the) Patriarch Michael the Great; the Order of Lights according to the Edessene tradition; the celebration of the Holy Eucharist on Christmas eve as well as on the evening of Thursday of the Passion Week; the Order of Good Friday according to the tradition of the Forty Martyrs in Mardin; a second Order according to the tradition of St Gabriel in Tur Abdin; the Order of Easter according to the traditions of the Monasteries of Mar Barsoum and Mar Hananya, another order for Easter according to the beautiful established tradition of the Monastery of St Gabriel.[8]

The present services of the principal feasts of the year reflect several traditions or 'orders', namely of Edessa, Amid, Mardin, Tikrit, Mosul and the monasteries of Tur

---

[7] Bar Salibi, *Against the Melchites*, p. 34.

[8] Ignatius Aphram Barsoum, *The History of Syriac Literature and Sciences*, p. 29.

Abdin.[9] These centres represent two major liturgical traditions: Tur Abdin in South Eastern Turkey and Mosul/Tikrit in Iraq. Tur Abdin was the seat of the Syrian Orthodox Patriarch of Antioch until the First World War and Mosul was that of Maphrian, the Syrian Orthodox primate in the Persian territory.[10] The two traditions are popularly known as 'Western and Eastern'.[11] According to the Patriarch Ignatius Barsoum, the 'Western rite' represents the liturgical traditions of Antioch, Edessa, the famous monastery of Qinnesrin and Melitene, and the 'Eastern rite' follows the traditions of Seleucia-Ctesiphon and Tikrit. The Eastern tradition shares a number of features with the East Syrians.[12] In their early stages of development, the Western rite was more 'Antiochene' and the Eastern was 'Edessene'. In fact the liturgical traditions of Edessa were also influenced by Antioch. However, a synthesis seems to have begun with the translation of the anaphora of St James into Syriac and it gained momentum under Jacob of Edessa (d. 708), Moses Bar Kepha (d. 903) and reached its climax in the twelfth century under Michel the Syrian (d. 1199), the compiler of the Syrian Orthodox Pontifical.[13] The synthesis was more or less complete by the thirteenth century.

The Greek Legacy

The Syrian Orthodox liturgy was opened to Greek influence throughout its development and synthesis. The so-called 'New and Correct Recension' of the Syriac anaphora of Saint James (wrongly attributed to Jacob of Edessa) claimed the authority of the Greek manuscripts. Greek antiphons of Severus of Antioch were translated into Syriac in the early sixth century by Paul of Edessa and were later revised by Jacob of Edessa. The manuscripts of the baptismal liturgy or several of the special services of the festivals proudly claim to be translations of the Greek original. The Syrian Orthodox Church was always proud of its Antiochene heritage and tried to maintain an unbroken link with it. This would explain the preference for the Greek sources. Even the 'Syro-Hexapla' was preferred over the Peshitta Old Testament in most of the monasteries of Tur Abdin.

The translation of Greek hymns and the adaptation of Greek elements entered into a new phase in the tenth century. In the late tenth century, north-west Syria was

---

[9] Ibid.; Samuel Athanasius, Introduction to *Ma'de'dono*, p. 6.

[10] 'Maphrian' literally means 'a begetter, progenitor, or prelate'. He was the Syrian Orthodox counterpart of the East Syrian patriarch, whose traditional seat was Tikrit and was later transferred to Mosul. The Malankara Orthodox Church claims that the Catholicate which was established in India in 1912 was the 're-establishment of the 'Catholicate' (i.e. Maphrianate) of Tikrit/Mosul.

See 'Maphrian', in J. Assfalg. and P. Krüger, *Petit Dictionnaire de l'Orient chrétien*, Paris, 1991, p. 366. A.P. Urumpackal, *The Juridical Status of the Catholicos of Malabar*, Rome, 1977.

[11] On the two traditions: Ignatius Aphram Barsoum, *The History of Syriac Literature and Sciences*, pp. 22–23; S. Brock, *Hidden Pearl*, III, pp. 34–35.

[12] B. Varghese, 'Some common elements', *The Harp* 13 (2000), 65–76.

[13] J.M. Vosté has published a Latin translation: See. J.M. Vosté, *Pontificale iuxta ritum Ecclesiae Syrorum Occidentalium*, Vatican, 1941.

conquered by the Byzantines, who occupied it for just over a century (964–1084). Until the tenth century, the Byzantine Orthodox Patriarchate of Antioch (or 'the Melkite Church') continued to follow the Antiochene liturgical rites. Thus the Syrian Orthodox and the Byzantines share several prayers. The best example is the entrance hymn *ho Monogenes* and its Syriac version *Ihidoyo*. The Syriac anaphora of the 'Twelve Apostles'[14] and the Byzantine anaphora of St John Chrysostom have several prayers in common, which probably go back to a fourth-century Antiochene archetype.[15] The oldest manuscripts of the baptismal liturgies of both the Churches contain further common material. The Byzantine re-conquest of north-west Syria in the late ninth century had a lasting impact on the liturgical history of the Churches of the region. The Constantinopolitan rite came to replace the old Antiochene and Jerusalem rites. The Greek Orthodox Church of Antioch ('Melkites') abandoned several features they had formerly shared with the Syrian Orthodox Church.[16] In the tenth and eleventh centuries several Greek canons were translated into Syriac for the use of the Melkite Churches, where Syriac was the liturgical language. The Syrian Orthodox Church adopted some of these hymns under the name of 'Greek canons' (see below). In the thirteenth century, Bar Hebraeus justifies this adaptation. After having described the contributions of Ephrem, Isaac of Antioch, Balai and Severus of Antioch towards the enrichment of liturgical hymnody, Bar Hebraeus continues:[17]

> Furthermore, at the time of the holy Jacob of Edessa and of the excellent George of the Arab Tribes those canticles which are called 'the Greek canons' were introduced by a certain Damascene author, whose name was Cyrene bar Mansur[18] and by a certain monk, who among them, was surnamed Aba Qusma,[19] the inventor of Quqlia, viz. canons which are more delightful than those composed by the former. Since this Cyrene, though belonging to the partisans of the Council of Chalcedon, did not apply himself to mentioning in his songs the points of dispute by which the schism had originated, his canons began to be introduced into our Church in East and West, as we learn from the holy Lazarus bar Sabta.

The most remarkable element that the Syrian Orthodox have adopted from the Byzantines might be the *octoechos*, or the liturgical music in eight modes. Severus of Antioch, whose name has been often associated with the *octoechos*, has probably nothing to do with its origin.[20] The Syrians were used to the 'septenary' system,

---

14 No longer used in the Syrian Orthodox Church. Syriac text with Latin translation, *AS* I–2, 212–27.

15 See H. Engberding, 'Die syrische Anaphora der Zwölf Apostel und ihre Paralleltexte einander gegenübergestellt und mit neuen Untersuchungen zur Urgeschichte der Chrysostomosliturgie begleitet', *OC* 34 (1937), 213–47; G. Wagner, *Der Ursprung der Chrysostomosliturgie*, Münster, Westfalen, 1973.

16 See S. Brock, *The Hidden Pearl*, III, pp. 34–35.

17 Bar Hebraeus, *Ethicon*, pp. 62–63.

18 John of Damascus.

19 Cosmas of Mayuma, the adoptive brother of John. Both names are often connected with the composition of 'Greek canons'.

20 See A. Cody, 'The Early History of Octoechos in Syria', in N. Garsoian et al., *East of Byzantium, Syria and Armenia in the Formative Period* (Washington, DC, 1982), pp. 89–113 (with bibliography).

rather than the 'octonary'. Thus the 'septenary' system is attested by most of the lectionaries before the early eleventh century.[21] Recent studies have demonstrated that the eight modes came to be used in the Syrian Orthodox Church by the eleventh century.[22]

On the other hand, the Syriac poetical genres such as *madrosho, sugito* and *memro* seem to have served as a model for the Greek *kontakion* and the early Greek hymnography.[23] However, the elaborate liturgical use of hymnody is a characteristic of the Antiochene tradition, of which the Byzantines and the Syrians are the heirs. Still, in the Syrian offices the importance of hymnody is even greater than in the Byzantine tradition.

Distinctive Features

Among the Christian Churches, the West Syrians have the richest collection of anaphoras (about eighty are known). Though they invariably follow the structure of St James, in the wording of the individual prayers the anaphoras differ from one another. Sometimes even the structure has been disregarded. Thus the anaphora of Thomas of Harkal has a curious Institution narrative.

> When he befittingly took the form of a servant, as the one who has to fulfill the preparations for our salvation, *he took bread and wine* and sanctified and broke and gave to his apostles saying: 'Take, receive from it, believe and be assured that you eat my body and drink my blood for the remembrance of my death until I come'.[24]

The same type of Institution narrative is also attested in the anaphora attributed to the 'Patriarch John, Yeshu Bar Shusan the Scribe' (d. 1073).[25] Here three liturgical units of St James have been conflated: the blessing of the bread, that of the chalice and the introduction to the anamnesis. Most probably these two anaphoras represent an ancient model.[26]

The Syrian Orthodox and the Maronite Churches also share several common liturgical elements. The pre-anaphora and the baptismal liturgy as well as several of the liturgical celebrations of both the traditions have a common history. Though both share several of the anaphoras, the Maronites have a few anaphoras of their own. The

---

[21] Ibid., pp. 94–97.

[22] Ibid., pp. 93–94.

[23] A. de Halleux, 'Héllenisme et syrianité de Romanos le Mélode', *Revue de l'histoire ecclésiastique* 73 (1978), 632–41 or, in English, S. Brock, 'Syriac and Greek hymnography: problems of origins', *Studia Patristica* 16 (1985), 77–81.

[24] Syriac text in *Annapuro* (1932), p. 228.

[25] On the manuscripts, A. Raes, AS. I–1, p. xli.

[26] The Institution Narratives in the *Testamentum Domini* and *The Deir Balyzeh Papyrus* are probably the nearest parallels.

Maronite anaphora of St Peter (known as *Sharar* by its opening words) has several prayers in common with the East Syrian anaphora of Addai and Mari. Both may derive from a common Edessene original, or rather perhaps from an Edessene version of an early Antiochene anaphora. The Maronite Breviary (*Shehimo*) also contains several hymns that are used in the East Syrian Church.

A very powerful sense of mystery – first manifested in the Antiochene tradition – could perhaps explain the elaborate use of symbols, processions and gestures. However, as Fr I.H. Dalmais says, 'from the earliest times, it was characteristic of the Antiochene liturgy to give a big place to singing and processions in order to satisfy a people whose religious devotion was very demonstrative'.[27] In spite of its pervading sense of mystery, the Antiochene liturgy is intensively human, with its 'spontaneity and drama'.[28] The processions, hymns, gestures, people's acclamations and responses make the celebration 'lively' and ensure the involvement of the entire community in the *leitourgia*, the common work of the Church. This sense of community is reflected in every expression of the Antiochene *lex orandi*.

The Syrian Orthodox liturgy lacks the 'pomp' of the Byzantine celebrations. External conditions made such pompous celebrations rather difficult. Whether in the Byzantine Empire, or in the Sassanid Persia or in the Muslim states, the Syrian Orthodox Christians always lived under constraints. Throughout their history, they were a community struggling for survival. Therefore their churches were modest in size and architecture and were often too small for solemn processions, unlike the Byzantines. The processions that were once held with solemnity (for example the entrance procession) gradually disappeared or were limited to the space around the altar. Their music was also simple and was mainly aimed at ensuring the active participation of the people. The use of the *octoechos* did not affect the simplicity of the church music.

In spite of the hard conditions, literary activity and liturgical creativity continued to flourish until the thirteenth century. After the thirteenth century, especially the ruthless massacres of Christians under Tamerlane, Syriac Christianity entered a phase of speedy decline. The prelates, clergy and the monks were somewhat illiterate and theological and liturgical creativity were at their lowest ebb. The clergy found it rather difficult to understand the meaning and the richness of the liturgical texts composed in the golden age of liturgical creativity. New prayers or hymns were composed to suit the mind of the time. The newly composed liturgical texts, including the anaphoras, were often mediocre, in both their content and language. Beautiful poetical pieces were often abridged without the least respect for content. Most of the liturgical texts composed after the fourteenth century belong to this genre. The *Penkito* or Festal Breviary published from Pampakuda is an example.[29]

---

27 I.H. Dalmais, *Eastern Liturgies* (New York, 1960), p. 128.

28 Ibid., p. 60.

29 *Penkito*, 3 vols, Pampakuda, 1963.

Theological Foundations of *Leitourgia*

The West Syrian fathers have not given a definition of liturgy. Perhaps it is felt unnecessary to define something self-evident, and so intimate to one's experience. For the West Syrians, worship is the vocation of man, the very purpose for which he was created. He was created to live in communion with God, as a liturgical being. This idea is fundamental to understanding the meaning of *leitourgia*, as lived and expressed by the West Syrian tradition. Liturgy is not something external to Christian witness. It is not an 'accessory', but an essential element of the Christian tradition. It is the very expression of the Christian identity. According to the West Syrians, to be a Christian means to be a liturgical being. Worship is not a supplementary or practical discipline in the life of a Christian. It is the realization of his vocation. This has been expressed in vivid phrases in the liturgical celebrations.

> *You created me and placed your hand upon me.*[30] On Friday in the beginning God created Adam from the dust and breathed on him the Spirit and gave him speech, that he might sing praise to him, halleluiah and give thanks to his creation.[31]

Psalm 139:5 was given a very interesting interpretation in the Syriac tradition. The Syriac phrase [*You*] *placed your hands upon me* can also mean *you have ordained me* (*as a priest*). Thus, according to a widely accepted Syriac tradition, Adam was created as a priest, with a vocation to stand before God on behalf of the whole creation.[32] According to the hymn that we have quoted, Adam's vocation was to offer praise to the creator as a representative, as a 'priest' of the creation. The Fall consisted in his failure to fulfil his 'priestly' vocation. Instead of 'ministering' to God, that is, to stand before God in an attitude of trust and thanksgiving – the content of communion – he did not believe in God's promise. Thus the Fall was also a failure to fulfil his liturgical vocation. As we will see later, according to the West Syrians, the purpose of the Incarnation was to 'teach man true worship' and thus to restore the broken relationship.

Modern exegetes have admitted that Genesis 2:15 can also be translated as *Yahweh Elohim took man and placed him in the Garden of Eden for the worship and* [*its*] *keeping.*[33] This is strongly implied in the Peshitta version. Thus Adam's life in Paradise was a liturgical life, which consisted of 'watching, fasting, prayer and sacrifices of righteousness'. We find thus in a *qolo* addressed to the 'good thief', who was promised Paradise:

> O thief, tell us of the beauty of Paradise and show us the tree of life that we may pluck first fruits from it, watching, fasting and prayer and sacrifices of righteousness.[34]

---

[30] Ps. 139:5 (Peshitta), sung as a *petgomo* (verse from the Psalms) sung before a *qolo*.

[31] Friday, *Ramsho, Shehimo*, p. 218.

[32] See M. Wurmbrand, 'Homélie de Jacques de Saroug sur la mort d'Aaron', *OS* 6 (1961), 255–78.

[33] Paul Evdokimov, *La Nouveauté de l'Esprit. Etude de Spiritualité*, Abbayé de Belle Fontaine, 1975, p. 44.

[34] Tuesday, *Sapro, Shehimo*, p. 109.

Liturgy gives us 'the first fruits' of Paradise, a foretaste of the joyful life in the presence of God. Paradise was a 'sanctuary' where God was present, and Adam was led to the 'sanctuary' as a priestly guardian.[35] When he failed to fulfil his vocation, he was expelled from Paradise. Worship is the expression of our longing ('*nostalgia*') to live in communion with God, and to regain our former inheritance and dwelling place. The orientation towards the East has this meaning as well (see below).

---

[35] Paul Evdokimov, op. cit., p. 44.

CHAPTER 1

Liturgical Theology: Scope and Method

Christian theology is the search for meaning and the articulation of that meaning. As a theological discipline, liturgical theology aims at the elucidation of the meaning of the liturgy. The question addressed by liturgical theology relates to the faith as expressed, communicated and preserved in the *leitourgia* of the Church.[1] Since *leitourgia*, the common act of the Church, is the object of liturgical theology, naturally the reality of the Church comes into focus. The entire experience and vision of the reality, as well as the concerns of the Church, are at stake in its liturgy. Its hopes, vocation and self-understanding find their expression in it.

There are several features that the Christian 'cult' shares with other religions. However, as A. Schmemann has rightly pointed out, the specificity of Christian liturgy consists in its eschatological character.[2] The Christian tradition was almost always conscious of this unique feature of Christian liturgy. The content of Christian eschatology is the manifestation of the Kingdom of God, which consists of the dynamic presence and the permanent indwelling of God among men, thus establishing a 'community', a life of communion with us. The Kingdom, or our life with God, is a 'possession' as well as the object of hope and prayer. This tension between 'already' and 'yet to come' is an important problem in liturgical theology.

1. Sources

For the study of liturgical theology, the *ordo*, of which liturgical texts form an important part, serves as the primary source. The liturgical commentaries, mystagogical catecheses and liturgical homilies are the main witness to the *lex orandi* as it is understood in the Christian tradition. In the Syriac tradition, liturgical commentaries and homilies were often written in verses, known as *memre* or metrical homilies. Excerpts from them have been incorporated into Syriac hymnody. *Memre* served as a model and a source of inspiration for a large number of liturgical hymns. Thus the hymnography served as supplications as well as expositions of the doctrines. Several of the liturgical homilies served as the direct source for a large number of *sedre*, one of the most characteristic units of the Syrian Orthodox and Maronite liturgies.

In addition to these sources, West Syrian fathers like Severus of Antioch and Jacob of Edessa had expounded the meaning of the rites in some of their correspondence. A

---

[1] A. Schmemann, 'Debate on Liturgy: Liturgical Theology, Theology of Liturgy and Liturgical Reforms', *SVTQ* 13/4 (1969), 218.

[2] A. Schmemann, 'Liturgical Theology: Remarks on Method', in Thomas Fisch (ed.), *Liturgy and Tradition: Theological Reflection of Alexander Schmemann* (New York, 1990), p. 142.

few of them have been incorporated into the canonical literature.[3] In a sense, the function of the conciliar decisions and canons on liturgical questions was similar to that of the liturgical commentaries. They often throw light on the meaning of some of the practices and have served to correct certain customs, the contents of some of the prayers and to fix the structure of certain rites. To some extent, the liturgical commentaries and the canonical sources were responsible for the fixation of the *ordo*. (The best example is the canon 48 of the Council of Laodicea: 'Those who are baptized shall be anointed with the celestial chrism after their baptism and shall become participants in the Kingdom of Christ.') They often guarded the ordo against unwarranted reforms, additions or omissions. In the case of the anaphora, the commentaries were largely responsible for the fixation of the structure and the themes. However, in the case of the baptismal *ordo*, variations in the structure continued to exist down to the twentieth century.

2. Liturgical Theology and the History of the *Ordo*

The search for meaning is inseparable from the study of the historical evolution of the *ordo* and its interpretation. Thus the primary task of liturgical theology is to study the history of the *ordo* ('To establish the liturgical fact', as A. Schmemann says[4]).

Significant progress has been made in the study of the history of the Western and Byzantine traditions, but in the case of the non-Byzantine Eastern liturgies, our studies are still in the initial stages. Our knowledge of the history of the Syrian Orthodox baptism, pre-anaphora and anaphora has been advanced considerably.[5] In the case of the East Syrian liturgy, in spite of a few important studies on the anaphora of Addai and Mari, several questions remain unanswered.[6] Most of the studies on the East Syrian liturgy, especially those by Indian liturgists, are merely discussions of secondary literature and unproved hypotheses.[7]

Historical study is not merely concerned with the evolution of certain rites or the origin of certain prayers and hymns. The evolution of the understanding of the meaning of the 'liturgical facts' should be an important part of it. To some extent the new rites or prayers are the result of that evolution. (Often new rites or prayers were introduced as an imitation of other liturgical centres or traditions and were later interpreted in order to make them fit into the liturgical system of the borrower.) Historical study

---

3 See A. Vööbus, *The Synodicon in the West Syrian Tradition*, Vols I & II.

4 Schmemann, 'Liturgical Theology': Remarks, p. 144.

5 See references to A. Baumstark, S. Brock, G. Khouri-Sarkis, P. Gamayel and B. Varghese in the Bibliography.

6 See W. Maccomber, 'A History of the Chaldean Mass', *Worship* 51 (1977), 107–20; B.D. Spinks, 'The Original form of the Anaphora of the Apostles: A Suggestion in the Light of Maronite Sharar', *EL* 91 (1977), 146–61.

7 For a complete bibliography, see P. Yousif, *A Classified Bibliography of the East Syrian Liturgy*, Rome, 1990; S. Brock, *Syriac Studies: A Classified Bibliography (1960–1990)*, Kaslik, 1996.

should address the theological issues behind the origin of certain prayers or rites in order to understand how the liturgical phenomenon was lived, interpreted and transmitted.

Historical study should focus attention on the shifts in the meaning of certain elements. This would help us to understand the reasons for the disappearance or introduction of certain elements and their impact on liturgical theology. In the West Syrian liturgy, the disappearance of the deacon's role in the preparation rites was an important development. Similarly the disappearance of the reading of the Book of Life, or that of symbols like the *bema*, was of lasting consequence for the *lex orandi*. Similarly the introduction of new elements (elaborate preparation rites, dramatic blessing of the censer in the pre-anaphora, inaudible prayers, elaborate fraction ceremony (breaking of bread) with its symbolic association with the passion of Christ) had important consequences for liturgical theology. The function of historical study should be to evaluate the history of each element and the history of its meaning understood as part of a tradition.

Historical study should also take into account that diversity in liturgical practices once existed – and still exists – in the West Syrian tradition. Diversity in the structure of the anaphora still exists in the Coptic tradition. Thus Alexandrian and Antiochene types of anaphoras exist side by side. The prayers of the Alexandrine anaphora of Gregory of Nazianzus have been addressed to Christ, whereas the Eastern anaphoras are generally addressed to God the Father. Similar anaphora(s) seem to have existed among the West Syrians. Thus the instruction of Moses Bar Kepha is to correct the prayers of the anaphora if they are not addressed to the Father.[8] In the East Syrian tradition, there are striking differences between the Anaphora of Addai and Mari and the other two anaphoras (Theodore of Mopsuestia and Nestorius). The Armenians use the unmixed chalice and unleavened bread. These were not normally regarded as a violation of the *lex orandi* as shared by all the Oriental Orthodox Churches.[9]

Historical study could help us to establish the limits to the diversity that is possible or tolerated in the liturgical phenomenon. This would be helpful in two respects. First, it would provide valid insights for liturgical reforms, adaptations and our search for new liturgical forms. Second, it would be useful in ecumenical encounters, where difference in liturgical practices is one of the stumbling blocks.

3. The Theological Analysis of the Liturgical Fact

The second step consists of the theological analysis of the 'liturgical fact' established by the historical study.[10] The theological analysis is often coloured by the

---

[8] Bar Kepha, *Eucharist*, p. 90.

[9] I am mindful of the controversy between Bar Salibi and the Armenians, which was based on historical rather than theological reasons. See Bar Salibi, *Against the Armenians*.

[10] Cf. Schmemann, 'Liturgical Theology': Remarks, p. 144.

preoccupations that are foreign to the tradition that shaped the 'liturgical fact'. To a certain extent this is unavoidable, as we have to interpret it to others in a language comprehensible to them. Thus Western scholars are tempted to use the categories that are familiar to their readers in the West. The theological criteria of the West are sometimes inadequate to establish the theological content of the Eastern liturgies. Thus the chrismation, an essential element of the Eastern baptism, has been too hastily identified with confirmation. Since the theologians in the West still differ on the meaning of the latter, theological problems that are completely alien to the East are brought into Eastern baptismal theology.

4. Comparative Study of Liturgy

In spite of the cultural and linguistic differences, there is a considerable interdependence among the Eastern liturgies. The Syro-Antiochene tradition is largely indebted to the Hellenistic culture. Severus of Antioch (d. 538), the great organizer of the Syrian Orthodox liturgy, was a man of Greek culture.[11] In the ninth and tenth centuries, the West Syrians came under Byzantine influence, especially in the case of hymnody. Thus several 'Greek canons' found their place in the Syrian Orthodox liturgy. In modern times, the Byzantines and the Oriental Orthodox Churches have acknowledged the common theological, spiritual and liturgical traditions that they share.[12]

Mesopotamian liturgical poetry had played a decisive role in determining the style and content of the Byzantine Kontakion. In fact the Byzantine hymnographer Romanos was influenced by early Syriac hymnody, especially that by Saint Ephrem of Nisibis, the most noted representative of the Mesopotamian tradition.[13] The hymnographers from Crete and Cyprus were also open to Mesopotamian influence. Since the fourth century, Cyprus had a Syriac-speaking community of Monks.[14] Most noted among them was an East Syrian, Abbot Gregory of Cyprus (seventh century). The famous Byzantine hymn-writer Andrew of Crete (*c.* 660–740), who became bishop of Gortyna in Crete, was from Damascus. In 712 he became anti-Chalcedonian and went back to the Chalcedonians' side in the next year. The so-called *Monogenes* (attributed to Severus of Antioch by the non-Chalcedonians and to the Emperor Justinian by the Byzantines) and *Trisagion* are the creations of the Syro-Antiochene tradition. Their earliest history is related to the non-Chalcedonians of Antioch. The Byzantine anaphora of Saint John Chrysostom and the Syriac anaphora of the *Twelve Apostles* have a common origin. To sum up, one cannot ignore the role that the Mesopotamian tradition

---

11 On the liturgical contributions of Severus, see K.E. Mcvey (ed. and tr.), *George Bishop of the Arabs: A Homily on Blessed Mar Severus, Patriarch of Antioch*, CSCO 531.*SS* 217 (Louvain, 1993), pp. 2, 21.

12 See the agreed statement of the 'Joint Committee of the Theological Dialogue between the Orthodox Church and the Oriental Orthodox Churches' (met at Anba Bishoi Monastery, Egypt, 20–24 June 1989), in *Sourozh* 42 (Nov. 1990), 38–41; also in *SVTQ* 34/1 (1990), 78ff.

13 Cf. G. de Matons, *Romanos le Mélode* (Paris, 1977), pp. 3–4, 16–27.

14 Assemani, *Bibliotheca Orientalis*, I, pp. 170–72.

played in shaping the Byzantine 'liturgical fact'. Similarly, after the ninth century, the Syrian Orthodox liturgy had borrowed several elements from the Melkites, whose liturgical texts were translations from Greek. The Greek *ochtoechos* largely influenced the Syrian Orthodox *ochtoechos*, as it was used among the Melkites.

The Eastern liturgical theology should focus on the liturgical elements that are common to both the Eastern and Oriental Orthodox Churches. In fact both traditions have the same liturgical and spiritual sensibilities and approaches. Both have remained faithful to the *lex orandi* of the undivided Eastern tradition. This should be taken into account in establishing the 'liturgicalness' or 'liturgical fact' of Eastern Christianity.

5. Study of Liturgical Vocabulary

A discussion of liturgical vocabulary is important for liturgical theology. Liturgical and theological vocabulary reflects the theological concerns of the community that created it. In a sense, the vocabulary indicates the 'theological content' or 'coefficient' of liturgical celebration (see our discussion of *teshmeshto, rozo* and *qurobo* in Chapter 3). Liturgical terminology marks the linguistic limits up to which we can go in the articulation of the *lex orandi*. Study of vocabulary should bring out the norms used by a tradition in the choice of words, expressions and images, as well as the meaning attributed to them. As we shall see, most of the Syriac liturgical vocabulary and images derive from the Syriac versions of the Bible, especially the Peshitta. Similarly in the case of the Syriac versions of the Bible, the vocabulary might have been carefully selected to meet liturgical needs as well. The implications of this in the translation of the Bible, liturgical texts, and patristic literature as well as in the composition of new liturgical forms need to be explored.

6. Liturgical Theology and the Biblical Exegesis

The role of the liturgical tradition or *lex orandi* in shaping early biblical exegesis is evident. The ultimate aim of biblical exegesis – at least in the East – was the exposition of the hidden meaning of the Word of God and the 'building up' of the Body of Christ. The Word was 'mystically broken'[15] in order that the faithful should share in the divine life that it reveals. The divorce between biblical exegesis and the *lex orandi* of the Church is a post-Enlightenment development.

Biblical exegesis, on the other hand, served as the model for liturgical exposition, and has often left its traces of influence on prayers and hymnody. It has also often provided a norm for the composition of prayers and hymns.

---

[15] Cf. 2 Tim. 2:15; also the Intercessions of the anaphora of St James.

7. Question of Liturgical Reforms

Liturgical history is a history of liturgical reforms: the history of additions, omissions, adaptations and expansions. In the West Syrian tradition, the reforms often took place as a slow and indiscernible process. The intervention of an authority or conciliar decisions was rarely the main factor behind these reforms. The liturgical commentaries and the Synods exhorted or appealed for some changes, and were incorporated rather slowly by a process of assimilation. Thus the introduction of the post-baptismal anointing in the West Syriac tradition was a gradual process that began in the fourth century and became widespread by the seventh. Similarly, the disappearance of the reading of the Book of Life (originally read before the anaphora), under the influence of St James Liturgy, was a very slow process. The planning and imposing of liturgical reforms 'from above' almost never took place in the Syrian Orthodox tradition. Liturgical anarchy or controversies were rather rarely reported in its history. The only noted liturgical controversy in the Syrian Orthodox Church was that regarding the use of the expression 'heavenly bread' in the formula of fraction that was reported in the eighth century.[16]

Liturgical history should point out the major liturgical reforms that took place in the history of Christianity. Their historical context and subsequent development should be carefully brought out. The suppression of the Agape, the transfer of the eucharistic celebration from the evening to the morning, the use of fixed formulae, the emergence of the parishes under the liturgical presidency of presbyters and the emergence of historical liturgies are a few such developments that mark major shifts in the understanding of the liturgical fact. The theological synthesis should draw lessons for today's liturgical reforms, often done with little respect for the *lex orandi* of the tradition from which a particular Church was born. Such a synthesis has ecumenical implications.

8. Theological Synthesis

Then there arises the question of a synthesis in liturgical theology. It should consider the following. How does the liturgy express the fundamental doctrines of the Christian Church, especially the Trinity, the Church itself, eschatology and the 'life of the world to come'? (These are the 'themes' of the Nicene Creed, the touchstone for all doctrinal formulations.) What is the meaning of liturgy in relation to our vocation and God's plan for humanity? How is it related to the revelation and its articulation in the Bible and in the tradition?

---

16 Bar Salibi, *Com. Eucharist*, ch.16, p. 85, note 1.

Leitourgia in the West Syrian Mystagogical Tradition

The liturgical commentaries represent an important stage in the development of liturgical understanding. Their aim was to bring out the *rozo* or the theological meaning of the liturgical celebrations. They attest how the Church viewed liturgy as the expression of her faith, her *lex credendi*. The orientations and concerns of the commentaries have been largely reflected in several liturgical texts, especially in the anaphoras composed in the second millennium, as well as in a good number of *sedre*. Thus the commentaries are important as witnesses to the *lex orandi* of a particular period and as a decisive factor in shaping its subsequent expression. To a large extent, the commentaries were responsible for the stability of the liturgical rites against unwarranted reforms. They were also decisive in fixing the structure and the content of the *ordo* and in realizing liturgical uniformity. In the West Syrian tradition, the commentaries seem to have played a major role in the reception of the anaphora of St James as normative.

1. Beginning of the Mystagogia

Since the beginning of Christianity, *mystagogia* or the exposition of the meaning of the liturgical celebrations, especially those of Baptism and Eucharist, was an integral part of the Christian *kerygma*.[1] *Mystagogia*, an introduction or an initiation to the mystery, has two dimensions: celebration of the mystery and its interpretation. They are inseparable. The meaning of a rite is communicated to the faithful primarily by the prayers of the celebration. But an understanding of the rite grew up in the Church along with the development of the liturgy. By the third century, the tradition to give symbolic interpretation to the rites became normal. In the fourth century, we find a distinction between the catechetical homilies addressed to the Catechumens and the

---

[1] On the *mystagogia* of the early Church, see Réné Bornet, 'Les commentaires byzantines de la divine liturgie du VIIe au Xe siècles', *Archives de l'Orient chrétien* 9, Paris, 1966, ch.1; Enrico Mazza, *Mystagogy. A Theology of Liturgy in the Patristic Age*, Peublo, New York, 1989. The major work on the history of patristic and medieval exegesis is: Henri de Lubac, *Histoire et esprit. L'intelligence de l'Ecriture d'après Origène*, Théologie 16, Paris, 1950; idem, *Exégèse médiévale. Les quatre sens de l'Ecriture*. Pt I, Vol.1–2; Pt II, Vol.1–2, Théologie 41, 42, 59, Paris, 1959–64. The Byzantine mystagogical tradition has its origin in the Syro-Antiochene tradition. See R.Taft, 'The Liturgy of the Great Church: an Initial Synthesis of Structures and Interpretation on the Eve of Iconoclasm', *Dumbarton Oak Papers* 34–35 (1980–81), 45–75; Paul Meyendorff, *St Germanus of Constantinople on the Divine Liturgy* (SVSP, New York, 1984), pp. 23–52.

mystagogical catechesis delivered to the neophytes.[2] The subject of the first was the basic Christian doctrines as expressed in the Creed, along with a partial exposition of the baptismal rites, whereas in the second type of homilies, the sacraments of Baptism, Chrismation and Eucharist were explained. The only West Syrian catechetical homilies known to us are those of Severus of Antioch.[3] Though the West Syrian festal homilies have followed the style of Severus, his catechetical homilies left few traces of influence on the commentaries on Baptism.

The West Syrian commentaries on sacraments, with a few exceptions, belong to the category of 'mystagogical commentaries'. West Syrian writers had a special preference for the sacraments of Baptism, Myron and the Eucharist.[4] However, they had written commentaries on different rites, such as Ordination, Consecration of the Church, Monastic Profession or Funeral.

2. Typological and Allegorical Commentaries

By the fourth century, typological and allegorical methods became widespread for biblical and liturgical interpretation. The distinction between these two types of explanation is important in understanding the history of West Syrian liturgical interpretation.

Typology seeks to explain the meaning of an event in the salvation history by relating it to another event whose inner meaning is fundamentally similar.[5] Thus the redemption achieved by Christ can be seen as the fulfilment of the Exodus, and the Eucharist can be seen as actualizing the work of Christ, and pointing to the final accomplishment in the world to come. Saint Ephrem, Aphrahat and Jacob of Serugh followed the typological method of commenting on the mystery of the liturgy. The West Syrian commentaries on Myron, as well as several *sedre*, also followed this method.

Typology is concerned with events as entities.[6] But allegory is more concerned with the details of events or things, and its interpretation of them can be unrelated to

---

[2] Major studies on the early catechetical homilies are: H.M. Riley, *The Christian Initiation: A Comparative Study of the Interpretation of the Baptismal Liturgy in the Mystagogical Writings of Cyril of Jerusalem, John Chrysostom, Theodore of Mopsuestia and Ambrose of Milan*, Studies in Christian Antiquity 17, Washington, 1974; E.J. Yarnold, *The Awe-Inspiring Rites of Initiation: Baptismal Homilies of the Fourth Century*, Slogh, 1971.

[3] See François Graffin, 'Les catéchèses de Sévère d'Antioche', *OS* 5 (1960), 47–54; J. Gribomont, 'Les catéchèses de Sévère d'Antioche et le Credo', *Pd'O* 6–7 (1975–76), 125–58; I.H. Dalmais, 'Source baptismale et le mystère pascale d'après les homélies de Sévère d'Antioche sur la préparation quadragésimale et l'entrée au baptême', *Pd'O* 6–7 (1975–76), 349–56.

[4] Cf. B. Varghese, *Les onctions baptismales dans la tradition syrienne*, CSCO 512, Louvain, 1989.

[5] Cf. Hugh Wybrew, *The Orthodox Liturgy*, New York, 1990, p. 63; Bornet, *Les commentaires*, pp. 42–45.

[6] Wybrew, *Orthodox Liturgy*, p. 64; Bornet, *Les commentaires*, 42–45. R.P.C. Hanson, *Allegory and Event. A Study of the Sources and Significance of Origen's Interpretation of Scripture*, London, 1959, gives the following definition: 'Typology is the interpreting of an event belonging to the present or the recent past as the fulfilment of a similar relation recorded or prophesied in Scripture. Allegory is the interpretation of an object or person or a number of objects or persons as in reality meaning some object or person of a later time, with no attempt made to trace a relationship of "similar situation" between them' (p. 7), quoted by Bornet, p. 44, n. 3.

any fundamental similarity of meaning. Its symbolism tends to be arbitrary. In the allegorical interpretation, the mystery of Christ present in the Eucharist began to be broken down into various aspects. Cyril of Jerusalem's mystagogical Catecheses and Saint John Chrysostom's Catechetical Homilies attest the first stage of a tendency to associate different parts of the liturgy with different moments in the life of Christ. Thus Chrysostom says that the altar represents the manger of Bethlehem and that the incarnation as well as the passion is made present in the Eucharist.[7] Though Cyril's method is primarily typological, he had a preference for the allegory.[8] Thus, according to him, in the liturgical ceremonies, the imitation (*mimesis*) of the historical events in the life of Jesus takes place in an image or in similitude; but salvation is communicated to us in truth.[9] Thus Baptism is a symbol of the Passion and Resurrection. The triple immersion represents the three days that Christ remained in the sepulchre (*MC*.II:4,6). The Chrismation is the 'antitype' of Christ's anointing by the Holy Spirit in Jordan (*MC*.III:1–2).

The first systematic allegorical explanation is found in Theodore of Mopsuestia's Catechetical Homilies.[10] Though he uses typology in his exegesis of Scripture, Theodore does not attempt to relate the Eucharist to any Old Testament prefiguration. For him, the Eucharist is the memorial of the historical life of Jesus, especially of His death and resurrection. Thus he relates the different aspects of the passion and death with successive stages in the celebration. The procession with the bread and wine represents Christ's journey to the crucifixion. The deacons stand for the angels who consoled Him during His passion. The deposition of the bread and wine on the altar represents Christ's burial. The coming of the Holy Spirit in the epiclesis symbolizes the return of Christ's spirit to His body. The fraction recalls the manifestation of the risen Lord.

With Theodore, we find a tendency to explain the doctrinal meaning of the prayers and the rites. The liturgical ceremonies evoke the mysteries of the faith. Thus the threefold immersion evokes the mystery of the Trinity.[11] The Eucharist is 'the ineffable image of the Economy of Christ'.[12] When he comments on the initial Trinitarian blessing, Sanctus or the *Holy things to the Holy*, Theodore refers to the Trinitarian doctrine. This approach has been continued by the West Syrians, namely Jacob of Edessa, George of the Arabs and Moses Bar Kepha. Theodore's discussion of the

---

[7] Bornet, *Les commentaires*, pp. 75–80; on Chrysostom's Mystagogy, see Mazza, *Mystagogy*, pp. 105–49.

[8] Bornet, *Les commentaires*, pp. 73–75.

[9] *Myst. Cat.* II:5 : '[In baptism] we did not really die, we were not really buried, but were not really crucified and raised again; but our imitation was in a figure, and our salvation in reality.'

[10] A. Mingana (ed.), *Commentary of Theodore of Mopsuestia on the Lord's Prayer and on the Sacraments of Baptism and the Eucharist*, Woodbrooke Studies 6, Cambridge, 1933; Bornet, *Les commentaires*, pp. 80–82; Mazza, *Mystagogy*, pp. 45–104; R. Taft, 'The Liturgy of the Great Church: An initial synthesis of structure and interpretation on the eve of Iconoclasm', *Dumbarton Oak Papers* 34–35 (1980–81), 62–65.

[11] See the long comments on the baptismal formula and the threefold immersion in: Mingana, *Commentary*, pp. 58–67.

[12] Ibid., p. 85.

fraction is marked by his Christological concerns.[13] This has been further developed by Bar Kepha in terms of Syrian Orthodox Christology.

In their allegorical interpretation, the Antiochenes and the Alexandrians followed different approaches. Theodore is the representative of the former and Pseudo-Dionysius the Areopagite that of the latter.[14] The fourth-century christological disputes born of the Adoptionism and Arianism led to an emphasis on the pre-existent divinity of the Logos and his consubstantiality with the Father. The Alexandrians and the Antiochenes offered their own solutions to this problem. The Alexandrian response was more concerned with the divinity of the Logos, and it led to a weakening of Christ's mediatorship, as they had less to say about the historical economy of Christ's saving work.

The Antiochenes, on the other hand, put stress on Christ's high priesthood as pertaining to his humanity,[15] and emphasized the saving works during his human life. These two approaches had lasting impacts on liturgical interpretation. Both expounded the meaning of the liturgical rites with little or no reference to biblical typology. The Antiochenes interpreted the symbols or rites in relation to the saving work of Christ. But the Alexandrians tried to explain how the symbols or rites reveal the spiritual realities and lead us to union with the One.

Generally speaking, the West Syrian commentaries on Baptism and the Eucharist followed the allegorical method of liturgical interpretation as developed by the Antiochenes, with occasional allegorical explanations inspired by Dionysius. Apart from John of Dara, who was largely inspired by Dionysius, the West Syrians were faithful to Antiochene mystagogical tradition.

3. First Mystagogical Catecheses in Syriac

Fourth-century Syriac writers like Aphrahat or Ephrem have not left us any commentary on the sacraments. Ephrem's Hymns on Nativity, Epiphany, Lent or Passover are in fact liturgical commentaries in the form of poetic meditations, probably composed to be sung on the corresponding feasts or seasons.[16] The type of literature known as 'mystagogical commentaries' reached the Syriac tradition probably through the school of Edessa, where the homilies of Theodore of Mopsuestia were translated into Syriac in the fifth century or through the non-Chalcedonians who maintained continuous contacts with the Hellenistic tradition of the 'West'. The popularity of mystagogical

---

13 Ibid., pp. 105–106.

14 On Dionysius, see R. Roques, *L'Univers dionysien*, Théologie 29, Paris, 1954, pp. 245–302; Bornet, *Les commentaires*, pp. 65–72 (bibliography); Taft, 'Liturgy of the Great Church', pp. 61–62; Paul Rorem, *Pseudo-Dionysius*, Oxford, 1993, pp. 91–132; Andrew Loth, *Denys the Areopagite*, London, 1989, pp. 52–77.

15 Taft, 'Liturgy of the Great Church', p. 69. Cf. Theodore, *Commentary* (ed. Mingana), pp. 79–82.

16 On the liturgical works of St Ephrem, see Pierre Yousif, *L'Eucharistie chez Saint Ephrem de Nisibise*, *OCA* 224, Rome, 1984, p. 29.

commentaries in the West Syrian Church since its organization in the Syriac-speaking regions of the Roman–Persian Empires would suggest a non-Chalcedonian initiative in their introduction into the Syriac literature.

However, among the Syriac writers, it was Narsai who wrote a *memro* for the first time entirely dedicated to the sacraments, and he made use of the homilies of Theodore. We have four *memre* on Baptism and the Eucharist attributed to Narsai.[17] They were most probably composed for the instruction of the faithful. However, their composition in twelve-syllable metre suggests that they were intended for liturgical use as well.

4. First West Syrian Commentaries

Among the West Syrians, Jacob of Serugh was one of the first to write liturgical homilies in Syriac. His *memre* on Baptism, the Eucharist or dominical feasts are not commentaries in the strict sense. On Baptism, Jacob's three homilies are of particular importance: 'On the three Baptisms (of the Law, of John and of Christ)', 'On the Baptism of Christ' and 'An Exhortation on Baptism'.[18] There are four homilies of Jacob, which give us an idea of Jacob's Eucharistic theology: 'Homily on the Reception of the Holy Mysteries' (=Hom. 95), 'Another homily on the same subject' (=Hom. 42), 'On the Crucifixion' (=Hom. 53), and 'Homily on the commemoration of the dead and on the Eucharistic Bread (=Hom. 22).[19] Unlike his contemporary, Narsai, Jacob does not comment on the rites and the details of the celebration. His style is similar to that of Ephrem, and follows the typological method. Although Jacob was highly honoured, like Ephrem, and several of his works were incorporated into the prayers, his method of liturgical interpretation was not taken as the norm by the West Syrians. The only known mystagogical work that imitated his style and method is the 'Metrical Homily on the consecration of Myron by George, Bishop of the Arabs' (which was attributed to Jacob of Serugh in some manuscripts). The gradual introduction of the Greco-Antiochene liturgical rites and the method of liturgical interpretation might be the main reason for the gradual disuse of this type of

---

[17] Cf. R.H. Connolly (tr.), *The Liturgical Homilies of Narsai*, Cambridge, 1909. Homily 17 is probably not by Narsai.

[18] P. Bedjan (rd), *Homiliae Selectae Mar Jacobi Sarugensis*, 5 vols, Paris, 1905–10. Vol.I, 153–67; 167–93; 193–211. An abbreviated English translation of Jacob, Homily 7 on Baptism can be found in T.M. Finn, *Early Christian Baptism and the Catechumenate* (Collegeville, 1992), pp. 189–97. For a study, see S. Brock, 'Baptismal Themes in the Writings of Jacob of Saroug', *Symposium Syriacum 1976*, OCA 205, Rome, 1978, pp. 325–47; B. Varghese, *Les Onctions*, pp. 137–47. On the exegetical method of Jacob, see B. Sony, 'La méthode exégétique de Jacques de Saroug', *Pd'O* 9 (1979), 67–103.

[19] Hom. 95: Bedjan III, 646–63; Hom. 42: idem II, 209–27; Hom. 53: idem II, 447–610; Hom. 22: idem I, 535–50. French translation of Hom. 95: J. Van der Ploeg, 'Une homélie de Jacques de Saroug sur la réception de la sainte communion', in *Mélanges Eugène Tisserant, Vol. III, Orient Chrétien, IIe partie*, Studi e Testi 233, Vatican, 1964, pp. 395–418. English translation: R.H. Connolly, 'A Homily of Mar Jacob of Serugh on the Reception of the Holy Mysteries', *Downside Review* 28 (n.s. 8, 1908), 278–87 (only parts).

mystagogical literature in the Syriac tradition. With the liturgical reforms of Jacob of Edessa, Greco-Antiochene rites began to replace the original Mesopotamian liturgical tradition preserved by the non-Chalcedonians of Persia. In their commentaries on Baptism and the Eucharist, the West Syrians followed the style and method of the mystagogical works of the Greek Fathers, which was probably accepted as more convenient for instruction both in the parishes and in the monastic schools.

The first known West Syrian mystagogical treatise is a short commentary on Baptism and the Eucharist, attributed in the two oldest manuscripts to Saint John Chrysostom.[20] In a tenth-century manuscript, an expanded version of this work has been attributed to 'Dionysius'. This attribution has been known to Moses Bar Kepha and Dionysius Bar Salibi, who assumed that the author was 'Pseudo-Dionysius the Areopagite'.[21] However, the author(s) had compiled from different sources. The importance of this commentary is that it helped to establish an exegetical tradition and to popularize a method of liturgical interpretation that became an accepted part of the West Syrian tradition.

According to Dr Sebastian Brock, 'the commentary is likely to belong to the early fifth century (at the latest)'.[22] Although the kernel of the commentary could belong to the fifth or early sixth century, it was surely expanded in the course of its circulation. As we shall see, such expansion was normal practice among the West Syrians.

The 'fifth-century commentary' (as we shall refer to it henceforward) is most probably responsible for a tendency to break down the Eucharistic mystery into a series of rites that are commented upon as if they were independent elements. This was in fact a hitherto unknown method in the West Syrian tradition. The work shows no interest in biblical typology, traditionally followed by the early Syriac writers. The document or its core might have originated in a milieu that was influenced by the Antiochene tradition. Thus it follows a method similar to that found in the homilies of Theodore of Mopsuestia. Rites, prayers and liturgical objects are given an allegorical interpretation proper to the Antiochene method of liturgical exegesis. We shall quote a few examples:[23]

> The hearing of the Scriptures and their understanding is like bread and water by which everyone is nourished.
> The washing of the priest teaches the catechumens to wash their minds of all cares.
> The Peace, which the faithful give one another, removes and quenches enmity between them.

---

[20] Text published by Patriarch Ignatius Ephrem Rahmani, *I Fasti della Chiesa Patriarcale Antiochena*, Rome, 1920, pp. x–xiii. Critical edition with English translation: S. Brock, 'Some Early Syriac Baptismal Commentaries', *OCP* 46 (1980), 20–61; idem, 'An Early Syriac Commentary on the Liturgy', *JTS*, n.s. 37 (1986), 387–403 (hereafter: Brock, 'Commentary').

[21] Brock, 'Commentary', 396.

[22] Dr Brock has suggested this date on the basis of the absence of the post-baptismal anointing. But post-baptismal anointing is still absent in the writings of Philoxenos of Mabbug (d. 523) and Jacob of Serugh (d. 521). Cf. Varghese, *Les Onctions*, pp. 137–46, 162–69.

[23] Brock, 'Commentary', 391–92.

The Altar is the place of Christ's sepulchre.
The Veil above the cup and paten [is] a sign of the stone, which was placed above the sepulchre of our Saviour.
The curtains or coverings are a likeness of this firmament between us and that heavenly region.

There are passages reminiscent of Theodore's homily.[24] Thus the Eucharist is presented as a memorial of the passion and death ('offering') and resurrection of Christ:

(The Priest is) the likeness of the soul of our Saviour which made an offering before its Maker and was raised up.
The deacon is the likeness of the angels who appeared at the head and foot of Jesus Christ our Saviour.
Their bending down to the ground is a likeness of those guards.[25]

At least two passages recall the phrases of Pseudo-Dionysius. If they carry any traces of influence of the *Ecclesiastical Hierarchy* on the original redaction, we can credibly argue for a fifth-century origin.[26]

5. George, Bishop of the Arab Tribes

Two important liturgical commentaries have been attributed to Bishop George (d. 724). The first one, '*Memra* on the Consecration of Myron', is a twelve-syllable metrical homily that has not yet received proper scholarly attention.[27] George might have composed it to be sung during the consecration of Myron. The method and style are similar to those of Ephrem and Jacob of Serugh, and the author follows the traditional typological method of liturgical interpretation. George's *memra* is perhaps the last major commentary of this genre. In their treatises on Myron, the West Syrian Fathers always pointed out that the Myron and its consecration were prefigured in the Old Testament types. George also repeats this traditional argument:

The fathers and the righteous, the just and the saints,
Behold, the ancients have indicated the type of the anointing.
The doctors were delighted by it, as well as the just of the former (days).
It was veiled and hidden, arranged and placed in the prophecy.
The oil perfected the kings and the priests, according to the Law.
[And] it had sent good news to Noah the just, to the ark,
When it indicated: 'It is through the oil that your salvation has been granted'.
The mystery of the anointing seethed in the olive branch,
And he plucked and gave a leaf to carry to the just.

---

24 Theodore, *Commentary* (ed. Mingana), pp. 79–84 (ch.5).

25 Brock, 'Commentary', 391–92 (= R.27, 28, 31).

26 Ibid., p. 392 (R.33–34).

27 Syriac text: V. Ryssel (ed.), *Poemi Siriaci di Giorgio vescovo degli Arabi*, Atti della Accademia dei Lincei IV-9, Rome, 1892, pp. 46–80 (= Ryssel +line).

Christ and the oil were represented there mysteriously,
[And also] the Spirit of love, a news of mercy and salvation.[28]

Myron is consecrated on Thursday, the fifth day of Holy Week. For George, this is because the five senses of Adam were corrupted by his Fall. His symbolic interpretation of the number five very well illustrates his exegetical method:

As his five senses were destroyed by vanity,
On the fifth day, he destroyed them in a five-fold way.
And therefore Moses wrote five books,
So that through five, the five (senses) may win victory, and he perfected them.
After five generations, Israel returned from Egypt,
As his five senses were immersed in pleasures.
Five talents, as the mystery of the perfection of the five senses,
The lord gave to the good servant who traded.
He purified and cleansed the senses of the soul and the senses of the body.
And gladly, he entered into the joy of his master and became heir.
And through the virgins, our Lord depicted the chamber of light.
He found the five, lighting their lamps.
Therefore the Holy Church celebrates a feast today,
So that all the mysteries may be wisely gathered to her.[29]

The second work attributed to Bishop George is *An Exposition of the Mysteries of the Church*,[30] in which the author had incorporated many of the materials from the fifth-century anonymous commentary. Thus the style and method of the two commentaries known under the name of George are different. The question of the authenticity of their attribution to George is beyond the scope of this book. *The Exposition of the Mysteries* might be a treatise destined for the instruction of the clergy. However, George's *Exposition* was an influential document in the history of West Syrian liturgical commentaries.

George seems to have taken the fifth-century commentary as the basis for his work, and expanded the original text incorporating his own comments and materials derived from other patristic sources, especially the *Ecclesiastical Hierarchy* of Pseudo-Dionysius the Areopagite. He included several Alexandrian interpretations, as developed by Dionysius. For Dionysius, the contemplation (*theoria*) of the liturgical rites leads the soul to the spiritual, mystical realities of the invisible world: 'The sensible rites are the image of intelligible realities. They lead there, and show the way to them'.[31] In the Dionysian system, 'liturgy is an allegory of the soul's progress from the divisiveness of sin to the divine communion, through a process of purification,

---

28 Ibid., pp. 228–39.

29 Ibid., pp. 191–204.

30 Syriac text and English translation: R.H. Connolly and H.W. Codrington, *Two Commentaries on the Jacobite Liturgy*, London, 1913. Eng. tr., pp. 11–23.

31 Cf. *Ecclesiastical Hierarchy*, II, iii, 2 397 C.C. Luibheid, *Pseudo-Dionysius. The Complete Works* (New York, 1987), p. 205.

illumination, perfection imaged forth in the rites'.[32] This vision of the mystery of liturgy is reflected in a number of passages in George's *Exposition*:[33]

> The service of the Psalm before the mysteries, which is rendered with one chant, shows the one will of the whole congregation of the Church, and [their] union with God.
> The censer, which the deacon takes about the whole nave, signifies the care of God for all, and the condescension and sweet savour of Christ. The return again of the censer to the sanctuary signifies the fixedness and unwaveringness of the divine care, which remains as it is, without diminution: even as a lamp, which is not diminished by taking from it of many lights.
> The peace which the faithful give to one another puts away and quenches former enmity and wrath, and brings about peace and quietness, and love of one with another, and reconciliation with God and with the holy angels.
> The veil which is over the mysteries signifies the secretness and invisibleness of the power that is hidden in the mysteries. That it is removed by the deacons, signifies the coming down and manifestation of Christ to each one according to as he is worthy.
> The veils, or curtains of the sanctuary are a symbol of the screen which is between us and the hiddenness of the heavenly place.
> The dividing of the holy mysteries to the faithful signifies the gathering together of the faithful themselves, and their union with one another and with Christ, even as the prophet said concerning Him: 'I will divide Him among many; and to many He shall divide the inheritance (cf. Is. 53:12)': which is the bestowal of forgiveness of sins.
> The reception of the mysteries brings about for us a union with God the Word, the Son of God.

Unlike his *memra* on Myron, in his *Exposition of the Mysteries*, George does not use any typology. Following the method of the fifth-century commentary, he uses the Antiochene allegorical interpretation as well. Thus he says that the mixing of wine and water symbolizes 'the life-giving blood and water which flowed from the side of Christ'.

> The bending of the knee is a sign of our fall through the transgression of Adam. Our rising up from the genuflection is a sign of our redemption through the resurrection of our Lord. (30)

George's contemporary, Jacob of Edessa (+708), also followed the methodology of the fifth-century commentary. Though Jacob's literary works could precede those of George, we have considered George first because his *Exposition* is closer to the fifth-century document in its style.

---

[32] Taft, 'Liturgy of the Great Church', p. 61.
[33] Connolly, *Two Commentaries*, pp. 15–16.

6. Liturgical Commentaries of Jacob of Edessa

Jacob of Edessa (*c.* 633–708), who gave a definite structure to the Syrian Orthodox liturgy, has probably authored at least two works which belong to the category of 'liturgical commentaries': (1) 'Discourse on the Myron'[34] and (2) 'Commentary on *qurobo* addressed to George the Stylite of Serugh'.[35] The styles of the works are different. The 'Discourse on the Myron', in which the author uses a large number of Old Testament types, was probably a sermon delivered during the consecration of the Myron.[36] The 'Commentary on the *qurobo*' in its present form might be a summary of Jacob's larger work, which seems to have been lost. Different redactions of the commentary (or its summary) were widely circulated, often with interpolations. The texts published by Assemani (taken from Bar Salibi's Commentary), Patriarch Rahmani, as well as the text found in a British Library manuscript (Add.14496) are probably portions of a larger commentary by Jacob.[37] The Commentary addressed to George the Stylite, as it is found in the Berlin manuscript, consists of three parts: (i) commentary on liturgical objects, sanctuary, liturgical dress, and the role of presbyter and deacon; (ii) on the number of crosses made in the celebration of the Eucharist; (iii) a short commentary on the prayers of the Eucharist, ending with that on the Lord's Prayer.[38]

In the first part, the author has incorporated materials drawn from the fifth-century commentary. The methodology of this part was inspired by the Antiochene tradition. Thus, 'Sanctuary (*Madbeha*) symbolizes Heaven; and the children of the whole Church is the type of the whole creation'; 'The Antimension (*tablito*) is the type of the cross of our Lord; the fans are the symbol of six-winged Seraphim'; the cope (*paino*) of the presbyter 'symbolizes the cloak of the Prophet Elijah as well as the covering of the celestial powers'; 'The censor indicates Christ and the fire in it symbolizes His divinity'. At least one passage of the first part would suggest the influence of Pseudo-Dionysius. Thus he has incorporated a paragraph entitled 'The order of the nine hosts':

> The order of the celestial armies above in the heavens, has been established and ordered in three Churches. Similarly, Our Lord and His disciples have ordered three orders in the earthly Church. They are the symbol of the exalted armies.[39]

The comments on the censer were certainly added later, as the censer with chains was introduced in the West Syrian Church much later (probably after the Crusades). However, the text provides a good example to enable us to understand how the later

---

[34] Syriac text and English translation: S. Brock, 'Jacob of Edessa's Discourse on the Myron', *OC* 63 (1979), 20–36.

[35] Unpublished manuscript, Berlin Sachau 218, fol.178v–186v (English translation forthcoming).

[36] Varghese, *Les Onctions*, pp. 186–99.

[37] J.S. Assemani, *Bibliotheca Orientalis* I, 479–88; Eng. tr. in F.E. Brightman, *Liturgies Eastern and Western* (Oxford, 1896), pp. 490–94; Rahmani, *I Fasti*, pp. xix–xxv; BM Add.14496, fol.1v–3v.

[38] These three parts are found in different orders in Rahmani, Assemani and in BM Add.14496.

[39] Berlin Sachau 218, fol.179r.

Syriac writers introduced new interpretations into the ancient works and presented them as the original version. We shall quote the text:

> The incense: It symbolises the humanity; the lower part of the censer symbolises the earth, and its upper [lid] symbolises the heaven. Its three chains are the symbol and type of the Holy Trinity. The incense is brought to the nave symbolising Christ who descended from heaven and [similarly] the deacon goes around. The priest takes the incense and goes around the whole church, symbolising God who descended and went around the world, and perfumed the whole creation with the teaching of the Gospel and again ascended towards His Father.[40]

The first part of Jacob's commentary was obviously known to Moses Bar Kepha (perhaps in a different redaction). In fact Bar Kepha incorporated Jacob's interpretation of the *semantron* (= sounding board) and incense into his commentary without mentioning the source.[41]

The second part of the commentary addressed to the Stylite George is a rubric concerning the number of crosses to be signed during the Eucharist. This document, probably part of Jacob's larger commentary, had been widely circulated either independently or as part of the later commentaries on the Eucharist.[42]

The third part, entitled 'Beginning of the *qurobo*' is a short commentary on the prayers of the Eucharist from the initial *Gloria Patri* to the *Sancta Sanctis* and the Lord's Prayer. This might be a summary of a larger commentary. However, it gives an allegorical interpretation of the liturgical texts. The commentary was surely used by Bar Kepha, and its methodology has influenced him. Let us quote a few texts:

> Beginning of the *qurobo*: Then in the beginning the priest begins [saying]: *Glory to the Father, to the Son and to the Holy Spirit*,[43] symbolising the unity of the One nature and essence of the Trinity, showing that it is indivisibly separated and unconfusedly united. Now it is said of the Son, who in the time of His Economy and eternally is God.
>
> The peace which is given, fulfills the Word of Our Lord: *Leave your offering on the altar and reconcile with your brother* (Matt. 5:23–24). Similarly the spiritual beings are assembled here and they give peace with us, for peace was established between them and us by the death of the Lord.
>
> And the *Love of God the Father* shows the love in which God gave His Son for us, as said Paul. *The grace of the only-begotten Son* shows that because of the grace towards each man, He tasted death. *And the communion of the Holy Spirit* [shows that] the sacrifice is accomplished by the communion of the Holy Spirit. The priest says these three *shall be with you all*, and they answer *with you also*, as said Gregorios the Great: 'it is this peace that the priest receives'.

---

40 Ibid., fol.180r. Cf. Brock, 'Commentary', 393 (=D.34–35).

41 Connolly, *Two Commentaries*, pp. 25–26, 37.

42 Cf. Bar Kepha's Commentary on the Eucharist, in Connolly, *Two Commentaries*, pp. 70–71; B. Varghese (tr.), *Dionysius Bar Salibi: Commentary on the Eucharist* (Kottayam, 1998), 3:1; 4:1 (= text of Assemani and Brightman. See above, note 37.

43 The initial *Gloria Patri* disappeared by the ninth century.

And again he adds: *Let your minds be above*, [meaning] that let you minds dwell upon heavenly things (cf. Col. 3:1) and be purified from earthly things.

A similar allegorical explanation is found among the East Syrians since the time of Gabriel Qatraya Bar Lipah (sixth–seventh century).[44] In the third part, Jacob makes practically no typological interpretation. Though he followed the typological method in his homily on Myron, for the liturgical objects and on the role of the clergy, he preferred a modest allegorical interpretation, as developed by the Antiochenes. His interest in developing the doctrinal meaning of the prayers is reminiscent of the method of Theodore of Mopsuestia. As in the Mystagogical Catecheses of Cyril of Jerusalem, Jacob comments on the liturgical texts and Moses Bar Kepha has followed this method.

7. Commentaries of Moses Bar Kepha

The commentaries of Moses Bar Kepha (d. 903) on Baptism, the Eucharist and the Consecration of Myron represent a landmark in the history of the West Syrian mystagogical tradition. His commentary on the Eucharist is the first full-scale work of this genre. Bar Kepha had used the works of his predecessors, namely the fifth-century anonymous commentary (which he quotes under the name of 'Saint John'), the commentaries of Jacob of Edessa, Bishop George, and the Syriac version of the *Ecclesiastical Hierarchy* as well as a document entitled *The Breaking of the Bread*,[45] on which very little information is available. Bar Kepha's work, in spite of his free use of the previous commentaries, is a perfect blend of the Antiochene and the Alexandrine mystagogies. However, with a clear preference for the traditional Antiochene tradition of liturgical interpretation, he freely reproduced the sources, often combining materials of various provenances with his own modest comments. He comments on the whole of the anaphora, from the reading of the scripture to the concluding prayer. Though he describes carefully the symbolism of the liturgical objects and rites, he gives particular attention to the prayers of the anaphora, a method already attested in the homilies of Theodore of Mopsuestia. Bar Kepha points out the doctrinal content of the liturgical texts and rites.

Following the Antiochene mystagogical tradition, Bar Kepha is interested in explaining the historical origin of certain prayers and rites. Then he comments on the goal of the prayer and its doctrinal importance and finally gives the spiritual meaning, as was customary in the Alexandrian mystagogy. His interpretation of the Trisagion is the best example of his methodology:

---

[44] Gabriel Qatraya Bar Lipah, *Interpretation of the Offices*, in *Theodore of Mopsuestia, Narsai, Gabriel Qatraya Bar Lipah: Homilies and Interpretation of the Holy Qurbana*, Changanachery, 1977.

[45] On this document, see R.H. Connolly, 'The Book of Life', *JTS* 13 (1912), 580–94.

> It is right that we make these enquiries concerning *Holy art Thou, God.*
> First: who taught us to say it? Secondly: why we say it. Thirdly: to which of the
> Persons of the Trinity it is addressed. Fourthly: what we signify by saying *Holy
> art Thou, God.*[46]

The influence of Antiochene mystagogical tradition is reflected in his comments on
the procession:

> That the mysteries go forth from the altar, and go about the nave in seemly order,
> and return to the altar, makes known that God the Word came down and was
> made man, and went about in the world and fulfilled the dispensation for us, and
> then ascended the cross, and afterwards ascended to His Father.[47]

Since the time of Moses Bar Kepha, we find a tendency among the commentators to
give directives concerning 'correct liturgical practices'. Thus Bar Kepha asks the
clergy to abandon certain practices or to correct certain prayers that he considered as
'wrong or unnecessary'. In the ninth century, during the epiclesis, some Syrian
Orthodox clergy struck their hands upon their foreheads. John of Dara refers to it as a
normal custom.[48] This custom seems to have been so widespread that Bar Kepha had
to use rather strong words to censure it:

> Now many uninstructed priests here strike their hands upon their foreheads, not
> knowing that this has here no sort of appropriateness – unless it be perhaps that
> they are sorry for what they have done! Now it is not right for the priest to strike
> his hand upon his forehead, because the gifts of the Spirit are given in silence and
> not with noises. Secondly, again: because God the Word came down silently and
> quietly upon Mary, and was incarnate of her, and not with noises and disturbances.
> And so here also does He come down and unite Himself hypostatically to the
> bread and wine that are on the altar.[49]

Commentaries served as a means to introduce uniform prayers and rites. Thus Bar
Kepha asks the clergy who read his commentary to introduce a major change in the
anaphora: if the prayers of the anaphora, except the final thanksgiving prayer, are not
addressed to the Father, they should be corrected.[50] Similarly he gives important
directions concerning the breaking of the bread during the institution, and the fraction.[51]

Bar Kepha, like most of the West Syrian commentators, do not place any special
emphasis on the meaning of communion and its significance in the spiritual life. They
have almost never pointed to the participation in the body and blood of Christ as the

---

[46] Connolly, *Two Commentaries*, p. 26.

[47] Ibid., p. 43; cf. Theodore, Homily on the Eucharist, ch.5, in Mingana, pp. 85–86.

[48] B. Varghese (tr.), *John of Dara. Commentary on the Eucharist* (Kottayam, 1999), ch.4:14, p. 80.

[49] Connolly, *Two Commentaries*, pp. 61–62.

[50] Ibid., pp. 89–90.

[51] Cf. the directives on the breaking of the bread at the institution: ibid., p. 53; fraction: ibid., pp. 68–69.

climax and the goal of the Eucharistic celebration. For Bar Kepha, the Eucharist is a series of rites, each having its own symbolism, often independent of others. In his comments on the communion, he is more concerned with giving the symbolism of the cloths, with which the mysteries are covered, and the removal of the cover. Then he goes on to give the reason why the celebrant receives communion first. Regarding the meaning of communion, Bar Kepha simply repeats the brief comments of Bishop George (who in turn used the fifth-century commentary), adding nothing of his own.[52]

Bar Kepha shows an interest in the explanation of liturgical vocabulary, a tendency already found in Theodore.[53] Thus the commentary of Bar Kepha on the Eucharist begins with the explanation of six 'names' of the Eucharist: Assembly, Communion, Access, Oblation, Mysteries (*roze*) and Perfection of Perfections. His comments on these terms bring out various nuances of the meaning of the Eucharist. Similarly, in his commentary on Baptism, he comments on 'baptism, illumination and regeneration', the three 'names' of Baptism. With the consistency of the method and the originality of the ideas and the presentation, Moses Bar Kepha can be considered as one of the best 'liturgical theologians' on the Syrian Orthodox tradition.

The explanation of Bar Kepha became quasi-official or at least the most commonly accepted interpretation in the Syrian Orthodox tradition. Thus Dionysius Bar Salibi has reproduced almost entirely the work of Bar Kepha, and it served as one of the main sources for the *Book of Treasures* by Jacob Bar Shakko (+1241), and the *Light of the Sanctuary* by Bar Hebraeus (+1286).

8. Commentary Attributed to John of Dara

A commentary on the Eucharist has been attributed to John, Bishop of Dara (d. *c*. 825).[54] If the attribution is correct, the work must be anterior to the commentary of Moses Bar Kepha. But we have discussed the work of Bar Kepha earlier, because it belongs to a series of commentaries having the same style and mode of approach, and the culmination of a method of interpretation developed by the West Syrians. But the commentary of John of Dara is different in its style and methodology. Unlike Bar Kepha, John does not comment on the rites in the order in which they appear in the liturgy. In the work of John we can find for the first time an attempt to follow a rather

---

52 Ibid., pp. 87–88.

53 Connolly, *Two Commentaries*, pp. 24–25; Bar Kepha, *Commentary on Baptism*; K.A. Aytoun, 'The Mystery of Baptism by Moses Bar Kepha, compared with the Odes of Solomon', in Jacob Vellian (ed.), *Studies in Syrian Baptismal Rites*, Syrian Church Series 6 (Kottayam, 1973), pp. 1–15 (see p. 7). See Theodore, *Homily on Eucharist* (ed. Mingana), p. 95.

54 Text edited with French translation: Jean Sader, *Le 'De Oblatione' de Jean de Dara*, CSCO 308–309; SS 132–33, Louvain, 1970. English translation by B. Varghese (above, note 48). See also the important study by J. Sader, *Le lieu de culte et la messe syro-occidentale selon le 'De Oblatione' de Jean de Dara. Etude d'archéologie et de liturgie*, OCA 223, Rome, 1983.

Alexandrian method of interpretation as developed by Pseudo-Dionysius the Areopagite. Unlike Dionysius, John comments on the architecture, liturgical objects as well as the liturgical texts.

In his introduction, John presents the Eucharist as a sacrifice, an idea that was not so central in the early West Syrian commentaries. His concerns were also different from those of his predecessors. In the first chapter, in which he deals with the functions of the presbyters and deacons, his main interest was to insist that before entering the sanctuary, they should be ritually pure with strict sexual abstinence. This was in fact a concern of some of the canonical sources. None of the earlier commentators had discussed this problem.

Chapter two is on the symbolism of the liturgical objects and the church architecture. In a rather long paragraph on the 'napkin', John insists that it should be of linen or silk, and not of wool. He gives a long explanation on silk and the 'worm' that produces it. For John, the worm symbolizes Christ and he gives an allegorical interpretation that recalls early Syriac exegesis:

> That there shall be no napkin of wool on the table: when man had sinned, his vestment was a tunic, in which there was wool; that means, after having committed sin, man resembled wool, that is, he was disposed to be coloured with all [sorts of] faults and be corrupted by the shameful passions and be defiled like wool, that is by death, so that his sin shall be known by the separation of the soul and the body and thus completely be effaced from man.
>
> [The reason] that a napkin of silk shall be on the table of the sanctuary is again the same: the silk is by its nature not corrupted, and it lasts for long time. The silk is from the worm, so far as, when the worm produces silk, it has to die. Thus the spiritual worm, which is the body of God the Word, when it produced the silk – that is, the souls of the holy fathers from the dark depths of Sheol – for before the salvific cross, all the souls of the fathers were placed in the darkness – when God the Word came, who is called 'worm' by the prophet David (cf. Ps. 22:6), he brought them out of dejection in which they were placed. This is clearly known from the book of Gospels, which says: 'Many bodies of the saints were raised and they entered Jerusalem' (Matt. 27:52). And as the worm dies when it produces this material, so when He brought out the dejected from their darkness, God died, so that by His death, He could deliver all the mortals from the corruptive death, whose concern was to corrupt the souls.[55]

John's interest in allegory is evident from his interpretation of the Church:

> The holy of holies shows the Church of the Seraphims, Cherubims and the Thrones; the *qestromo*, the Church of the Lordships, Dominions and the Powers; the nave, the Church of the principalities and the Archangels and the court of the Holy Church. This is because, all which were in the Law of Moses are in the Holy Church, which are established so that their arrangement shall be triple. But also because, it has three gifts, namely perfection, illumination and purity. The perfection by its perfect creation, that is by the image and by the gifts of the Holy

---

55 Varghese, *John of Dara*, II:10, pp.36–37.

Spirit; and by illumination, that is by privation of ignorance, because it existed entirely in the divine knowledge. And by purity, that is by holy baptism, she was purified from all sins, defilements and wounds. Again when man sinned, he sinned in a triple [way]: by the soul, by the body and by the mind. But when God came, he saved him in a triple [way]: that is, by the mind, [soul and the body . . .]. That is why the Church is arranged in three parts: since the Church is for man and man was triply saved, it is meet that there should be three parts in the church also.[56]

Inspired by the methodology of Pseudo-Dionysius, John considers liturgical objects and rites as manifestations of spiritual realities, and he gives an allegorical interpretation to each of them:

The table of the sanctuary is of wood . . . indicating mystically that as the wood is destroyed by fire, the body of the Word offered on it shall destroy all sins and lawlessness incurred by the true faithful of the Church.[57]

That the *tablito* should be covered with a veil, symbolises the veil Moses put over his face, because he became shining by the gifts of the Holy Spirit and the sons of Israel could not look at him, for they did not have the holiness and chastity of Moses to look at his face . . . The veil spread over the *tablito* also shows the veil put over the holes pierced in the hands, feet and the opening of the side of our Lord Jesus Christ. Similarly over the celestial armies also secrecy and covering was imposed, so that they should not see the passions that God took upon Him.[58]

That the paten and the chalice should be placed on the veil, above the *tablito* symbolizes the superior essences and the celestial powers by whom God is sanctified and glorified.[59]

The anaphora over the mysteries symbolises the types and shadows placed from the old over the economy of God, which were to function for the salvation of men. Again, the anaphora indicates the word of the divine prophet David: *He made darkness His covering and it has surrounded His tent* (Ps. 18:11). *Darkness His covering* is the ignorance of all, [by which] none of His creatures knows what is the composition of God the Word, that is of the divinity with the humanity.[60]

For Dionysius and John of Dara, the divine mystery is revealed and communicated to us in and through symbols. Thus every liturgical object serves as a means of revelation, which helps us to perceive the depth of the mystery. Sometimes the allegorical interpretation becomes artificial and arbitrary. Thus an interesting explanation has been given to the symbolism of the spoon:

Why is a spoon placed on the mystical table? The spoon symbolises the Holy Spirit, through whom we receive the body of God the Word. The spoon symbolises also the nature of the holy angels, who are the first to know the hiddenness and the protection of God. The spoon again symbolises the hand of God which took the dust and formed and made man.[61]

---

56 Ibid., II:3, p. 30.
57 Ibid., II:7, p. 33.
58 Ibid., II:11, p. 38.
59 Ibid., II:12, p. 39.
60 Ibid., II:15, pp. 40–41.
61 Ibid., II:28, p. 51.

Similarly the 'purificator' (*mkaprono*) used for washing the fingertips of the celebrant is the symbol of the 'womb of the holy virgin'. The sponge used for wiping the fingers is the symbol of 'the holy body of the Church, which absorbs the spiritual waters upon which the Holy Spirit descends', or of 'the bodies, which are deprived of God.'[62]

Such fanciful interpretations were sometimes adopted by the West Syrian commentators after the thirteenth century. The most striking example is the explanation given to the transfer of the sponge and the spoon from the left side of the paten and chalice to the right. In fact, here the priest wipes his fingers on the sponge, takes it, kisses and places it on his right side. But several commentators of the modern period, without understanding the real motif of the act, have interpreted it as a symbol of the second coming of Christ in a flash.[63]

The commentary of John of Dara is perhaps the most original one written by a West Syrian author of the Abbasid period. The methodology, though inspired by Dionysius, is consistent and well thought out. His ideas were perhaps too abstract, and his style was probably unfamiliar to the West Syrians of the Abbasid period. This might be why his commentary did not get much attention. The West Syrians seem to have preferred the unsophisticated and direct style of Moses Bar Kepha, which was in continuity with a tradition of liturgical interpretation, developed in Antioch in the fourth century. Thus, in the twelfth century, Dionysius Bar Salibi faithfully continued the same tradition in his commentary, which he claims to have written on the basis of the 'works of the ancients'.[64]

The following exegetical methods seem to have been influential in shaping West Syrian mystagogical tradition: (i) the early Syriac exegetical method followed by Aphrahat and Saint Ephrem, which was developed in a milieu having close contact with the Jewish rabbinical traditions; (ii) the Antiochene tradition as found in the works of Saint John Chrysostom and Theodore of Mopsuestia; (iii) the Alexandrian method of liturgical interpretation as developed by Pseudo-Dionysius the Areopagite.

We can discern six stages in the development of the West Syrian tradition of liturgical interpretation.

1   An early stage of catechetical homilies (for example Severus of Antioch), which was in continuity with the Antiochene catechetical tradition. By the middle of the sixth century, this tradition seems to have been extinct, as the Syrian Orthodox Church was struggling for survival in a Chalcedonian Byzantine Empire and in a Sassanid Persia where organized conversions were virtually impossible.

2   An early stage of metrical homilies (*memre*) in continuity with the early Syriac tradition, also extinct by the beginning of the eighth century. George, Bishop of the Arabs, was probably one of the last mystagogues to follow this style. However,

---

62 Ibid., II:27, p. 50.

63 Cf. Mathews Mar Barnabas, *A Devotional Study of the Holy Qurbana*, New York, 1999, p. 96.

64 Bar Salibi, *Commentary on the Eucharist*, 1:1, p. 2.

the prose homilies (*turgome*), also inherited from the early Syriac tradition, continued to be used as a model down the centuries, and they have played a decisive role in the development of *sedre*.

3   A period of short commentaries which follow the Antiochene methodology, blended with modest Alexandrian allegorical explanations.

4   A final synthesis in the ninth century largely determined by the Antiochene tradition with some sympathy towards the Alexandrian allegory (for example Moses Bar Kepha).

5   A ninth-century attempt by John of Dara to use the method of Dionysius, which did not gain ground.

6   A period of fanciful allegorical explanations that arose during the decadence of the Syrian Orthodox Church after the thirteenth century.

The Syrian Orthodox commentators, with the exception of John of Dara, tried to maintain continuity with the Antiochene tradition by using the same method, schema, themes and terminology. As to the terminology, we find a few words constantly repeated: 'represent', 'signify', 'symbolize', 'typify', 'symbol' (*rozo*), 'type' (*tupso*), or 'sign' (*oto*). Obviously Saint Ephrem and Moses Bar Kepha or Bar Salibi did not use these words in the same sense. However, the word *rozo* (mystery or symbol) needs careful study, for it is at the centre of the West Syrian liturgical theology and a key to understanding it.

There are similarities in the approach of various commentators. They are not concerned with questions such as: 'What happens to the elements?' or 'How and when does it happen?' For them a liturgical celebration contains a *rozo*, a meaning, for it manifests the presence of God and offers a foretaste of 'things to come'. The symbols, which are an integral part of the celebration, provide a vision, a manifestation. Each symbol represents, indicates, stands for or stands in the place of something. The epiphany of the 'events that took place, and that will take place' (Theodore) takes place in space and time, veiled by symbols.

It is significant that the ancient Church maintained continuity between biblical and liturgical interpretation. This means that the Church understood its prayers and liturgical rites as expressions of the Word of God. In the East, especially in the Syriac tradition, prayers and hymns were primarily of biblical inspiration. Liturgical celebration was understood as a revelation, the 'showing forth' of the Word of God addressed to man. In the Old Testament, *dabar*, the Word of God, is a *parole* as well as an *act*, which contained a meaning, a life-giving message addressed to man inviting him to live in communion with God. Similarly, liturgy is a *word*, a life-giving message, a revelation, an invitation addressed to the world to live in communion with God in Christ.

The use of allegorical and typological interpretations cannot be simply discarded as 'pre-scientific' or as 'irrelevant for today'. What appears to be 'outdated' according to the norms prescribed by post-Enlightenment rationalism was an effective means to preserve the 'liturgicalness' of the West Syrians for several centuries, especially during their most difficult times. The allegorical and typological interpretations have left a quasi-permanent mark on Eastern liturgical theology. First, they have followed a method that was widely accepted for biblical exegesis. Second, they presuppose that liturgy is a 'revelation' of saving truths, which needs exposition. Liturgy is understood as a celebration, a showing forth of the 'mystery' of the Church's faith. It offers a glimpse of the meaning of everything in relation to the Word of God or its interpretation. The use of symbols and gestures is an 'allegorization', a visible and tangible expression of the liturgicalness. Allegory or typology serves as a language to communicate depth of meaning. In a sense it is a 'sacramental' language, indicating the limits of our rationality.

This does not mean that liturgical theology can still make use of this method. Allegorical interpretation has a danger, for it often focuses attention on the accessories, instead of the essential meaning of the liturgy. Thus often the meaning of individual rites and elements has been given undue emphasis at the expense of the meaning of the celebration as a whole. This leads to a risk of the compartmentalization of the *leitourgia*. Liturgy has often been seen as a series of rites, gestures or an 'array' of symbols, each of which has a meaning in itself, independent of others.

To a certain extent a similar risk is implied in some of our modern approaches to liturgical theology. A few elements have been singled out and discussed, independent of the Church's *lex orandi*. The discussions on liturgical presidency, or on the communication aspect of liturgy, are examples of such compartmentalization.

CHAPTER 3

Liturgical Vocabulary

The use of specific liturgical terms implies a standardization of some of the fundamental ideas. For example, words such as *leitourgia, sacrifice, sacrament, celebration, offering*, and *Eucharist* denote some of the fundamental meanings of the Christian liturgy. Translation of a word into another language cannot always bring out the shades of meaning of the original. The best example is the Aramaic word *raz* (Syriac *rozo*), which has been rendered into Greek as *mysterion* or into Latin as *sacramentum*. Though *mysterion* is the nearest equivalent of *rozo*, it does not convey some of the basic nuances of Aramaic. Similarly in the case of modern languages, the German *Gottesdienst* is closer to the meaning of Greek *leitourgia*. But *worship* in English or *culte* in French do not convey the meaning of the original. Classical languages have preserved a tradition of thought which is often difficult to render in modern European languages without the risk of the loss or distortion of meaning.[1]

Each liturgical term deserves to be studied in detail, for every word contains a past, bears within it the history and the tradition of the Church. Each term reflects the mind of the praying community, with all its nuances.

Unlike the Byzantines and the Latins, the Syrians have no technical term with an exclusive meaning (similar to *leitourgia*) to denote the liturgical phenomenon. The Syrians use a variety of terms to refer to the liturgical celebrations or to their constituent parts. Most of the Syriac liturgical terms have been borrowed from the Syriac versions of the Bible, especially from the Peshitta. Thus the terms reflect more or less faithfully the meaning of the original Hebrew or Greek. A brief survey of the most commonly used words can illustrate the nuances implied in the Syriac understanding of liturgy. Each word adds shades of meaning that complement each other.

1. *Rozo*

In the liturgical context the word *rozo* has usually been translated as 'mystery', 'sacrament', or less often as 'symbol'. In fact, the word *rozo* or its root *raz* is used in a variety of senses in the Syriac liturgical texts and the commentaries, reflecting various aspects of the liturgical phenomenon.

The word *raz* is a Persian loan word in the Aramaic and Hebrew and appeared first in apocalyptic texts.[2] In the Old Testament, *raz* first appears in the Aramaic of Daniel (early second century BC), where it was used to designate the secret meaning of a

---

[1] See Paul Imbs, 'Du langage humain à la parole de Dieu', *LMD* 53 (1958), 9–22.

[2] See Raymond E. Brown, *The Semitic Background of the Term 'Mystery' in the New Testament*, Facet Book, Biblical Studies-2 (Philadelphia, 1968), p. 6.

dream that God reveals to Daniel (2:7–18; 27–30; 4:6). Here it has a sense of eschatological mystery, 'a veiled announcement of future events, predetermined by God, whose unveiling and real meaning are reserved to God alone and the one inspired by his spirit'.[3] The meaning of *raz* is very close to that of Hebrew *sod*, which means 'heavenly assembly', where decisions and decrees concerning the destiny of man are made. Prophets were admitted to this secret heavenly assembly to hear its decrees. Thus *sod* conveys the notion of intimate friendship.[4]

In the Qumran texts, the word designates the plans or decisions of God concerning the eschatological age, both salvation and judgement.[5] In the Wisdom of Solomon (2:22), the expression 'mysteries of God' refers to the saving designs of God, an idea reflected in the New Testament. These ideas were influential in shaping the New Testament concept of mystery.

In the New Testament, the Greek word *mysterion* (*rozo* in Syriac) refers to the mystery of the Kingdom of God (Matt. 13:11; Mark 4:11; Luke 8:10). Saint Paul uses the word more than twenty times. However, three passages are representative: Rom. 16:25–26; Eph. 1:9–10 and Col. 1:26. In these texts the *mysterion* (or *rozo*) (used in the singular) refers to revelation, manifestation, making known, imparting a saying. The mystery consists of God's will revealed in Christ 'to unite all things in him, things in heaven and things on earth' (Eph. 1:9–10). This mystery was hidden for ages and generations, but now made manifest to his saints' (Col. 1:26).

The 'mystery' in the New Testament expresses the 'drama of human redemption', 'the drama of truth', to use the words of Clement of Alexandria.[6] This idea is fundamental to understanding the meaning of the Syriac word *rozo*.

Rozo *in Liturgical Use*

In its liturgical use, the word *rozo* (pl. *roze*) has a variety of meanings.[7] It can mean 'a secret, an agreement, a council, anything having a mystical meaning, a type, figure, sign, symbol or likeness'. In the liturgical context, more often it means 'a mystery, the Holy Eucharist, a sacrament, or a mystical (theological) signification'. Its root *raz* means 'to conspire, to be shown forth mystically', and the passive derivatives (*Ethpaal* and *Ethpeel* conjugations) mean 'to be instructed, to be initiated into mysteries or spiritual realities, to symbolize, to celebrate, to be shown forth (in a sacrament), to signify, to point to, or to narrate'. No other Syriac word seems to contain the various nuances of the liturgical phenomenon. It should be noted that *rozo* is never used in a limited sense, as in the case of the Latin word *sacramentum*.

---

3 Ibid., p. 8.

4 Ibid., pp. 2–6.

5 See Art. 'Mystery', in John L. Mckenzie, *Dictionary of the Bible* (Bangalore, 1998), pp. 595–98; here, p. 597.

6 See, Vaselin Kesich, *The First day of the New Creation: The Resurrection and Christian faith* (SVSP, New York, 1982), p. 43. It should be noted that the term *mysterion* is firmly linked with the Christian Kerugma and is never used by St Paul to refer to any cult either Hellenistic or Christian.

7 Cf. J. Payne Smith, *A Compendious Syriac Dictionary* (Oxford, 1979), pp. 26, 524, 536.

A. *Early use:* Odes of Solomon *and the Syriac* Acts of Judas Thomas

(a)   The earliest use of the word outside the Bible is attested in the *Odes of Solomon*, in which the following verse is placed on the lips of Christ (8:10):

> Keep my mystery (*tar roz*), you who are kept by it;
> Keep my faith, you who are kept by it.

This is the sole use of the word in the *Odes*. Probably the word refers to faith, if this verse can be taken as an example of poetic parallelism.[8]

(b)   In the liturgical sections of the Syriac *Acts of Judas Thomas*, the word is used ten times (eight times in the plural and twice in the singular). Christ is called 'revealer of the hidden mysteries'.[9] The Holy Spirit is 'the revealer of the hidden mysteries',[10] or 'the revealer of the mysteries of the chosen among the prophets',[11] or 'the revealer of the mysteries of the Exalted'.[12] The Father reveals 'the mystery/mysteries of His First Born (his Son) to the Prophets by the Spirit of Holiness'.[13] The apostle Thomas is called 'sharer in the holy mysteries of God (or sharer in the holy counsel of God: *bar rozaw*)'.[14]

The most significant use of the word *rozo* (for a theology of liturgy) is found in the *Song of Praise of Thomas*:

> To be praised are you, the Son of life, accomplishing the will of your Father, who have reconciled your creatures, so that they worship, in you, Him who sent you, and become partakers in your counsel (or partakers in your mysteries: *bnai rozaw*).[15]

Here the word *rozo* refers to God's plan for our salvation. Christ has reconciled us with God and made us the worshippers of God the Father, and we have become 'partakers in the divine counsel'. This would mean that worship introduces us into an intimate relationship with God, an idea already implied in the Hebrew word *sod* and the Aramaic *raz*.

Apparently, the *Acts of Judas Thomas* makes a distinction between the singular and the plural forms. The singular form *rozo* refers to the 'mystery of the Son' or to the 'mystery of the cross', that is, the mystery of the incarnation. The plural refers to the

---

8 A similar passage is found in the catechetical lectures of Cyril of Jerusalem: 'Guard the mystery for Him who gives the reward'. *Procatechesis*, 12 (*NPNF* VII, 4).

9 Prayer of the Apostle at the bridal chamber. W. Wright, *The Apocryphal Acts of the Apostles* (London, 1871; reprint Amsterdam, 1968): Vol.I (Syr.), p. 179; Vol.II (Eng.), p. 154 (= Wright, *AAA*).

10 Baptism of the King Gundaphorus: Wright, *AAA* I, p. 193; II, p. 166.

11 Baptism of a certain woman: Wright, *AAA* I, p. 218; II, p. 189.

12 Ibid.

13 The song of praise of Thomas: Wright, *AAA* I, pp. 280, 281; II, pp. 246, 247.

14 Wright, *AAA* I, p. 214; II, p. 185.

15 Wright, *AAA* I, p. 282; II, p. 250.

whole economy of salvation. In the later liturgical texts, this distinction has been more or less regularly kept.

(c) In the fourth century, especially in Aphrahat and Ephrem, *rozo* was used in a wider sense. Thus it was used for any religious symbol (especially Old Testament types), for the sacramental rites, and in the plural for the Eucharist.[16]

B. The liturgical commentaries   The commentary of Moses Bar Kepha (d. 903) on the Eucharist provides an example of the different senses in which *rozo* or *raz* has been used in later times.

> The Exposition of Moses Bar Kepha that is the Explanation of the mysteries (*roze*) of the oblation (*qurob qurbono*) . . . [It is called] 'Mysteries' (*roze*), because Christ delivered them secretly (*rozonoit*) to the company of His disciples in the upper chamber. Secondly, because after He had delivered them to the disciples, He revealed to them the mystery (*rozo*) concerning His passion. [It is called] 'Perfection of Perfections', because without it not one of the divine mysteries (*roze alohoye*) is perfected; for he who is baptized is not perfected except he receive the mysteries (*roze*); so also he who is blessed [to be] a deacon or a presbyter, with it, he is perfected and completed.[17]

Here Moses Bar Kepha uses the plural form *roze* in four different senses.

1   The theological meaning of the Eucharistic celebration or the liturgical theology (cf. the title).
2   The entire Eucharistic celebration (*roze* is one of the names used for it).
3   The celebration of the 'sacraments', namely Baptism and Ordination, which includes the celebration of the Eucharist.
4   The Body and Blood of Christ.

The singular form *rozo* refers to the 'hidden meaning' of Christ's passion and *raz* (used as adverb) means 'secretly'. Elsewhere Bar Kepha uses the verb in the sense 'to symbolize' or 'to signify' the mystery of the passion.[18]

In a fifth-century anonymous commentary (published by S. Brock), *roze* refers to the entire Eucharistic celebration as well as to the consecrated bread and wine.[19] In the Commentary attributed to Jacob of Edessa (d. 708), the singular form (*rozo*) is

---

[16] E. Beck, 'Symbolum-Mysterium bei Aphrahat und Ephraem', *OC* 42 (1958), 19–40; S. Brock, *Luminous Eye: The Spiritual World Vision of St Ephrem* (Rome, 1985), pp. 37–65.

[17] R.H. Connolly and H.W. Codrington, *Two Commentaries on the Jacobite Liturgy* (London, 1913), pp. 23–25.

[18] Ibid., p. 53: '[as] the priest takes the bread and breaks it . . . He declares and signifies (*mraz*) that Christ was broken on the cross . . .'. On the fraction Bar Kepha writes: '[as] he unites and fits together the two halves of the bread . . . He symbolizes (*mraz*) and shows by that Emmanuel is one . . .' (p. 67). In both cases, *raz* refers to Christ's passion, which has been liturgically symbolized.

[19] Brock, 'Commentary', pp. 387–403, see D52; 56.

used either in the sense of 'symbol' or as a synonym for 'type' (*tupso*).[20] The verb *raz* is used in the sense of 'to depict' or 'to indicate'.[21]

In his brief *Exposition of the Mysteries (roze) of the Church*, George, Bishop of the Arabs (d. 724) deals with Baptism, the Eucharist and the Consecration of Myron.[22] On one occasion George uses the word *roze* to refer to the entire Christian tradition, which includes the Bible, the liturgy and the doctrines. Thus commenting on Baptism, he writes: 'The beginning of the mysteries (*roze*) of the Christians is true faith.'[23]

George uses the singular form in the sense of 'symbol': 'That he is dipped three times is a mystery (*rozo*) of the three days Our Lord was in the tomb'.[24] Here *rozo* refers to the 'symbolization' of the salvific death of Christ.

Elsewhere George writes: '[The priest] portrays spiritual images by a mystery (*rozo*)'.[25] When Moses Bar Kepha quotes this text, the plural form *roze* is used.[26]

C. The West Syrian anaphoras and other liturgical texts   In the West Syrian anaphoras, *roze* usually refers either to the Eucharistic celebration as whole or to the body and blood of Christ. However, it is used in a much wider sense. Thus in the anamnesis of the anaphora of Jacob of Edessa, the economy of salvation celebrated in the Eucharist is called *roze*: 'The awe-inspiring mysteries (*roze*) of Your wonderful deeds, O God the Word, we see with the eyes of our minds'.[27] The anamnesis of several of the anaphoras uses the word *roze* in this sense.

Thus the word *rozo/roze*, as used in the anamnesis, often refers to a celebration of the death and resurrection of Christ. In the anaphora of Mar Julius we find: 'Whenever you celebrate (*mkahnin*) this mystery (*rozo*), you perform the memory of my death and resurrection until I come'.[28]

In most of the cases, the word *rozo* (or *roze*) denotes a liturgical/sacramental celebration or a symbol, which is an integral part of that celebration. The use of this word for the entire economy of salvation or for the entire Christian tradition has liturgical implications. It refers to the doctrinal tradition as well as to the message of the Gospel as these are interpreted and meditated in a liturgical context. In the early Church, catechetical lectures were delivered as part of the canonical hours or as part

---

20 Also in St Ephrem. See above, note 9.

21 Berlin Sachau 218, fol.178b–186b.

22 Syr. text and Eng. tr., Connolly and Codrington, *Two Jacobite Commentaries*.

23 Ibid., p. 1. In the *Penkito* similar usages can be found. Thus in the Prooimiun of the third hour on the fifth Sunday after Easter we find: 'O [Lord] how wonderful are your promises and your mysteries (*roze*) that you have handed over to the earthly beings. And how glorious and honoured are the things that you have entrusted by word through the preachers of your Gospel'. Pampakuda Manuscript 200, p. 48. Malayalam translation (ed. 1969), p. 85.

24 Ibid., p. 14.

25 Ibid., p. 17.

26 Ibid., p. 35.

27 *AS* III-1, p. 58.

28 *AS* III-1, p. 86. See the anamnesis of the anaphora of *Mathai Ro'yo*: 'Whenever you celebrate (*metarzin*) through them, you commemorate my death and resurrection'. *Anaphora* (P-1986), 170.

of a Eucharistic celebration. In the Syriac East, the Western type of theological faculties are of quite recent origin. Theology was taught in communities, which followed strict monastic discipline and the celebration of the Holy Eucharist, and the canonical hours were important parts of the curriculum. The doctors or noted teachers of theology were usually called *marzone* (those who initiate into the mysteries; celebrants of the mysteries; instructors).[29]

The word *marzone* (from *rozo*) implies that the teaching of theology and the celebration of the mysteries are inseparable. In this context the meaning of the words of Evagrius become clear ('If you pray in truth, you are a theologian; if you are a theologian, you will pray in truth'). Liturgical celebration is a theological act, and the teaching of theology is a 'liturgical act'.

It is better not to limit the meaning of the word *raz* to 'mystery' in the sense of a secret or hidden thing. In its liturgical use, *rozo* and its derivatives refer to the mystery of the death and resurrection of Christ. It can either be a celebration, an action or an object. Thus in the anamnesis of the West Syrian anaphoras, it refers to the celebration of the death and resurrection of Christ. According to George, Bishop of the Arabs, the three-fold dipping is a mystery (*rozo*) of the three days in the tomb. For Jacob of Edessa, the sounding-board is the symbol (*rozo*) of the wood of the cross, and the breaking of the bread symbolizes (*mraz*) the passion of Christ.

In these texts, the action or an object (that is, a liturgical symbol) is an integral part of a celebration. Their symbolism is rooted in the mystery of the death and resurrection of Christ, which is being liturgically enacted in the Eucharist or in Baptism. Thus in the consecration of the baptismal water we find: 'Almighty God, show forth (*hawo enun*) these waters . . . , the waters which symbolize (*metarzin*) the death and resurrection of Your Only-Begotten Son . . .'.[30]

Thus *rozo* or *raz* is a celebration, or rather a showing forth, of the mystery of the death and resurrection of Christ, in which our salvation and hope are rooted.

In the Sanctus of the anaphora of Mathai Ro'yo the word *raz* is used in the sense of 'to narrate' ('May we narrate – *narez* – your properties with the threefold hymns . . .').[31]

As we have noted, *raz* can also mean 'to conspire; to do united efforts or action', which is very close to the meaning of *leitourgia* (common work). The word *raz* thus can refer to a united action of the Church, the Body of Christ, in which we are initiated into the Kingdom of God or incorporated into Christ. In this sense, *rozo* as a celebration manifests the mystery of Christ and his Kingdom. It reveals the 'mystery that was hidden to the ancients', which consists of the gathering together of all in Christ and standing before God. Thus *rozo* is the means of our access to the presence of God.

---

[29] A word derived from *rozo*. For the use of the word, see the anaphora of Saint John Chrysostom (or John of Haran), Fifth Diptych: 'Remember O Lord the skillful teachers, and true instructors (*marzone* = true priests).'

[30] Athanasius Yeshu Samuel, *The Sacrament of Holy Baptism according to the Ancient Rite of the Syrian Orthodox Church of Antioch* (1974), p. 62. See also the anamnesis of the anaphora of Mathai Ro'yo, above, note 28.

[31] Anaphora (P-1986), p. 169.

Rozo is a token of something promised; it is the token of the Kingdom of God ('How wonderful are your promises and your mysteries – *roze* – that you have handed over to the earthly beings').[32] It is in this sense that the word is used in the Syriac translation of Theodore of Mopsuestia's first homily on Baptism: 'Every mystery (*rozo*) is in fact an indication through signs (*otwoto*) and symbols (*roze*) of invisible and ineffable things'.[33] Then Theodore continues: 'In a mystery (*rozo*) there are signs (*otwoto*) of things that will take place or have already taken place'.[34]

A sixth-century *Exposition of the Mysteries* attributed to Narsai represents the classical understanding and the use of the word *rozo*:

> Lofty, in truth, and exalted is this mystery (*rozo*) that the priest performs in the midst of the sanctuary mystically (*rozonoit*). Mystically (*rozonoit*) the Church depicts the glorious mysteries (*roze*); and as by an image (*yuqno*) she shows to all men these things that have come to pass. Those things, which came to pass in the death of the Son, she commemorates by the Mysteries (*roze*); His resurrection also from the dead she reveals before all. A mystery mystically shows (*mrazaz*) that which has come to pass and that which is to come about: but the Church shows mystically (*marzoze*) in the Mysteries (*roze*) only that which has come to pass.[35]

Thus *rozo* is primarily an act of the Church, the Body of Christ. It is a 'showing forth', through a liturgical celebration, of the passion, death and resurrection of Christ.[36] This meaning of the word *rozo* is applicable to every liturgical celebration of the Church, as well as to its various elements, such as a gesture, an object, or even its theological meaning. *Rozo* is a symbolization, a showing forth of the unity of all in Christ (cf. Eph. 1:9–10). *Rozo* manifests the world to come, in which the entire creation will be restored to the condition that God has willed. The word underscores the eschatological nature of the Church, liturgy and the entire Christian experience. It carries the dual connotation of something both hidden and revealed, a riddle and a revelation together. Similarly a liturgical celebration, or a symbol that is integral to it, conceals and reveals the divine presence. As Paul says, 'For now we see in a mirror dimly' (1 Cor. 13:12). *Rozo* 'dimly' reveals the divine presence. Prayers, hymns,

---

32 Promiun, fifth Sunday after Easter, third hour, Pampakuda Manuscript 200, p. 48.

33 Theodore, Hom. XII, 2, R. Tonneau and R. Devreese (eds), *Les Homélies catéchétiques de Théodore de Mopsueste* (Vatican, 1949), p. 325; A. Mingana, *Commentary of Theodore of Mopsuestia on the Lord's Prayer and on the Sacraments of Baptism and the Eucharist*, Woodbrooke Studies VI (Cambridge, 1933), p. 17.

34 Ibid.

35 Eng. tr. R.H. Connolly, *The Liturgical Homilies of Narsai* (Cambridge, 1909), (hom. 17), pp. 1–2. Syriac text: A. Mingana (ed.), *Narsai Doctoris Syri, Homiliae et Carmina* (Mosul, 1905), Vol.I, p. 271. The author of the homily does not explore the eschatological dimension of *rozo*. According to S. Brock, hom. 17 is 'almost certainly not by Narsai himself, but must date from the 6th century'. S. Brock, *A Brief Outline of Syriac Literature* (Kottayam, 1997), p. 36.

36 See Paul Verghese, 'Relation between Baptism, Confirmation and the Eucharist in the Syrian Orthodox Tradition', *SL* IV-2 (1965), 82–83.

gestures and liturgical symbols like icons, cross and incense are integral to the act of 'showing forth'. Each participates in the dynamic presence of God in its own way. From this arises the problem of liturgical symbolism.

Symbols are integral to liturgical and sacramental celebrations. An icon or a cross is used not simply to direct our imagination during the prayers. They are always erected with a prayer of consecration, asking God to manifest them as a means of grace and salvation. Thus they serve as a material centre in which there reposes a divine power, an energy, for they point to the archetype. The creation is potentially a 'symbol' that points to the existence, wisdom and glory of God (Ps. 19:1–2). As a result of the Fall, it was subjected to 'the bondage of decay'; but it looks forward to 'obtain the glorious liberty of the children of God' (Rom. 8:21). When we sanctify a material object and dedicate it to a liturgical use, as children of God, we proclaim that it has been freed from the 'bondage of decay' and that it henceforth participates in the 'glorious liberty', which is salvation and sanctification. As people become 'sons of God', 'christs' and 'pneumatophores', the material world shares in their destiny and becomes symbols of spiritual realities. As the priest of creation, man offers the 'first-fruits' of creation to God as *eucharistia*, as a means to live in communion with Him. This explains the use of light, incense, bread, wine or oil.

It is significant that the word *mysterion/rozo* has been used in the Gospels to refer to the mystery of the Kingdom. A *rozo* is the manifestation of the Kingdom of God. Indeed, the experience of the Kingdom consists of the radical newness of humanity in Christ, as a result of the indwelling of the Holy Spirit. Communion with the Triune God, or participation in the divine life, will be granted to us, when we will be 'christified' and 'pneumatized'. The life-giving Word of God will guide us to the waters of life. This experience of the Kingdom, an anticipation of the eschatological fulfilment, is already accessible in the Body of Christ.[37] It is in the liturgical acts that this experience is made accessible to us. Its accessibility is not limited to a few of the liturgical celebrations, namely, the sacraments. It is available in every liturgical act in a manner proper to it, for every celebration is rooted in the unique mystery of Christ. A liturgical celebration is a *rozo* of the Christ event, and consequently that of the Kingdom. The act of assembling – the primary act in liturgy – is the *rozo* of the unity of all in the Kingdom of God. It is a manifestation as well as a foretaste. Thus the word *rozo* provides a key to understanding the relationship between Church, Kingdom and the liturgy.

2. Teshmeshto

The Syriac word *teshmeshto* is the nearest equivalent of *leitourgia*, and it contains the different connotations of the Greek. It has been applied to all the ministries and offices within the Church in which it manifests itself and fulfils its nature and vocation. Thus

---

37 J. Meyendorff, *Byzantine Theology* (New York, 1974), p. 191.

teshmeshto refers to a liturgical celebration as a whole in the sense of *ordo* (*tekso*). (for example, *teshmeshto d-denho* = order/service of the Epiphany). The word *teshmeshto* can also signify a part of a celebration (for example, the funeral liturgy consists of four parts and each of them has been called a *teshmeshto*).

The word *leitourgia* occurs six times in the New Testament, and it has been always rendered as *teshmeshto*.[38] The verb *leitourgein* has been translated as *shamesh*[39] (or as *ethkashap* = to supplicate or intercede[40]). The *teshmeshto* and its root *shamesh* have been used to translate the Greek words *diakonia*[41] or *diakonein*.[42]

In the Old Testament, the Hebrew word *aboda* (= service or adoration: *latreia* and *leitourgia*) has been rendered as *pulhono* (= work or service).[43] However, its meaning is similar to that of *teshmeshto*.[44]

The content of the word does not imply mere slavish service, but rather a relationship based on love and trust. It implies the discharging of a work or a responsibility entrusted to a trustworthy servant.[45] It denotes the disposition of availability, a proximity to the sovereign, an attitude of humble and loving readiness to obey and to fulfil his will. The meaning of the word cannot be understood in terms of 'service' or 'servile duty'. It implies an honour, a privilege, and a special favour to approach God and to stand before him. The opening prayer of the preparation rites of the Eucharist very well illustrates this idea: 'Make us worthy, O merciful and benevolent Lord God, with knowledge and awe and spiritual discipline to stand before Thee in purity and holiness, and to serve (*shamesh*) Thee as Lord and Creator to whom worship (*segto*) is due from all; Father, Son and Holy Spirit, forever'.[46]

The word *teshmeshto* (and *shamesh*) is also used in the sense of priestly ministry.[47] It is in this sense that it has generally been used in the West Syrian liturgical texts.[48] *Teshmeshto* is the fulfilment of our priestly vocation. The Church as the royal priesthood gathers together and performs the *teshmeshto*, primarily to be with God as His people and to be His witnesses in the world. This is presented in one of the oldest prayers of the Preparation rites:

---

38 Luke 1:23; 2 Cor. 9:12; Phil. 2:17; 30; Heb. 8:6; 9:21.

39 Rom. 15:27; Heb. 10:11.

40 Acts 13:2. *Ethkashap* is the *Ethpaal* conjugation of *kshp* (= to supplicate). The Greek word *leitourgos* (occurs five times in the NT) has been rendered as *mshamshono* (= deacon): Rom. 13:6; 15:16; Phil. 2:25; Heb. 1:7; 8:2.

41 Luke 10:40; Acts 6:1; Rom. 10:30; 2 Cor. 8:1–6; 9:1; 12ff. etc.

42 Luke 17:8; 12:37; 22:26; John 12:2; Acts 6:2 etc.

43 The verb *plah* has been used in Gen. 2:15.

44 In 1 Chr. 23:22 *shamesh* has been used to render *aboda*.

45 According to A.H. Herbert, the content of the word *aboda* does not suggest merely slavish service, but rather a relationship, especially in faithfully discharging the work given to a servant. A.H. Herbert, *Worship in Ancient Israel* (London, 1963, 3rd edn), p. 1.

46 Athanasius, *Anaphora*, p. 3.

47 In Luke 1:23, Heb. 9:21 and 10:11 it refers to the Old Testament cult.

48 For example the prayer that the celebrant says as he puts on the liturgical vestments: 'clothe me with choice garments that are fitting for the service (*teshmeshto*) of Thy glory and for the praise of Thy holy name . . .'. Athanasius, *Anaphora*, p. 10.

Account us worthy, O Lord God, that having our hearts sprinkled and cleansed
from all evil, we may enter into Thy great and exalted Holy of Holies. May we be
enabled to stand in purity and holiness before Thy Holy altar, and in true faith
offer (*kahen*) reasonable and spiritual sacrifices unto Thee, O Father, Son and the
Holy Spirit.[49]

Liturgy (as *teshmeshto*) means to stand near God and enjoy His presence. (This idea
is implied in the vision of the heavenly liturgy that the Book of Revelation presents.[50])
Teshmeshto is an act of communion, a life in the presence of God, seeking and seeing
His face. This idea is fundamental to understanding the spirit of West Syrian liturgical
celebrations.

3. *Qurobo*; *Qurbono*

In Syriac the meaning of these words is more or less the same. Thus both mean *oblation*,
offering, *gift*, and *the Eucharistic liturgy*. But *qurobo* also means *the consecrated
bread, access*, or *being brought near*. Similarly, *qurbono* often refers to the consecrated
bread. Though the words have been used to refer to sacrifice, they have a much broader
sense. The Syriac word for sacrifice is *debho*: the Eucharist has been called *debho* in
a figurative sense. Though the sacrificial meaning is common, it is not the key concept
to understanding the Eucharist.

Moses Bar Kepha's commentary on the Eucharist begins with discussion of 'six
names' of the Eucharist: Assembly (*knushyo*), Communion (*shawtoputo*), Access
(*qurobo*), Oblation (*qurbono*), Mysteries (*roze*), Perfection of Perfections (*gmirut
gmiruto*).[51] He gives the following definition of *qurobo* and *qurbono*.

[It is called] 'Access' (*qurobo*) because by it they that were far off and they that
were near, and they of heaven and they of earth, have been brought near
(*ethqarabw*) to one another, as Paul has said: 'In him we have access' (*qurobo*):[52]
that is, the people and the peoples, heavenly and earthly beings. [It is called]
'Oblation' (*qurbono*), because He was made an oblation to God the Father for our
sins, as the apostle said: 'He who offered himself for us' (Heb. 9:14), etc. And in
the Law of Moses also they used to call *qurbono* those sacrifices which were
offered for sin.[53]

Though Bar Kepha distinguishes between the meanings of *qurobo* and *qurbono*, each
has the same connotation. Both are derived from the root *qareb* (to offer, draw near).
This would imply that sacrifice is more than 'immolation' or 'slaughter of a victim'.

---

[49] Ibid., p. 9. This prayer has now been placed as the opening prayer of the second service of the
Preparation rites, and has also been found in the East Syrian Preparation rites. See Brightman, *LEW*, 270.

[50] Rev. 5:8–14; 6:9–11; 7:9–17.

[51] Expression borrowed from Dionysius the Areopagite, *EH* III, I, 424C.

[52] Eph. 2:18.

[53] Connolly and Codrington, *Two Jacobite Commentaries*, pp. 24–25.

It is an access to the presence of God through an act of offering. It was probably in this sense that the Epistle to the Hebrews understood 'the sacrifice of Christ' (Heb. 10:12). *Qurobo* or *qurbono* is an access to the presence of God in Christ. The entire *leitourgia* of the Church is a *qurobo*, an offering as well as an access to the Trinitarian mystery. The other terms that Bar Kepha uses underscore the different aspects of this relationship.

Even the sacrificial connotation should be understood in the broader perspective of the history of salvation. Theologians have often associated sacrifice and sin rather too closely, thus limiting the meaning of the salvific death of Christ to a few concepts such as atonement, satisfaction, propitiation and the appeasing of divine wrath.[54] In its spiritual sense, sacrifice is a means of restoring creation to divine order. It re-creates relationships between men and between God and man. This idea is most probably implied in *qurobo*. A relationship ('nearness or access') is created through the act of offering. The Eucharist is an 'assembly', an act of assembling. The assembly is manifested as the Church, because of its 'nearness' to the Trinitarian community. A new relationship is manifested, for the community has been assembled as the 'Church of God', the officially called-out community, the manifestation of the Kingdom of God, as the assembly of 'the Last Days'. The New Testament graphically affirms the reality and depth of this relationship by using a variety of expressions.

4. Other Important Terms

Sluto *(prayer)*

The word *sluto* can refer to a liturgical hour or to a liturgical formula, or simply to a 'prayer'. In the Peshitta version of the Psalms, it is used in the sense of the Hebrew word *tephillah* (Ps. 141:1; 143:1). Its root *slo* or *sali* means 'to slope', 'to lean towards' or 'to be prone to'. Thus *sluto* can also mean reconciliation, and readmission to communion. A prayer is an act of 'loving inclination'.[55] Thus prayer as such is readmission into God's presence and is an act of communion with Him.

Taudito *(Confession, Praise, Thanksgiving, Religion, Doctrine)*

The root of the word *taudito* (*awdi*) means 'to confess, acknowledge, profess, assert, to believe, or to praise'. The Ethaphal form *ettawdi* means to be confessed, acknowledged, declared, accepted, recognized, to be preached, or to be praised. Its derivatives occur several times in the Hebrew Psalms.[56] The word *tawdito* has been

---

54 Constantin Galeriu, 'The Structure of sacrifice', *SVTQ* 30 (1986), 45.

55 O. Cullmann: 'Prayer is the loving inclination towards God in which we bring our needs before him as a child brings them before its parents', O. Cullmann, *Prayer in the New Testament* (London, 1995), p. 33.

56 Ps. 118:1; 122:4; 136:1–3; 138:1–2 etc.

used to render the Hebrew *todah*.[57] The shades of meaning that the word contains are of great importance for liturgical theology. Praise, thanksgiving and doctrine are inseparable.

Dehlo *or* Dehelto *(Fear, Awe, Worship, Religion)*

These words have been used in a general sense. The word *pulhono* also has a similar meaning (worship, religion, service), and this word, or its derivatives, has been used in the Old Testament to render the Hebrew *abodah*. This implies that the essence of a religion is worship, its most regular and authentic expression.

The use of a rich vocabulary illustrates the variety of meanings ascribed to the liturgy. However, the meaning of our worship of God cannot be reduced to a few concepts or terms that have been classified in post-Enlightenment dictionaries. Each word reflects the depth of the mystery. The variety of vocabulary used for praising or singing is striking. The major theme of the Syriac hymns is often the meditation of the unfathomable divine mystery and the philanthropy which enables man to offer glorification followed by a humble supplication: 'make us worthy to glorify you forever!' For rhythmic or rhetorical reasons, a variety of terms is often used in prayers or hymns. The opening prayer of the *Ramso* of the feast of the Nativity provides an example:

> Make us worthy, Lord God, to glorify (*shabah*) you without investigation, and to bless (*barek*) you with the blessed Cherubim without doubt, and to exalt (*ramrem*) you with the principalities without hindrance, and to celebrate (*'ad'ed*) [the feast] with the heavenly beings without blame, and to shout (*yare* = *to sing*) to you without hesitation with the innocent shepherds, and to worship (*sged*) you with the Malgians without alteration, and with your mother to rejoice unceasingly in you. Now and forever, Amen.[58]

---

57 Lev. 7:12; 13; 15; 22:23.
58 Pampakuda MS 13, p.143. cf. Malayalam Tr. pp.139–40.

CHAPTER 4

Liturgy as the Expression of Doctrine

It is axiomatic that doctrinal tradition for Easterners is not merely an intellectual system. Doctrine is inextricably bound up with liturgical action.[1] In the East, for the broader masses of the faithful, the liturgy is a 'plastic representation of Christian doctrine'.[2] In worship the faithful see and experience their faith or the faith of the Church. Schleiermacher's remark about the liturgy as 'representative action' is true of Eastern Christianity.[3]

In the prayers, fundamental doctrinal themes are regularly evoked with the aim that they are constantly received and re-received by the consciousness of the worshipping community.[4] The repetition of certain themes is not merely a pedagogical motif. It is, rather, a proclamation, a witness to the Church's experience of God and its certitude regarding the meaning and goal of life. In and through the liturgical celebrations, the Church proclaims its right vision (*orthodoxia*) of God to the world and invites the world to join in the right glorification. The right vision enables us to approach God with confidence and to offer him praises. The doctrines open our eyes to see the goal of life beyond the material world and to pray for the realization of God's eternal plan for us. Thus doctrine orients our celebration and provides the right vision regarding everything. Doctrine is, in a sense, a guide to preserving the faithful from going astray. It helps us to discern error that turns us away from truth.

The tradition of expressing the doctrines in liturgical texts was obviously inherited from Judaism. The prayers of Judaism were not merely petitions or its doxology triumphal words. The Jewish tradition carefully narrated the *mirabilia dei* in its doxologies (*berakoth*). The great things that God has done for the fathers, or the community, were evoked not for the sake of God, but for each member of the community, so that he might understand who Yahweh is, whom he worships.[5]

Along these lines, the early Church always insisted on the intrinsic relationship between doctrine and the Eucharistic liturgy. Thus Irenaeus of Lyons wrote: 'Our doctrine agrees with the Eucharist and the Eucharist confirms our doctrine.'[6] The Eucharistic prayers were first composed in the interests of doctrinal, not liturgical, uniformity. The Eucharistic prayer itself, with its account of salvation history, is the proclamation of the community's common faith. In later centuries, the introduction

---

[1] C. Scouteris, 'Doxology, the language of Orthodoxy', *The Greek Orthodox Theological Review* 38 (1993), 153–62.

[2] S. Zankov, *The Eastern Orthodox Church* (London, 1929), pp. 102–103.

[3] Ibid.

[4] Constantin Andronikof, *Le sens de la liturgie. La relation entre Dieu et l'homme*, Théologies, Paris, 1988, pp. 125–38 (= ch.9: Dogme et Liturgie).

[5] Carmine de Sante, *Jewish Prayer. The Origins of Christian Liturgy* (New York, 1991), pp. 33–131.

[6] Irenaeus, *Against the Heresies*, IV, 18, 5, *SC*.100 (1965), p. 611.

of the Nicene Creed further emphasized the doctrinal dimension of the liturgy. The prayers of all the sacramental and liturgical celebrations were carefully composed within the limits of orthodoxy, so that they should express the mind of the Church. Prayers were always carefully formulated, selected and introduced in the liturgy, to imprint the faith of the Church in the minds of believers. Thus doctrines are 'lived', that is, expressed, celebrated and transmitted in and through the liturgy. By introducing doctrinal themes into the doxology, the Syrians intended to communicate to the faithful the traditional vision of the Trinity and incarnation and thus to preserve it in and through the liturgical life. For the Syrian Orthodox Church, during its most difficult period under Islamic rule since the seventh century, liturgical gatherings were the primary places where doctrines were explained, meditated on, prayed about and appropriated.

Dogmatic definitions are not final and definitive statements which exhaust the being of God. They serve as 'windows, which open into a world of inexhaustible richness and amazement'.[7] The 'gaze' through the windows of words and concepts enables us to yearn for communion with God and realize it through worship. Our words and thoughts are a finite opening towards the infinite; they are able to evoke the memory of God in us and to foster within us a spiritual life, which can ultimately lead us to salvation.[8]

Christianity is not a philosophical school for speculating about abstract truths. It is essentially communion of the whole man with the living God.[9] Communion means a life of love and adoration with the living God, that is, to participate in his life, which has been offered to man out of his infinite love. Doctrines convey glimpses of that life and exhort man to respond to the divine love and to appropriate the life of love. Doctrines convey the Christian experience of 'the community of saints'. The faithful are convinced of the veracity of the Church's witness to ultimate reality, for example, the eschatological promises of Christ, the fulfilment of each and every thing in the Kingdom of God, become a reality. They are made present and the faithful are assured of their veracity. In the liturgy, in the presence of the Triune God, everything becomes evident and transparent. Liturgy becomes an 'anamnesis', a showing forth of the things to come as well as the handing over of an experience.

Doctrines are articulations of the right vision of the Church, the 'praying thoughts' of the community that worships God in 'Spirit and in Truth'. As Nicolas Lossky observes, the doctrinal formulations summarize the essential things related to our salvation:

> Dogma has always had a single aim – to reorient the Church towards what is strictly necessary: the reality of the Incarnation of Christ with all its consequences for the whole created world and the salvation offered in the risen Christ.[10]

---

[7] A.M. Allchin, *The Kingdom of Love and Knowledge. The Encounter between Orthodoxy and the West* (London, 1979), p. 200.

[8] Cf. D. Staniloae, *Theology and the Church* (New York, 1980), p. 73.

[9] Ibid.

[10] N. Lossky, 'Liturgy and liturgical art from an Ecumenical Perspective', *Sourozh* 36 (May 1989), 37–38.

Doctrines represent the unanimous certitude of the Church concerning truth. We share in that knowledge of truth that the Church possesses and we are raised by faith to the contemplation of truth and the vision of God.[11]

According to the patristic tradition, doctrinal difference implies a 'defective' vision of God. It means that the vision has been blurred by pride and refusal to share in the catholic and liturgical experience of which doctrine is a reflection. Thus a 'heretic' is simply unable to worship 'in Spirit and in Truth'. If a man persists in heresy, it means that he refuses to participate in the right vision of God and thus to offer right glorification. This is the theological basis for excommunication. One who professes a different teaching is excluded from liturgical *koinonia*, and thus he is given an opportunity for repentance. This idea has had a profound influence on the Eastern tradition as whole.

In a sense, doctrinal statements imply a true agreement of many to stay and pray together. This might be one of the reasons for the introduction of the Nicene Creed into the liturgical *ordo*. This concept of 'agreement' is equally true in the case of liturgical texts, whose function includes the confession of the orthodoxy of the community. Doctrines provide a basis for unity of the worshippers. The unity of faith implies a change in our attitude. We consent to see the realities through the eyes of the 'great clouds of witnesses'. We are united by faith to be of 'one heart and soul' (Acts 4:32).

The Christian truth is of equal value and importance for all the faithful, both learned and ignorant, clergy and laity. The saving truths, as articulated in the doctrinal statements, determine the fate of all mankind. As Vladimir Soloviev has rightly observed, '[The doctrinal truths] are vital practical truths, accessible to all and pointing to all the only way of salvation and of direct approach to the Kingdom of God'.[12]

Eastern theologians always point to the soteriological dimension of the doctrines. Thus the noted Eastern Orthodox theologian John Zizioulas writes:

> [The] dogmas are principally soteriological declarations; their object is to free the original *eikon* of Christ, the truth, from the distortions of certain heresies, so as to help the Church community to maintain the correct vision of the Christ-truth and to live in and by this presence of truth in history. The final intention of all this is to lead to communion with the life of God, to make truth into communion and life.[13]

Doctrinal statements are incorporated into doxology, in order to protect the community from distortions of the truth, so as not to endanger the truth's soteriological content.[14]

Whether in its preaching, biblical expositions, doctrinal formulations or liturgical celebrations, the Church points out the ways to salvation. In its liturgical celebrations,

---

11 Cf. The anamnesis of the anaphora of Mar Isaac requests that at the Last Judgement, 'we may be made worthy of your contemplation (*theoria*) and to be rejoiced'. *Annapuro* (1986), p. 242.

12 V. Soloviev, *God, Man and the Church* (Greenwood, 1874), p. 165.

13 J.D. Zizioulas, *Being as Communion* (SVSP, New York, 1985), pp. 116–17.

14 Ibid., p. 117.

the Church proclaims its doctrines on the saving truths, its certitude of God and his Kingdom. She aims precisely to release man from his 'narcissism' and effectively to unite him with his fellow human beings and thus to restore the integrity of true life in God.

1. Abba, Father! Liturgy and the Trinitarian Doctrine

The most striking common characteristic of the Eastern Christian liturgies is their Trinitarian emphasis.[15] For the Eastern Christians, the Trinity is 'the unshakeable foundation of all religious thought, of all piety, of all spiritual life, of all experience'.[16] Unlike the medieval and post-medieval western theology, the East held the revelation of God the Holy Trinity as the basis of all Christian theology. Liturgy has its foundation in the revelation of the triune God, a 'community' of three divine hypostases that exists in mutual love and adoration.

In the New Testament, the redeeming death of Christ has been pictured as a *leitourgia* offered to God 'through the Eternal Spirit' (Heb. 9:14). Those who are united with Christ 'pray in the Holy Spirit' (Jude verse 20; Eph. 6:18). In the Spirit, the members of the Body of Christ address God 'Abba, Father!' (Gal. 4:6; Rom. 8:16). Christians pray in the Spirit who himself 'intercedes for us with sighs too deep for words' (Rom. 8:26).

The fact that the mystery of the Trinitarian life has been presented in terms of *leitourgia* means that the liturgy introduces us to that mystery, which consists of a life of mutual love and adoration. Trinitarian life, as it has been revealed in Christ, means a creative availability of one hypostasis *vis-à-vis* the other two. Thus the three have one will and their actions are simultaneous and concomitant. This life of communion has far-reaching implications for the life and destiny of man, who has been created to live in communion with God. Communion with God means living in love and adoration of God. The Fall consists of failure to fulfil the will of God, or rather a refusal to trust the life-giving Word of God. The Word of God ceased to be the guiding principle in the life of Adam. He trusted 'a word of lie' rather than the Word of God. Man denied the company of God. The disintegration or fragmentation of the human community was the result of alienation from God. The Old Testament narrates God's efforts to restore the communion. The goal of the Incarnation was the reintegration and the restoration of the unity of humanity in Christ. The unity of humanity is achieved, manifested, continued and sealed in the worshipping community, the Church, the Body of Christ. Worship offers man the possibility to live in communion with God, the possibility that he refused, with the Fall, to accept. He was offered the possibility of living in the light of the Word of God and thus to have a foretaste of eternal life. This fundamental idea is vividly expressed in West Syrian prayers.

---

[15] See Nicholas Zernov, 'The Worship of the Orthodox Church and its Message', in A.J. Philippou (ed.), *The Orthodox Ethos. Studies in Orthodoxy*, Vol.I (Oxford, 1964), p. 116.

[16] V. Lossky, *The Mystical Theology of the Eastern Church* (London, 1957), p. 65.

The Incarnation has made us the sons of the Heavenly Father and given us the possibility to address him as 'Abba, Father'. The Holy Spirit leads us to the Son and through him to the Father. The goal of the Incarnation was to restore our relationship with the Triune God, which was impaired as a result of the Fall. As a prayer of the *Shehimo* puts it:

> Glory to the holy Father, who sent his holy Son and he descended and dwelt in a pure and holy womb in a holy manner; he came in our image and likeness, that we might become like him; he became a son of man that he might make us sons of his Father and partakers of his holy Spirit.[17]

In other words, the goal of the Incarnation was to deliver us from false worship and to lead us to the true and perfect worship of the Holy Trinity. Thus in a prayer of the Service of Pentecost we read:

> Christ Our God, by Your loving kindness, full of mercy and compassion towards us who were worshippers of the adversary and the rebellious demons, You turned us from the worship of idols and made us perfect and true worshippers of the Holy Trinity.[18]

Christ made us true worshippers of the Holy Trinity. In a litany of the same service we find:

> We, who through idolatry had become worshippers of the adversary and through the acknowledgement of the Holy Trinity have been made true worshippers by You, who are one of the Holy Trinity.[19]

The work of the Apostles consisted precisely in bringing the human race to the knowledge of the Holy Trinity:

> We thank You, O Lord God, Father of all mercies, for . . . You filled them [the apostles] with the Holy Spirit . . . Thus You sanctified, exalted and sent Your holy apostles to bring the human race to the knowledge of the Trinity, one triune God, baptizing them in Your holy name, O Holy Father, and in that of Your Only begotten Son and Your Holy Spirit, by whom and with whom, we also worship, praise and glorify the Holy Trinity, one true God, now and forever and ever.[20]

The Trinitarian foundation is always emphasized in the prayers of the West Syrian Church. Thus a liturgical celebration invariably begins with a confession and glorification of the triune God: 'In the name of the Father and of the Son and of the

---

[17] Wednesday, *Sapro*, *Shehimo*, 153. See also the First Service of Pentecost (*Sedro*): 'Because You were pleased, O God the Father, to restore man who was created in Your image, and who of his free will slid into idolatry, You sent Your Word and Your Son for our reformation.' *Ma'de'dono*, 319.

[18] Second Service (inaudible prayer), *Ma'de'dono*, 345.

[19] Pentecost, First Service, Litany, *Ma'de'dono*, 327.

[20] Pentecost, First Service (inaudible prayer), *Ma'de'dono*, 329.

Holy Spirit, one true God, to whom be glory and upon us mercy and compassion for ever and ever. Amen.' When the West Syrians begin their daily prayer each morning and evening, they place their daily cycle under the protection of the Trinity.

The liturgical celebrations are interposed at regular intervals with a Trinitarian glorification: 'Glory to the Father, Son and to the Holy Spirit.' This is followed by the people's response: 'From eternity to eternity' (cf. Ps. 90:2; 89:53 Peshitta). This reminds us that the foundation and the goal of worship is the glorification of the Trinity, and the people express their consent with their response. Almost every prayer is concluded with a Trinitarian doxology: 'we will offer praise and thanksgiving to You and to Your Father [or *Your Son* if it is addressed to the Father] and to Your Holy Spirit, for ever and ever'. The Trinitarian invocation is required because outside the Trinitarian faith, it is impossible to know Christ, to recognize in Jesus the Incarnate Lord, one of the Holy Trinity.

Thus the prayers regularly recall that our worship is directed to the triune God. This idea is often vividly expressed: 'Sanctify our souls by Your divine gifts, and grant wisdom to our intellects that we may understand the true and supreme worship of the consubstantial three Persons of the Godhead, now and forever.'[21]

The whole of life, therefore, is an offering, a *leitourgia* offered to the Holy Trinity, 'who is understood as one and confessed and proclaimed as three'.[22] The revelation of God as Trinity – a community of three divine persons existing in mutual love and adoration – is an invitation for a *leitourgia* and consequently for communion. The Father has been revealed as 'the monarch', 'cause' or 'principle of divinity', which means that he is the centre of adoration for which his Son redeemed humanity in the Spirit. The Trinity is a 'liturgical mystery', or a 'liturgical life'. The inner Trinitarian movement has been expressed in terms of an 'eternal worship', and our worship in the Body of Christ, in the Spirit, introduces us to that movement. In the words of Pseudo-Dionysius the Areopagite, 'all the hierarchic operations', which include the liturgical celebrations, are aimed at 'passing the light of God' on to us.[23]

It is in and through worship, that is, the sacrifice of our whole being, that we become imitators of Christ, who offered himself to God the Father. The concluding prayer (*Hutomo*) of the first part of the preparation rites (*tuyobo*) summarizes the meaning of worship:

> O Pure and spotless Lamb, who offered Himself to the Father, an acceptable offering for the expiation and redemption of the whole world, make us worthy that we may offer ourselves to Thee a living sacrifice well-pleasing unto Thee after the manner of Thy sacrifice for us. May we be accounted worthy to offer

---

[21] Ibid., p. 315.

[22] The anaphora of Mar Eusthathios, Prayer of the Imposition of the hands (before *Sancta Sanctis*), Pampakuda (1986), p. 188; also *Promiun-Sedro, Annapuro* (1986), 43; cf. Pentecost, *Lilyo*, Second *Qaumo*, *Crown III*, 200.

[23] 'And the objective, the prime purpose of each sacrament is to impart the mysteries of the Deity to the one being initiated', Pseudo-Dionysius, EH, III:1, *PG* 3, 425 A. Again: 'It is true of course that all the hierarchic operations have this in common, to pass the light of God on to the initiates.' Ibid., 425 A–B.

unto Thee, O Lord, sacrifices of praise and thanksgiving for a savour of spiritual sweetness. Let all our thoughts and words and actions be whole burnt offerings unto Thee. Grant us, O Father, Son and Holy Spirit, to appear before Thee without blemish all the days of our life, and ever be well-pleasing to Thy Godhead.[24]

Liturgy is the coming closer to God.[25] It is a continuous *qurobo*, that is, gathering together before the throne of God. Thus a prayer has, implicitly or explicitly, a triadic structure, and each prayer is a proclamation of God as one in three. As Kallistos Timothy Ware puts it, 'We think the Trinity, speak the Trinity, breathe the Trinity'.[26]

2. The Trinitarian Structure of the Anaphora

In the East, the anaphora has a triadic structure.[27] This is true of the Syriac anaphora of St James as well as the other West Syrian anaphoras. The Trinitarian dimension is emphasized by beginning the anaphora with a Trinitarian benediction: 'The love of God the Father, the grace of the only-begotten Son and the communion of the Holy Spirit be with you all, my brethren, for ever and ever.'

The benediction recalls that the faithful have assembled before the triune God. As Moses Bar Kepha says, this is not a prayer, but a declaration of the loving-kindness of God.[28] The priest recalls that the assembly has entered the threshold of the heavenly court.[29] This has been further emphasized with the *Sursum Corda*: 'Let our minds and our understanding and our hearts be above where our Lord, Jesus Christ, sits at the right hand of God the Father.'

The Sanctus that follows affirms the awareness of the presence of the triune God. The West Syrian commentators see the Sanctus primarily as a Trinitarian doxology. Thus Moses Bar Kepha writes: 'By singing three times *Holy, Holy, Holy*, they [the Seraphim] signify that this God who had no beginning and has no end, is three Persons. By saying *Lord*, they show that these three Persons are one in nature and one Lord.'[30]

The Post-Sanctus (of St James) describes the divine economy and the redemption of man as the common work of the divine persons:

---

[24] Athanasius, *Anaphora*, p. 9.

[25] The Syriac word for Eucharist is *qurobo*, which comes from the root *qareb* (to come near, to approach, to offer).

[26] Kallistos Ware, *The Orthodox Way* (rev. edn, New York, 1995), p. 38.

[27] See B.Varghese, 'West Syrian Anaphora as an Expression of the Trinitarian Doctrine', *The Harp* 4 (1991), 215–23.

[28] 'it is not a prayer, but [declares that] by reason of His love God gave His Son for us'. Bar Kepha, *Eucharist*, p. 46; See Bar Salibi, *Eucharist*, 10:1.

[29] '[The priest] commits them to the Holy Trinity'. Bar Kepha, *Eucharist*, p. 46.

[30] Ibid., p. 49; Bar Salibi writes: 'First, the priest remembers the intelligent creatures, heavenly ranks, Cherubim and Seraphim, and [then] bids [us] to shout with them the threefold Holy to the Trinity.' *Eucharist*, 11:1.

> In truth you are holy, O King of the worlds and giver of all holiness. Holy is your Son, our Lord Jesus Christ, and holy is your Holy Spirit who searches out your deep things, O God the Father. You are almighty terrible, good, partaker of sufferings and especially towards your creation, who made man from the earth, having bestowed upon him the delight of paradise. But when he had transgressed your commandment and fallen, you did not disregard, you did not leave him, O good [one], but did chasten him as a father fair of mercies; having called him through the law, you did educate him through the prophets, and finally you did send your only begotten Son himself to the world, that you might renew your image; who when he had come down and was become incarnate of your Holy Spirit and of the holy, virgin, and blessed Mary, and had conversed with man, having accomplished (*dabar*) everything for the salvation of our race.[31]

As we shall see in the next chapter, some of the early West Syrian anaphoras have further expanded the Post-Sanctus to express the chistological concerns of the time. However, the general tendency was to use the Post-Sanctus as a means to give a summary of the Trinitarian doctrine. The anaphora of Dionysius Bar Salibi provides an example:

> Holy is the Father who is begetter, not begotten; holy is the Son who is begotten; holy is the Holy Spirit who proceeds from the Father and takes from the Son. One is the true God who redeemed us through his mercies and compassion.[32]

The West Syrian anaphoras owe their structure and themes of prayers to the Liturgy of St James, whose structure seems to have been fixed in the context of the theological controversies of the fourth and fifth centuries. The central part of the anaphora can be divided as follows: (a) Sanctus and Post-Sanctus; (b) Institution and Anamnesis; (c) Epiclesis. This arrangement would suggest that the very structure of the anaphora has a Trinitarian foundation. As we have noted, the Sanctus is the glorification of the Father, the source and principle of the Trinitarian mystery. In the anamnesis, the whole mystery of Christ is recalled. In the epiclesis, the Church, the Body of Christ, asks the Father to send the Holy Spirit upon the Church (the mystical body of Christ) as well as upon the offerings (the sacramental body and blood of Christ).

3. Prayers Addressed to the Father

It is significant that all the prayers of the West Syrian anaphora, except the concluding prayer, are addressed to God the Father. The Church, the Body of Christ, gathers together in the Spirit of sonship, and offers the Eucharist. Christians dare to call God 'Our Father', because he has authorized us to do so in Christ, and we have been given the 'Spirit of sonship'. True Christian prayer is always Trinitarian. Trinitarian invocation

---

[31] O. Heiming, *AS* II-ii, 142–44.

[32] *Annapuro* (1986), p. 134.

is required because outside the Trinitarian faith, it is impossible to know Christ, to recognize in Jesus the incarnate Lord, 'One of the Holy Trinity'.

In a sense, the Lord's Prayer is a Trinitarian invocation. Whether in Baptism or Eucharist, the function of the Lord's Prayer is to bring out the Trinitarian dimension of the liturgical celebration. Thus Moses Bar Kepha explains the meaning of the Lord's Prayer:

> God is said to be our Father by reason of baptism. For because we and Christ have been born from the one womb of divine (*moronoyto*) baptism, we have hereby become His brethren, and sons of His heavenly Father . . . Hence God is called our Father, because He begot us from baptism by His Holy Spirit.[33]

Commenting on the words 'Thy kingdom come', Bar Kepha writes: 'Again, thus: *Thy kingdom come*: that is, He calls "the kingdom" the help and succour of the Holy Spirit. Pray ye, He says, that God the Father may grant you the help of the Holy Spirit . . .'.[34]

Thus the Lord's Prayer is the prayer of the children, addressed to the heavenly Father to grant the Holy Spirit. Its aim is precisely to lead us to communion with the triune God.

Even the prayer addressed to the Son does not contradict this principle for the following reasons:

1 The actions of the Trinity are 'concomitant' and ' simultaneous'. A *promiun* of the Service of Pentecost puts it thus: 'Whenever the Father is mentioned, the Son and the Spirit are of Him; and when the Son is mentioned, the Father and the Spirit are acknowledged in Him; and when the Spirit is mentioned, the Father and the Son are included'.[35]

2 The 'Christ event' is an integral part of the economy of the Holy Trinity. It is the expression of the saving will of the Triune God. Thus in the final thanksgiving prayer of the Syriac anaphora of St John Chrysostom (or John of Haran) we find: 'Jesus Christ, our God, You were sacrificed for us by Your will, and that of Your Father, and that of Your Holy Spirit, You have given us Your Atoning Blood to drink . . .'.[36] It is important to note that, in the West Syrian anaphoras, the final thanksgiving prayer is always addressed to Christ. The prayer that we have quoted underlines the fact that the prayers are addressed to the Second Person of the Holy Trinity, and is in harmony with the triadic structure of the anaphora.

3 Every prayer of the anaphora (including the final one addressed to the Son) concludes with a Trinitarian glorification: 'We may glorify You and God the Father who begot You and Your all-holy and Good and Adorable and life-giving Spirit,

---

[33] Bar Kepha, *Eucharist*, pp. 74–75.
[34] Ibid., p. 80.
[35] *Ma'de'dono*, 317 (First Service).
[36] *Annapuro* (1986), pp. 151–52.

of one substance with You, now and forever, world without end.'[37] The titles and the acclamations of the Father and the Holy Spirit used in the liturgical texts presuppose both interpersonal and economic relationships between the three divine hypostases. Therefore they should not be considered as purely Christ-centric. In the liturgical texts, in spite of a few prayers addressed to the Son, the chief emphasis has always been placed on the threefold saving activity of God (cf. 1 Cor. 6:11).

The anamnesis of the West Syrian anaphora also follows this principle. Though the first part of the anamnesis has been addressed to the Son, it is concluded with a supplication addressed to the Father: 'For your people and your inheritance we pray to you, and through you to your Father, saying . . .'.[38]

As we shall see later, the epiclesis is also presented in a Trinitarian framework. The Church, the Body of Christ, implores God the Father to 'send Your Holy Spirit upon us and upon the offerings'.

4. Eucharist and the Communion with the Holy Trinity

Our unity in Christ leads us to communion with the triune God. In and through the participation in the Body and Blood of Christ, we have been granted communion with the Holy Trinity, the final and ultimate goal for which we have been created. The meaning and significance of the Eucharistic communion cannot be understood apart from the Holy Trinity. Commenting on the Trinitarian benediction that precedes the *Sancta Sanctis*, Moses Bar Kepha states:

> *The priest: May the grace of the Trinity, holy, uncreated and eternal and equal in essence be with you all* – That is, he says this to them: These mysteries which have been consecrated and completed and perfected for you, and which you are about to receive, they have been bestowed upon you by the grace of the Holy Trinity, since they are not without or apart from the Trinity, but are one of the Persons of the Trinity, that is the Son become incarnate.[39]

In the anaphora of Saint James, this is further emphasized by the Trinitarian acclamation during the *Sancta Sanctis*, which is an invitation to communion:

> One Holy Father. One Holy Son. One Holy Spirit. Glory be to the Father, and to the Son and to the Living Holy Spirit, Who are One, forever and ever.
> The One Holy Father with us, Who, by His mercy, created the World. (People: *Amen.*)
> The One Holy Son with us, Who, by His own precious sufferings redeemed the world. (*Amen.*)
> The One Holy Spirit, with us, the Perfecter and Fulfiller of all that has been and all that will be. May the Name of the Lord be blessed for ever and ever. (*Amen.*)

---

37 Athanasius, *Anaphora*, p. 61.
38 Ibid., p. 40.
39 Bar Kepha, *Eucharist*, p. 86.

In Syriac, the people's response is '*aman Amen* (*With us Amen*)'. Thus their consent to the Trinitarian acclamation has been most emphatically expressed.

In the Eucharist, the Father has made us worthy to partake of the heavenly table as well as of the Holy Spirit. Thus, in Christ, we have been made worthy of partaking in the Trinitarian life. This is stated in the thanksgiving prayer of the anaphora of St James:

> We give thanks unto Thee, O Lord, for the abundance of Thy mercy wherewith Thou hast accounted us worthy to partake of Thy Heavenly table. Grant, my Lord, that our participation in Thy Holy mysteries be not a cause for our condemnation and that being accounted worthy to partake of Thy Holy Spirit we may find a share and an inheritance with the righteous from ever.[40]

---

[40] Athanasius, *Anaphora*, p. 61.

CHAPTER 5

Liturgy as the Expression of Christology

1. The Christological Foundation

The Christian liturgy has its foundation in the Incarnation of the Second Person of the Holy Trinity. Incarnation is an act of God's philanthropy, to restore us to communion with himself. God became man in order to restore God's image in man that was impaired by the Fall. The liturgical texts regularly evoke the meaning and goal of the incarnation in vivid phrases. A Hymn of the Book of Common Prayer (*Shehimo*) summarizes the goal of Incarnation:

> Glory to the Holy Father, who sent his Holy Son and He descended and dwelt in a pure and holy womb in a holy manner. He came in our image and likeness, that we might become like Him; He became a son of man that He might make us sons of His Father and partakers of His Holy Spirit.[1]

The West Syrian writers repeatedly say that the goal of Incarnation was to 'teach us true worship'. For them, the salvation or the filial relationship with God means a relationship of love and adoration. This has been presented in a *sedro* of the Feast of the Annunciation. After having narrated the divine mercy, which has realized the Incarnation and the Annunciation, the *sedro* continues:

> You have removed the perdition and proclaimed forgiveness to the lost. You have taught the created tongues your glorification, and the lips of the earthly the praise of your greatness. You have filled the heaven with wonder and persuaded the earthly for the glorification of your divinity.[2]

We have been redeemed from idolatry and brought to the true worship, which is the way of salvation. Thus we find in another *sedro*:

> King of Kings . . . , Saviour of our human race and the One who renews our nature, You came down from the throne of majesty because of Your divine love, while You were sitting on it with Your Father, and Your life-giving Holy Spirit and exalted by the heavenly armies. You have put on humility and are clad the likeness of flesh for our salvation. And on account of us, the debtors, You came down to the earth full of thorns, in order to redeem us from idolatry. From the vanity of idolatry, you have gathered us and attracted us to the worship of You, and Your Father and Your Holy Spirit.[3]

---

[1] Wednesday, *Sapro*, *Shehimo*, 153.

[2] Annunciation, *Lilyo*, Second *Qaumo*, Pampakuda MS 13, p. 66.

[3] Sunday of the Visitation of Mary to Elizabeth, *Sedro*, *Ramsho*, Pampakuda MS 13, p. 77.

Worship is an integral part of God's salvific work. In his love for mankind, 'God the Word of glory became man to make us gods by grace'.[4] Christ has shown us the way of life for the kingdom.[5] The way of life consists of a life of prayer. The Father had sent his Son in order to teach us to pray: 'Praise to the Father, who by the Son taught us to pray; worship to the Son who prayed in passion for us; thanksgiving to the Holy Spirit who receives prayers and responds to all fair requests.'[6]

In the East, especially in the Syriac tradition, salvation is understood in terms of healing, renewal and restoration. Philoxenos of Mabbug writes:

> The goal of His coming is the following: To purify the soul from evil and to bring it back to its original condition. He has given His commandments as medicinal plants and as the remedies for the purification of the spiritual nature.[7]

'The Commandments' surely include the commissions: 'Baptize', 'Do this in remembrance of me' and 'Pray continuously'.

The healing imagery was a favourite one for the Syriac writers. Christ is presented as the 'remedy' for the disease of humanity that the heavenly physician has sent:

> The mercy of God which is spread over the creation sent to every man a remedy according to his disease; for the grievous disease of the Egyptians, it sent Joseph; for the greed of the house of Ahab, Elijah the prophet; for the great city of Nineveh, it sent Jonah the preacher; and when he saw that the world had rebelled against the yoke of repentance, he sent his only Son and redeemed it by his cross.[8]

Worship and the sacraments are part of the remedies used by the good and heavenly physician. They have been 'instituted' by him as means of salvation and healing for humanity: 'David prophesied and said: the Lord will come and heal the broken-hearted; our heart was broken by sin and Christ healed it by the waters of baptism, . . . blessed is he who heals it.'[9]

Everything taught or done by Christ has a single aim: to heal, that is, to save us from the infirmities of fallen humanity. Christ, the heavenly physician, healed the lepers and the blind as a sign of the 'healing' of humanity from the disease of sin and death:

> Glory to the heavenly physician who descended from the heights to the depths, that he might heal the diseases and the sickness of the race of Adam; the lepers met him and were cleansed, the blind and they saw the light, and the sinful woman who approached him received forgiveness.[10]

---

4 *Sedro*, Sunday, third hour: 'God the Word of glory, who became man in your love for mankind; that you might make us divine by your grace . . .'. *Shehimo*, 347.

5 'God the Word, who came in your love and became man, and trod for us the way of life to the kingdom.' Thursday, *Ramsho*, *Shehimo*, 171.

6 Thursday, *Sutoro*, *Shehimo*, 182.

7 Philoxenos, *Letter to Patricius: 3*, *PO* 30, 747.

8 Wednesday, *Sutoro*, *Shehimo*, 133.

9 Monday, *Ramsho*, *Shehimo*, 34.

10 Monday, *Sapro*, *Shehimo*, 66.

The healing or salvation consists of teaching the way of worship. Thus an *enyono* ('response') of the *Ramsho* of the White Sunday says:

> Out of love, you became man for the sake of man who died and was lying in corruption, and by your passion in the flesh, you calmed the passions of the human nature, and you taught the nations which you redeemed to praise you and to say, 'Bless the Lord, all you servants of the Lord, and offer thanks to Him and to exalt him and give him glory for ever and ever'.[11]

The apostles were associated with the healing ministry. A *sedro* of the Pentecostal cycle says: 'Praise to You, True Physician, Lord Jesus Christ, who sent medicines by the hands of your holy apostles to heal all the diseases of man.'[12]

When we pray, we pray in Christ, as members of the body of Christ. As Origen says, one who prays participates in the prayer of Christ:

> One who prays participates in the prayer of God's Word who lives among those who know not the Word, who is absent from no one's prayer. The Word prays to the Father in union with the believer whose Mediator he is. Indeed, the Son of God is the high priest of our offerings and our advocate with the Father. He prays for those who pray; he pleads for those who plead.[13]

This patristic vision of prayer has left its traces of influence on some of the West Syrian liturgical texts. Thus a prayer of the Great Lent exhorts the penitent: 'Take heart, you who pray; do not be lazy. Add your prayer to His [prayers] that has [great] power. For, on account of his [prayer] yours is being accepted.'[14]

The medicine that the apostles had given to the nations was the true worship of God:

> O Glorious Name which the apostles carried in the inhabited world by their words and deeds, by You they gathered a chosen people from the nations into one Church and brought to You true adorers who worship Your sovereignty in the Spirit and they shed abroad all over the world the fragrance of Your death.[15]

The Church continues the healing ministry that has been entrusted to the apostles and the liturgy is part of the mission of healing; it is a medicine prescribed for our healing. In the Church, in its liturgical and sacramental celebrations, we receive Christ, 'the Medicine for the forgiveness of offences sent by the Father to heal our wounds'.[16]

---

[11] *Crown* III, 53.

[12] Friday after Pentecost, *Lilyo*, First *Qaumo*, *Sedro*, *Crown* III, 222.

[13] Origen, *On Prayer*, 10. Eng. tr. A. Cunningham, *Prayer. Personal and Liturgical. Message of the Fathers of the Church*, Vol.16 (Washington, 1985), p. 143.

[14] Friday, *Lilyo*, First *Qaumo*, *Bo'uto*, *Great Lent*, 115; Mal. tr. (1997), p. 195.

[15] Feast of the Twelve Apostles, *Ramsho*, *Etro*, *Crown* III, 543.

[16] Third Sunday after the feast of the Cross, *Ramsho*, *Etro*, *Crown* III, 423–24. See the opening prayer of fifth Sunday after the feast of the Transfiguration, *Ramsho*: 'O Herb of the Pardon of our faults, You were sent from the father to heal our wounds.' *Crown* III, 364.

A hymn of the Feast of St Peter and St Paul evokes the same idea in a different way:

> Like farmers, Peter and Paul, chosen apostles, were sent to the world. And like the sun they lighted the whole earth covered with darkness. They taught to worship in Spirit and in truth and built churches. They made to shine a great light, the true light, and faith in the Father and the Son and in the Holy Spirit, whom all creatures worship. And nations and peoples and tribes now sing praise to Him.[17]

Thus the whole liturgical tradition has its foundation in the economy of salvation. This is suggested in the first epistle of Clement (ch.40): 'He [Christ] has enjoined offerings [to be presented] and service to be performed [to him], and not thoughtlessly and irregularly, but at the appointed times and hours.'[18]

Christ, the *leitourgos par excellence*, is the *raison d'être*, model and the goal of worship. In him, worship is given a new dimension. It is henceforth a filial relationship, an act of communion. In Christ, our prayers and the Eucharist become a sacrifice. 'Sacrifice' is a 'sacramental language', and it denotes our reconciliation with God the Father, through our participation in Christ. It denotes our drawing near to God in Christ. In Christ we are introduced into the presence of God the Father. Incarnation has provided the possibility to approach God as children, and to call upon him 'with unashamed faces' (*parhesia*). This is the meaning of the expressions such as 'participation in the divine life' or to 'abide in Christ'. Our participation in Christ ('the anointed one') means that we participate in his anointing. Thus the Holy Spirit abides in us; we have been made 'pneumatophores'. Everything that the Spirit touches is restored and sanctified, and a 'touch of eternity' has been conferred. The creation is potentially 'pneumatophore', that is, capable of manifesting the glory of God to serve as a *rozo,* a symbol, pointing to the Creator.

2. Prayers Addressed to Christ

Even though the Eucharistic prayer has a Trinitarian structure, it is Christo-centric in formulation, giving great weight to the phrases on the second person of the Holy Trinity. The Christological dimension was sometimes expressed by addressing the anaphora to Christ.[19] The Eucharistic prayers in the Syriac *Acts of Thomas* and the

---

[17] *Lilyo,* Second *Qaumo, Crown* III, 537.

[18] *Ante Nicene Fathers* X (5th edn 1969).

[19] Joseph Jungmann's conclusion that the prayers of the anaphora were always addressed to the Father was widely accepted. According to him, the prayers addressed to Christ were introduced in the fourth century (J. Jungmann, *Place of Christ in Liturgical Prayer*, London, 1989). But recently, A. Gerhards has demonstrated that the prayer addressed to Christ was always one of the norms of Christian liturgical prayers. Gerhards, 'Prière adressée à Dieu ou au Christ? Relecture d'une thèse importante de J.A. Jungmann à la lumière de recherche actuelle', in A.M. Triacca and A. Tistoia (eds), *Liturgie, Spiritualité, Cultures. Conférences Saint Serge* (Rome, 1983), pp. 101–14.

Greek anaphora of Gregory Nazianzen are examples of this type.[20] In the Syriac tradition, there seem to have existed Eucharistic prayers addressed to Christ. The anaphoras of Addai and Mari (Post-Sanctus) and Peter Sharar (Post-Sanctus and Anamnesis) still preserve prayers addressed to Christ. Similarly, the Post-Sanctus and the Anamnesis of the anaphora given in *The Testament of Our Lord* follow the same pattern. However, under the influence of the anaphora of St James, the West Syrians might have revised the prayers of the anaphora. The Commentary of Moses Bar Kepha on the Eucharist gives the impression that prayers addressed to Christ existed in the West Syrian anaphoras as late as the ninth century. Thus he directs a major change in the anaphora: if prayers of the anaphora, except the final thanksgiving prayer, are not addressed to the Father, they should be corrected.[21]

The traces of the prayers addressed to Christ are still found in the Syrian Orthodox Eucharistic celebration. The alternate prayers for the ante-pax on Maundy Thursday and Holy Saturday are still addressed to the Son.[22] Similarly, in the Syriac anaphora of St James, the anamnesis has been addressed to Christ, whereas in Greek St James and in the Apostolic Constitutions, it is addressed to the Father. The Syriac anaphora of the Twelve Apostles, which has several parallel texts in the Greek anaphora of St John Chrysostom, also has an anamnesis addressed to the Son.[23]

The Post-Sanctus enumerates the great things that God the Father has done by sending his only-begotten Son for the salvation of humanity.[24]

> In truth you are holy, O King of the worlds and giver of all holiness. Holy is your Son, our Lord Jesus Christ, and holy is your Holy Spirit who searches out your deep things, O God and Father. You are almighty, terrible, good, compassionate and especially towards your creation, who made man from the earth, having bestowed upon him the delight of paradise. But when he had transgressed your commandment and fallen, you did not disregard, you did not leave him, O Good [one], but did chasten him as a father fair of mercies; having called him through the law, you did educate him through the prophets, and finally you did send your only begotten Son himself to the world, that you might renew your image; who when he had come down and was become incarnate of your Holy Spirit and of the holy, virgin, and blessed Mary, and had conversed with man, having accomplished everything for the salvation of our race. (*The Institution Narrative follows*.)[25]

---

[20] It should be noted that the anaphora of Gregory Nazianzen (still used in the Coptic Church) is not an Alexandrian type, but Syro-Antiochene. See Q. Gerhards, *Die Gregor von Nazianz (329/30–c.390) zugeschriebene griechische Anaphora und ihre Stellung in der Geschichte des Eucharistiegebets*, LQF, Münster, Westfalen, 1982.

[21] Bar Kepha, *Eucharist*, pp. 89–90.

[22] Prayers given in Athanasius, *Anaphora*, p. 33. On both days, Kiss of Peace is not given as a sign of mourning.

[23] The anaphora of the Twelve Apostles, in R.C.D. Jasper and G.J. Cuming, *Prayers of the Eucharist. Early and Reformed* (Collegeville, 1990), p. 126.

[24] The economy of salvation is the theme of the Post-Sanctus in the Antiochene type of anaphoras. See M. Arranz, 'L'économie du salut dans la prière du Post-Sanctus des anaphores de type antiochien', *LMD* 106 (1971), 46–75.

[25] Heiming (ed.), *Anaphora of Saint James*, AS II-1, 142–44.

Thus the Post-Sanctus, with its emphasis on the will of the Father and its accomplishment in the Incarnation of the Son, serves as an introduction to the account of the Eucharistic Institution, and the anamnesis that follows. Sometimes West Syrians have expanded the Post-Sanctus by giving additional emphasis to the mystery of Christ. The anaphora of Timothy of Alexandria provides an example for using the Post-Sanctus as a means to communicate the 'miaphysite' Christology:

> In truth you are holy and blessed by all, O God the Father, and holy and blessed by all is your only begotten Son our Lord Jesus Christ, who was born ineffably before the world, who eternally holds the throne at the right hand side of your majesty, and your Holy Spirit who is [also] holy and blessed by all, through whom all things of the earth and heaven are sanctified. And those who are near to you in heaven offer glory and honour, to your name and [you are] honoured by all, O King of the worlds. We therefore, your servants, [who have] many sins, while answering with the heavenly armies, we praise, glorify, and bless and ask you for mercy [and say] our Saviour and God, have mercy upon us, reveal your merciful face to us and save us. For you are the one who had mercy upon our race and sent us your only begotten Son, Lord, who is our Saviour Jesus Christ, illuminator, benefactor, and redeemer of our souls and bodies, who was proclaimed by his prophets in the ancient days, when he was about to dwell among us, came in the end of time and took himself our humanity; the Word became flesh; he neither took change nor alteration, but by the Holy Spirit he was conceived by Mary, the ever-virgin and holy Mother of God. [He took] a body having a rational and intelligent soul, in true and hypostatic unity, which was not an imaginary apparition. Without separation or division, he truly took a human body and soul and all that a man has and in all things he resembled us except sin. He did not merely dwell among men, but while being perfectly God the Word, he perfectly took flesh and became man. His divinity did not become humanity; but he remained in his divinity and took completely the human nature. He was not two, but one King, one Christ, one Lord, one God the Word incarnated who is revealed to us. He dwelt among men, affirmed the earth and blessed it; he restrained the waves of the sea. He was known with his deeds, revealed in power, conquered the human passions and put an end to the transgression of law, converted the erring, and destroyed the power of death from us, which had conquered man in the beginning, and showed him to be invincible in the end. Through the [human] body he caught hold of [death] and that which was caught was destroyed. Through his death, he restored the glory of man who was destitute from glory. (*The Institution Narrative follows.*)[26]

The Christological introduction to the Institution Narrative is theologically consistent with the meaning and content of the liturgical units that follow. The long introduction aims at bringing out the soteriological implication of the Christological doctrine. The doctrine becomes normative by its soteriological implication and its reception by the Church through its liturgical application.

---

26 Anaphora of Timothy, *AS* I-1, 16–18. Cf. 'Anaphora of the Patriarch John I', in H. Fuchs (ed.), *Die Anaphora der monophysitischen Patriarchen Johannan I* (Münster, Westfalen, 1926), pp. 12–16.

3. Meaning of the Institution Narrative

It is in the Institution Narrative that the Christological content of the anaphora finds its concrete expression. Since the Middle Ages, the theologians of the West were increasingly interested in the meaning and function of this liturgical unit, and had seen it in terms of consecration. Consequently, the Institution Narrative was seen as the 'formula' that marks 'the moment of consecration'. There emerged a theology of consecration at the expense of pneumatology. To a large extent, liturgical theology has been held up by the issues raised by these discussions.

In the Syrian Orthodox tradition, the account of the Institution is a historical narrative, rather than a consecratory formula.[27] In the Institution, the Church commemorates and narrates the institution of the Eucharist by Christ in the culmination of his public ministry, so revealing the meaning of his salvific death. According to Dionysius Bar Salibi, in its celebration the Church proclaims the origin of the Eucharist and the reason for its offering:

> Here [the priest] narrates the mystical story and makes commemoration of the priestly sacrifice that our Lord accomplished in the upper room, in the evening in which he was about to surrender for us. After having celebrated the Old Testament Passover, he fulfilled the high priestly order, and entrusted this service to his disciples.[28]

Moses Bar Kepha says that the Institution is not a prayer, nor a request, but a narrative. Therefore he censures any '*Amen*' after the signing of the bread:

> But . . . we must know that when the priest says here 'and for life everlasting', it is not right he should give occasion to the people to answer 'Amen'; for it is not a prayer, or a request, but this place is a narrative; and it is on account of a prayer that the people ought to answer 'Amen'; but not on account of a narrative.[29]

The narrative of the Last Supper is in fact an 'anamnesis', a showing forth of the events that took place in the upper room. The liturgical gathering, the manifestation of the apostolic community in space and time, participates in those events. The faithful have been gathered around the table of Christ, where Christ himself presides. In the person of the priest, Christ himself pronounces the sacramental words. In one of his letters, the Patriarch Severus of Antioch (d. 538) writes:

---

[27] See my study, *St James*, pp. 28–30. Cf. Isaq Saka, *Fushoq Qurobo* (Zahle, Lebanon, 1963), p. 73, quoted by G. Khouri-Sarkis, *OS* XII-2 (1967), 160 (article by A. Cody, n.11). See the review of this book by Khouri-Sarkis, *OS* XI-3 (1966), 380–87. Khouri-Sarkis argues that, for the Syrians, the words of Institution have consecratory value. *OS* XII-2 (1967), 160–63. According to P. Rodopoulos (*The Consecration of the Gifts of the Holy Eucharist* [Greek], Thessalonike, 1968), the words of the Institution possess only a narrational rather than a consecratory character, pp. 252, 250. We owe Theodore Stylianopoulos for this reference. See *The Good News of Christ* (Brookline, 1991), p. 65.

[28] Bar Salibi, *Eucharist*, 12:1, p. 65.

[29] Bar Kepha, *Eucharist*, p. 56.

You should know that the priest who offers, represents the great God and our Saviour Jesus Christ; for he in fact celebrates the memory of the sacrifice which he himself instituted, and of that which he himself began in the mysterious supper.[30]

In another letter addressed to Misael the deacon, Severus says:

It is not the offerer himself who, as by his own power and virtue, changes the bread into Christ's body, and the cup of blessing into Christ's blood, but the God-befitting and efficacious power of the words which Christ who instituted the mystery commanded to be pronounced over the things that are offered. The priest who stands before the altar, since he fulfills a mere ministerial function, pronouncing his words as in the person of Christ, and carrying back the rite that is being performed to the time at which he began the sacrifice for his apostles, says over the bread, 'This is my body which is given for you: this do this in remembrance of me' while over the cup again he pronounces the words, 'This cup is the new testament in my blood, which is shed for you' (Luke 22:19–20). Accordingly it is Christ who still even now offers, and the power of his divine words perfects the things that are provided so that they may become his body and blood.[31]

The words of Severus do not imply that his teaching was similar to the Latin doctrine of consecration by the 'Words of Institution'. In fact, these letters were addressed to those who attributed a special sanctity to the Eucharist offered by certain monks and bishops (a 'misconception' still prevalent in some milieux in the East). Severus corrects them and points out that the sanctity of the Eucharistic celebration does not depend on the quality or saintliness of the celebrant, as Christ himself sanctifies the offering. However, Severus insists on the role of the Holy Spirit:

It is not the man who offers the sacrifice, but Christ completes it through the words uttered by the offerer and changes the bread into flesh and cup into blood, by the power, inspiration and grace of the Holy Spirit.[32]

The West Syrian writers always pointed to the presence and the operation of the Spirit as the essential condition for the consecration. However, they almost never identified any particular element as the moment of transformation. Institution and Epiclesis are mutually complementary. Bar Salibi writes:

[The priest] recites the words that our Lord said in the upper room when he accomplished the mystery. By these [words], he indicates that he is the one who consecrates now as well as these elements which are placed on the altar, by the

---

[30] Letter 105, To Caesarea the Hypatissa, *PO* XIV, 256.

[31] Severus, *Select Letters*, II-1, 238. In another letter Severus says: 'For it is Christ himself and his mysterious words which he pronounced over the bread and the cup of blessing that completes the rational and bloodless sacrifice, not the priest who stands before the altar' (ibid., 245). As Paul Evdokimov says, in the East, the priest's relation to Christ is not one of substantial identity – which is true only of the Eucharistic gifts – but of iconic correspondence. See O. Clement, 'The Eucharist in the Thought of Paul Evdokimov', *Eastern Church's Review* (1975), 113–24, here p. 121.

[32] Letter to Ammian and Epagathus, Severus, *Select Letters*, II-1, 234–35.

will of the Father and by the operation of the Spirit, through the priest who signs crosses and recites the words. It is not the one who ministers, but the one who is invoked on the mysteries who consecrates. Again the bread receives the first sign (*rusmo*) of consecration through the signing (*hatmo*) of the crosses. It symbolizes the mystical consecration which was accomplished on that evening in the upper room. Again the sign (*hatmo*) of the crosses symbolizes him who consecrates the offered gifts by the will of his Father and by the operation of the Spirit.[33]

It is significant that the consecration has been associated with the Institution as well as with the Epiclesis. This seems to have been inspired by two theological presuppositions: one, the operations of Son and the Spirit are concomitant and simultaneous; and two, in the Incarnation, the role of the Spirit is precisely manifest in Jesus as the anointed one and to bring the economy of salvation to its completion. As we shall see in the next chapter, according to the Syriac theologoumena, the Spirit who manifests Jesus as the Son 'manifests' the bread and wine and the Body and Blood of Christ. In fact, the very term 'Christ' implies the dynamic presence of the Spirit in the Person and work of the Son. This fundamental doctrinal vision has far-reaching consequences for the sacramental and the liturgical theologies.

4. Anamnesis and the Mystery of the Incarnation

The anamnesis, which begins with the Post-Sanctus, is an integral part of the narration of God's loving-kindness towards humanity.[34] After having narrated the mission of the Son to restore the image of God and the Institution of the Eucharist 'for the remission of sins and the eternal life',[35] the anaphora continues to evoke the death, resurrection, ascension, the Second Coming and the Last Judgement. Thus the whole economy of salvation beginning with the creation and its fulfilment in the Parousia has been evoked.

> Remembering therefore, O Lord, your death and your resurrection on the third day from among the dead, and your ascension into heaven and your position at the right hand of God, and your terrible and glorious second coming wherein you are about to judge the world in righteousness and reward everyone according to his deeds: we offer you this fearful and bloodless sacrifice, that you would not deal with us according to our sins, nor reward us according to our iniquities, but according to your mildness and love for mankind, blot out our sins, your suppliants. For your people and your inheritance beseech you, and through you to your Father, saying: [*People: Have mercy upon us, O God, Father Almighty.*][36]

The reference to the Second Coming and the Last Judgement in the anamnesis is significant. In a sacramental celebration, we commemorate past events as well as the

---

[33] Bar Salibi, *Eucharist*, 12:4, p .65.

[34] See, B. Varghese, *The Syriac Version of the Liturgy of St James*, p. 32.

[35] Cf. the concluding phrases of the blessings over the bread and wine in *St James*.

[36] Anamnesis: St James, *AS* II-1, 148. Cf. Athanasius, *Anaphora*, p. 40.

events to take place.[37] In the anamnesis, the whole economy of salvation is recalled, celebrated, 're-presented' or made 'contemporaneous'. The Eucharistic assembly becomes 'co-participant' in the events that are celebrated. In fact the Eucharist as a whole is an anamnesis of the 'economy of salvation'. As Jacob of Edessa says, 'The [content] of the whole Eucharist (*qurobo*) is to remember and to recount all [things] which Christ has done for us.'[38]

Anamnesis was an essential element of the Jewish Passover ceremony. Commenting on the anamnesis required by Exodus (ch.12), Rabi Gamaliel says, 'In each generation each man shall consider that he himself has been delivered from Egypt.'[39] In the Eucharist, by making the anamnesis of Jesus Christ, we celebrate and consequently render present and operative what God has done, and what he will do and what he does for the salvation of the world. As J.J. von Allmen says, 'Jesus is there, with all his work; the church is there, with all her history, and the creation is there, with all its aspirations.'[40]

It is significant that anamnesis does not evoke the Pentecost. It means that only Christ is the object of the anamnesis. The Church celebrates the mystery of Christ and gives thanks to God the Father for Christ by narrating the economy of salvation. It enumerates the needs of the world and offers the 'fruits of the earth and the works of man' precisely in order to integrate them with the sacrifice and the eternal intercession of Christ.[41] The Church has been authorized to do so by his command: 'Do this in remembrance of me until I come.'

However, the anamnesis has been actualized in the power of the Holy Spirit, for Christ himself has said: 'The Holy Spirit whom the Father will send in my name, he will teach you all things and bring to your remembrance all that I have said to you' (John 14:26). Here we could perhaps find the theological basis for the Epiclesis that follows the anamnesis. Through the anamnesis (that is, the memorial or celebration) of the mystery of the Incarnation, the Church actualizes its participation in the eternal offering of Christ and his prayer for the sending of the Holy Spirit upon the entire creation. In Christ, having been identified with the prayer of Christ, the Church beseeches God the Father to send the Holy Spirit 'upon us and upon the offerings'.[42] The Spirit manifests the Church and its offerings as 'pneumatophores', the ultimate destiny of the entire creation in the Kingdom of God. (It is in this sense that the Church has been qualified as the 'foretaste of the Kingdom' or the Eucharist as the Messianic banquet.) This has been very well expressed in the structure of the anaphora

---

37 Cf. Theodore of Mopsuestia: 'We perform, therefore, this ineffable sacrament (*rozo*) which contains the incomprehensible signs of the economy of Christ, our Lord, as we believe that the things implied in it will happen to us.' (*Hom. On Baptism*, ed. Mingana, p. 20.)

38 Quoted by Bar Salibi, *Eucharist*, 3:4, p. 10.

39 Quoted in J.J. von Allmen, *Célébrer le Salut: Doctrines et pratiques du culte chrétien* (Paris, 1984), p. 15.

40 Ibid., p. 27.

41 See B. Bobrinskoy, 'Reflexions d'un théologien orthodoxe', *LMD* 121 (1975), 73.

42 Epiclesis of St James.

of St James. After having narrated the various phases of the economy of salvation realized in the person and work of the Second Person of the Holy Trinity, the Church beseeches God the Father:

> We also, O Lord, your weak and sinful servants receiving your grace give thanks to you and praise you for all things and by reason of all things. *People: Lord God, we glorify you, we bless you, we worship you and we beseech you for mercy. Have mercy upon us. [The Epiclesis follows.]*[43]

Christology and pneumatology are inseparable. Christ makes us 'pneumatophores' and the Spirit 'christifies' us. The anamnesis serves as the basis for our supplication for the pneumatization of the entire creation. Liturgical theology should explore the implications of the continuity between anamnesis and epiclesis.

5. Pre-Anaphora, *Ordo Communis* and the Post-Communion as Expressions of Christology

Although the anaphora has retained the Trinitarian structure, the prayers of the preparation rites, Pre-Anaphora, *Ordo Communis* and the Post-Communion, are largely inspired by Christological concerns. The general principle behind this development could be summarized as follows. In the earliest tradition, the Eucharistic prayers were composed to reflect Christological concerns. This was probably necessary because the person and work of Christ were the subjects of controversy until the middle of the fourth century. We have noted that some of the ancient Eucharistic prayers have preserved traces of this tradition. In the second half of the fourth century the discussions were shifted to the person and work of the Holy Spirit and the consubstantiality of the three divine hypostases. Thus the anaphoras were henceforth composed to give weight to the equality and the role of the three divine persons in the act of creation and redemption. In the second half of the fifth century, the Church was once again drawn into Christological controversies, namely the question of the union of divinity and humanity in Jesus Christ. The East Syrians, the Chalcedonians and the non-Chalcedonians had their own explanations regarding the mystery of the union. Each argued for the orthodoxy of their respective positions and simply condemned the others as 'Nestorian', 'Dyophysite' or 'Monophysite'. Each tradition articulated its vision of the Christological mystery in its liturgical texts. In the case of the West Syrians, the essentials of the anaphora remained more or less unchanged. Thus in the anaphora, the prayers were invariably addressed to God the Father, the source of the Trinitarian mystery. However, as we have seen, the anamnesis followed the ancient Christological model. This was probably held to be theologically correct, as the Son is the object of the 'anamnesis'.

---

[43] St James: concluding part of anamnesis. *AS* II-1, 148. Athanasius, *Anaphora*, p. 40.

But in the elements that were developed in the sixth century or later, the Christological controversy found its expression, especially in the hymns and prayers of the Pre-Anaphora and the *Ordo Communis*. The preparation rites and the Post-Communion, which attained their present form after the fourteenth century, also followed the same line.[44]

The Trisagion, an entrance hymn for the liturgical celebrations, was the first to be modified for Christological reasons. The Syrian Orthodox fathers had introduced the Christological ending 'He who was crucified for us (have mercy upon us)'.[45] In the East, the Trisagion was interpreted either as a theological hymn addressed to the Father, or as a Christological hymn. In Jerusalem, in Constantinople and in the West, it was taken to be addressed to the Trinity. But in Syria, some regions of Asia and Egypt, it was understood as a hymn addressed to the Son. Several Chalcedonian texts from Syria and adjacent areas (including Cyprus) followed a Christological interpretation.[46] In the context of the Christological controversy, the non-Chalcedonians of Antioch emphasized the Christological meaning by the addition of the phrase 'He who was crucified for us'. The modification of the Trisagion was unacceptable to the Chalcedonians and this led to heated controversies.

By the ninth century the so-called *Ihidoyo* (*Only begotten*) – the Syriac version of the *Monogenes* – was introduced to bring out the Christological dimension of the Pre-Anaphora.[47] In a sense, this was a legitimate development, as the reading of the scriptures, which was always understood in terms of Christology, follows the *Ihidoyo* and Trisagion. The Gospel is the proclamation of the 'living words of our Lord Jesus Christ'.[48] The Epistles that precede it are the 'good tidings of Jesus Christ' as preached by the apostles. The Old Testament lessons are always selected in relation to the mystery of Christ. The sermon – an essential element of the Pre-Anaphora – is the exposition of the mystery of Christ in relation to the readings.

Since the ninth century, *Promiun* and *Sedro* became essential elements of the Pre-Anaphora. A large number of them have been addressed to Christ. However, a Trinitarian doxology has been added to the *Sedre* to maintain the Trinitarian spirit of the celebration. After the sixteenth century, an invariable 'Prayer for pardon and grace' was inserted between the *Promiun* and *Sedro*, which is also addressed to Christ.

---

44 See B. Varghese, 'Early History of the Preparation Rites in the Syrian Orthodox Anaphora', in R. Lavenant (ed.), *Symposium Syriacum* VII (Rome, 1998), pp. 127–38.

45 Byzantine sources are unanimous in saying that the addition was made by Peter the Fuller, the Syrian Orthodox Patriarch of Antioch (+488). S. Brock, 'The Thrice-holy hymn in Liturgy', *Sobornost/ECQ* (1986), 24–34.

46 V.S. Janeras, 'Les byzantins et le trisagion christologique', in *Miscellanea Liturgica in onore de Cardinale Giacomo Lercaro*, T.II (Rome, 1967), pp. 469–99.

47 The Syrian Orthodox tradition attributes *Ihidoyo* to Severus of Antioch and the Byzantines to Justinian I. See D. Julien Puyade, 'Le Troparion *ho Monogenis*', *ROC* 2s. t.VII (=XVII, 1912), 253–58 (argued for the possible authorship by Severus). V. Grumel, 'L'auteur et la date de composition du Troparion *ho Monogenis*', *EO* XXII (1923), 398–418 (argued that Justinian might be the author). Its first attestation in the Byzantine Eucharist is in the ninth century. See R. Taft, 'Monogenis, ho', *ODB* II (1991), 1397.

48 Cf. the proclamations of the deacon and the priest before the reading of the Gospel: Athanasius, *Anaphora*, p. 22.

In the same period (ninth–tenth century), the fraction ceremony became more elaborate with the addition of a series of complex rites and prayers articulating the mystery of the passion. At least until the eleventh century, in several dioceses, the fraction was done with a rather simple formula: 'We break heavenly bread and sign the holy chalice in the name of the Father, Son and the Holy Spirit.'[49] By the twelfth century this was replaced with a longer formula, relating various gestures of the fraction ceremony to the passion, death and resurrection of Christ.

Since the fourth century, the Syro-Antiochene tradition has seen the fraction as a type of the passion and death of Christ. Theodore of Mopsuestia and Narsai are among the earliest writers to adopt this interpretation. Among the West Syrians, Moses Bar Kepha was probably the first to give an elaborate commentary on the fraction.

> [The priest] takes some of *presto* in his hands. And whereas he breaks it in two, he shows that God the Word truly suffered in the flesh and was sacrificed and broken on the cross. Whereas he takes some of the body and dips it in the blood, and brings some of it [the blood] and signs over the body, he shows that this Slain One was besprinkled with His blood in the upper room when He said, 'This is my blood', and on the cross when His side was pierced with a spear and there came forth from it blood and water, and He was besprinkled therewith. Again, whereas he brings some of the blood and signs the body, he makes a union of the soul with the body; and he shows that after the soul of the Word was separated from His body, His soul returned and united to His body: howbeit His Godhead was in no wise separated either from His body or from His soul, neither can it be separated. And that bread is the body of God the Word, but wine is His soul; for the blood is a symbol of the soul, as it is written: 'The soul of all flesh is the blood' (Lev. 17:11,14). But again, whereas, after he has signed [with] some of the blood over the body, he unites and fits together these two halves of the *pristo* one with another, he symbolizes and shows by this that Emmanuel is one, and is not divided into two natures after the union. Again, he shows that after He was sacrificed on the cross He made all to be at peace by the blood of His cross (Col. 1:20), and united and joined together heavenly with the earthly beings, and the People with the peoples, and the soul with the body. Again by fetching the *pristo* about in a circle, he declares and signifies that He was sacrificed on the cross for the sin of the circle of the world. Why does He bring some of the blood to the body and sign, and not bring some of the body to the blood and sign? And we say, because the blood is the soul; and it was the soul that came and was united to the body when He rose from the dead, and the body did not go and be united to the soul.[50]

Bar Kepha comments on complex rites which, most probably, existed in his days. The rites might have been inspired by the minute interpretations given to the fraction.[51] In other words, the Christological concerns found their ritual expression in the fraction ceremony. The present Syrian Orthodox fraction rites are essentially the same as the one described by Bar Kepha. It contains three elements:[52] a prayer attributed to

---

49 Varghese, *The Syriac Version of the Liturgy of St James*, pp. 40–41.

50 Bar Kepha, *Eucharist*, pp. 67–68.

51 Varghese, *St James*, pp. 42–43.

52 See Athanasius, *Anaphora*, pp. 49–50; Brightman, *LEW*, 97.

Dionysius Bar Salibi; a hymn (*bo'uto*) attributed to Jacob of Serugh (addressed to the Father narrating the passion of the Son); and brief prayers addressed to Christ. The long prayer, attributed to Bar Salibi, was probably inspired by the commentaries of Bar Kepha or Bar Salibi.[53] It is in fact a vivid presentation of West Syrian Christology:

> Thus truly did the Word of God suffer in the flesh and was sacrificed and broken on the Cross; and His soul was departed from His body, while His Godhead was in no way departed either from His soul or from His Body. And He was pierced in His side with a spear and there flowed out blood and water for the atonement of the whole world, and His Holy Body was stained therewith. For the sins of the whole world, the Son died on the Cross, and His soul came and was united with His Body. And he turned us from the wrong practice to the right deeds. By His blood He reconciled and united the Heavenly with the earthly beings, and the people with the gentiles, and the soul with the body. The third day, He rose again from the sepulcher, and He is one Immanuel, and is indivisible into two natures after the unity indivisible. Thus we believe and thus we confess and thus we confirm that this flesh is of this blood and that this blood is of this flesh.

The prayer is accompanied by a series of gestures that correspond to the phrases. First of all, the bread is broken into two halves (symbolizing the separation of the soul from the body). Then they are joined together (symbolizing the inseparability of the Godhead from the soul and the body in spite of death). One half is dipped in the wine and the other is signed with it ('the flow of blood and water') and then the two halves are once again joined together ('the soul united to the body'). The bread is turned in an anticlockwise direction ('he turned us from wrong practices'), and then raised ('resurrection'). Then one piece is cut off and dipped in the wine and the entire bread is moistened.[54]

Here we have an example of the ritualization of the symbolic interpretation given to the fraction with relation to the passion and death of Christ. In a sense, this is a 'visualization' of Christology. Obviously, the West Syrians have given interpretations that correspond to their Christology, and the complex rites might have arisen out of them. We have other examples of similar ritualizations, which we will discuss elsewhere in this book. As a principle of liturgical development, we could say that the commentaries have often given birth to rubrics or gestures.

6. Preparation Rites and Christological Concerns

In the Syro-Antiochene tradition since the end of the fourth century, the preparation of the bread and the wine has been interpreted in terms of the passion and death of Christ. Theodore of Mopsuestia is perhaps the earliest witness to this tradition. In his commentary on the Eucharist, Theodore writes on the offertory procession:

---

53 Varghese, *St James*, pp. 42–43.

54 This is but a general description of the gestures. Some of the minute details are left out.

It is the deacons who bring out this oblation . . . which they arrange and place on the awe-inspiring altar . . . We must also think of Christ being at one time led and brought to His passion, and at another time stretched on the altar to be sacrificed for us. And when the offering which is about to be placed [on the altar] is brought out in the sacred vessels of the paten and chalice, we must think that Christ our Lord is being led and brought to His passion.[55]

The preparation rites of most of the Eastern anaphoras have followed this tradition.[56] The Syrian Orthodox rites of preparation also associate the passion and death of Christ with the act of offering:[57]

The priest picks up the bread in both hands and says: He was led like a lamb to the slaughter, and like a sheep before the shearer, is dumb so He opened not His mouth in His humiliation (Acts 8:32; Is. 53:7). Lord, prepare it with Thy hands. May the Lord reign world without end.[58]

As he places the bread in the Paten and looking upwards, he says: O Thou first-born of the heavenly Father, accept this first-born from the hands of Thy weak and sinful servant.

He mixes water with wine in the cup, and says: *O Lord God, as Thy divinity was united with Thy humanity so unite this water with this wine.*[59]

As he pours the same into the chalice, he says: Our Lord Jesus Christ was crucified on the cross between two thieves in Jerusalem, and was pierced in His side with the spear, and there flowed out from Him blood and water to wash away the sins of all creation. And he who saw it testified, and his testimony is true; and he knows well that what he said is true that you also may believe (John 19:35).[60]

It is interesting to note that the Syrian Orthodox prayers have striking parallels in the Byzantine and East Syrian preparation rites. Syrian Orthodox theologians have seen the mixing of the wine and the water as a symbol of the union of the divine and the human natures. They were always very keen to defend their *miaphysis* Christology against the Byzantines and the East Syrians. The mixing of the wine and water provided a concrete example to illustrate the doctrine of composite hypostasis and the 'one incarnate nature of God the Word'. Thus this doctrine found its expression in the prayer that follows the mixing of water and wine ('as thy divinity was united with thy humanity so unite this water with this wine'). When we compare this prayer with the corresponding formulas in the East Syrian and the Byzantine preparation rites, the doctrinal motif of the West Syrians is evident. In the Byzantine Prothesis, the deacon pours the wine and water together into the chalice saying: 'Lord, Bless the Holy

---

55 Theodore, *Eucharist*, ed. Mingana, p. 85. According to Theodore, the deacons who arrange the bread and wine represent the angels who came and ministered Jesus before his passion (cf. Luke 22:43).

56 See Brightman, *LEW*, 148–49 (= Coptic tradition); 199–206 (Ethiopian tradition); 251–52 (East Syrian); 356–57 (Byzantine).

57 Athanasius, *Anaphora*, p. 6.

58 Cf. Byzantine tradition: Brightman, *LEW*, 356.

59 Cf. East Syrian tradition: Brightman, *LEW*, 251.

60 Also in the East Syrian tradition. Ibid., 251–52.

union.'[61] The East Syrian formula is more elaborate: 'Water is mixed with wine and wine with water, and let them be one: in the name of the Father and of the Son and of the Holy Spirit, forever.'[62]

Thus the widespread action of mixing water and wine has been interpreted by the West Syrians as a ritualization of their Christology. In this regard their approach is perfectly in continuity with the patristic tradition, which has always interpreted liturgical rites or symbols in relation to the person and work of Christ.

---

61 Brightman, *LEW*, 357.
62 Ibid., p. 251.

CHAPTER 6

Pneumatology of the Liturgy

In the economy of salvation, the activity of the Son and the Holy Spirit is 'complementary and reciprocal'.[1] Following the pneumatology of the Cappadocians, the Christian East, especially the Syro-Antiochenes, have always insisted on the unity of the operations of the Son and the Spirit.[2] The redemptive work of the Son cannot be considered apart from the Holy Spirit's work of sanctification.[3] The Church, the Body of Christ, in which the redemptive work continues, is a communion of the Holy Spirit, and Christ is the centre of this *koinonia*.

The Athanasian aphorism ('The word took flesh that we might receive the Spirit'[4]) very well summarizes the Eastern understanding of salvation, which is true of the Syriac tradition as well.

1. Pneumatological Foundations of Liturgy

The Pentecost has placed the Church in a new situation. Henceforth she lives in the Spirit and worships God 'in Spirit and in Truth', which makes her the new Israel and the bride of Christ (Rev. 21:1–2). In fact the uniqueness of the new dispensation is the possibility to worship 'in Spirit and in Truth'. The Spirit inspires the Church to pray ('The Spirit and the Bride say "Come"': Rev. 22:17). Indeed, the Spirit inspires us to address God as 'Abba, Father!' (see above, Chapter 5). As the East Syrian writer Sahdona (seventh century) says, 'the Holy Spirit breathes the memory of God into man'.[5] The Spirit grants him the fear of God,[6] and makes him a 'temple of God', a dwelling-place of the Holy Trinity. In other words, he becomes a temple, 'a place of incessant prayer', or 'a liturgical being'. He regains the privilege and vocation that he lost because of the Fall. The image of God, which implies a relation of communion with God, was impaired by the Fall. It has been restored in the Spirit. Man regains the freedom (*parhesia*) to stand before God and to worship him.

Worship in the Spirit is the one that always pleases God. A hymn of the *Shehimo* (Monday morning) points to its significance:

---

[1] Timothy Ware, *The Orthodox Church* (Penguin Books, 1975), p. 234.

[2] See the beautiful study by Emmanuel-Pataq Siman, *L'expérience de l'Esprit d'après la tradition syrienne d'Antioche*, Théologie Historique 15 (Paris, 1971); John Breck, 'The Two Hands of God. Christ and the Spirit in Orthodox Theology', *SVTQ* 40/4 (1996), 231–46.

[3] Ware, *Orthodox Church*, pp. 234–35.

[4] St Athanasius, *On the Incarnation and against the Arians*, 8. *PG*.26: 996C.

[5] *Le Livre de la Perfection*, ed. A. de Halleux, *Martyrius (Sahdona). Œuvres spirituelles, III, CSCO*.200, SS.86 (tr.), p. 16.

[6] In the Third Service of Pentecost (*Sedro*), the Spirit is called 'the Spirit of piety'. *Ma'de'dono*, p. 351.

God is a Spirit and seeks those who worship in the Spirit; blessed is he who worships Him in Spirit and in truth; the prophets worshipped Him in Spirit and the apostles in the Holy Spirit; and behold, the Church and her children worship and sing praise.[7]

The Spirit, who inspires human beings to praise God, inspires the angels as well: 'Glory to the Father who sent his Son for our salvation; adoration to the Son born in the flesh from the Virgin Mary; thanksgiving to the Spirit who sent the watchers to sing praise to the King born in the flesh'.[8] The Spirit himself teaches prayers. Thus in the *Shehimo*, in a dialogue between the Church and David, we find:

Tell me, King David, what is the praise which you sing by day and by night? Halleluiah is the praise, which the watchers and the angels sing. The Holy Spirit taught it to me and I taught it to the priests, and behold the churches and the monasteries sing with one accord, halleluiah, glory to the Lord.[9]

The idea of 'praises taught by the Spirit' recalls the 'praises and hymns of the Spirit' of which St Paul speaks (Col. 3:16 *Peshitta*).[10] Praise is the sole content of angelic worship. Worship in the Spirit can mean worship along with the angels, who adore God with spiritual songs and praises.

Pentecost is the accomplishment of the salvific work of the Holy Trinity. The Incarnation rendered humanity capable of receiving the Holy Spirit. In a sense, the coming of the Paraclete is the main purpose of the redemption of man in Christ.[11] By the coming of the Holy Spirit, we have become 'sons of the kingdom of God',[12] that is, sons of the heavenly Father and 'partakers of his Holy Spirit'.[13]

The Spirit is 'always at the side of the Holy Church to help her'.[14] This help is manifold, and includes the gift of the faith in the Holy Trinity:

When the Holy Spirit, Giver of life and full of all beauty dwells in the holy apostles in a manner proper to God alone, He honours them with a divine knowledge of the diversity of languages, and teaches children of men to believe . . . in one God who . . . is three persons, but these are one nature and in essence.[15]

---

7 *Shehimo*, p. 61.

8 Revelation to Joseph, *Lilyo*, Third *Qaumo*, *Crown* I, 105; 112.

9 Monday, *Lilyo*, Third *Qaumo*, *Shehimo*, p. 52.

10 The Peshitta version of Rom. 8:26 (the Spirit 'prays for us') and 8:27 (the Spirit 'prays for the saints') and Eph. 6:18 ('Pray at all times in the Spirit') were decisive in shaping the Syriac understanding of prayer. Cf. Robert Beulay, 'La prière continuelle chez les Spirituels Syro-Orientaux', *Notre Vie Liturgique. Etudes Inter-Religieuses* 3 (2000, CERO, Lebanon), 87–111; see 107ff.

11 See Nikos A. Nissiotis, 'The Importance of the Doctrine of the Trinity for Church Life and Theology', in A.J. Philippou (ed.), *The Orthodox Ethos. Studies in Orthodoxy*, Vol.I (Oxford, 1964), pp. 32–69, here p. 55.

12 'On this day the Holy Spirit descends from heaven to mingle with the sons of men that they may become sons of the kingdom.' Pentecost, *Lilyo*, Second *Qaumo*, *Crown* III, 201.

13 Wednesday *Sapro*, *Shehimo*, 153. (Text quoted above.)

14 Pentecost, *Ramsho*, *Enyono*, *Crown* III, 189.

15 Ibid.

The Spirit, who taught 'fishermen to proclaim the mysteries',[16] helps us and enables us 'to offer spiritual fruits of praise well pleasing to God'.[17] This is the meaning of becoming temples for the dwelling of the Holy Spirit.

The Spirit teaches the mysteries of God and persuades us to worship the triune God. He prepares the Church and through it the whole creation for the final gathering up of all things in Christ (cf. Rom. 8:20–23; 1 Cor. 15:28; Eph. 1:10). The Spirit is present in the Church, in each Christian ('the anointed one') as a ceaseless call and an irresistible drive towards the unity of all in Christ, the final *koinonia* of all with the triune God. In the Spirit, who is the foretaste of the blessedness of the kingdom and the guarantee of our inheritance (Eph. 1:14), believers truly possess the things to come and already enjoy them.[18] Worship in the Spirit brings us to the presence of the eternal God and the place and value of everything is revealed in relation to the eternity of God.

The West Syrians consider worship as a gift of the Spirit, the sign of his living presence in human beings. Thus in the concluding prayer of the third service of Pentecost (addressed to the Spirit), this gift is invoked.

> Grant that we may keep in ourselves Your divine gifts and offer You continually pure worship all the days of our lives. Make us pure shrines for Your glory and for the dwelling of Your glorious divinity.[19]

The Lord himself has promised: 'When the Spirit of truth comes, he will guide you into all the truth' (John 16:12). This surely includes the way of prayer. Thus the Spirit who dwells in us will teach us to pray.

> We acknowledge that we have gained and learned by You to offer worship to You in Spirit and in truth ... Make us worthy, by Your loving-kindness and Your grace, to become pure shrines for Your ministry and holy temples for the dwelling of Your glory. So that ... We may raise up glory and thanksgiving and offer prostrate adoration to You, O Spirit Comforter and the Sanctifier of our souls, and to the Father from whom You proceed, and to the Son from whose own You take, now and for ever.[20]

The Spirit makes us shrines, meaning that we become a place of incessant prayer. In fact sanctification by the Spirit means that the Spirit makes us liturgical beings. Our filial relationship with God also implies a liturgical life. Through our incorporation in Christ, we participate in his prayer, and the Spirit who eternally dwells in Christ becomes our unction which penetrates our being. We are entirely 'Christified' by the Spirit who enables us to cry 'Abba, Father!'

---

16 Pentecost, *Lilyo, Crown* III, 199.

17 Pentecost, *Ramsho, Sedro, Crown* III, 190.

18 See Abhishiktananda, *Prayer* (SPCK, New Delhi, 1993), p. 14.

19 *Ma'de'dono*, p. 365.

20 Ibid., pp. 363–64 (Third Service, Inaudible Prayer).

2. Prayers Addressed to the Holy Spirit

In general, prayers directed to the Holy Spirit are rather rare in the West Syrian tradition, another characteristic that it shares with the Byzantine and the other Eastern traditions. Prayers are usually addressed to God the Father (for example the anaphora), to the Son or to the Holy Trinity. The reason may be that the Person of the Holy Spirit is the most mysterious, the least known of the three.[21] As a *sedro* of the service of Pentecost says, the Holy Spirit is the one 'who declares, but cannot Himself be expressed in words', or the Spirit 'exceeds quality' and is 'beyond quantity'.[22]

The liturgy of Pentecost contains a series of prayers addressed to the Holy Spirit.[23] They throw light on the mysterious personality and the work of the third Person of the Holy Trinity. The main ideas that these prayers contain could be summarized as follows.

1 The Spirit is consubstantial with the Father and the Son. Though he is mysterious, his Person is distinct from that of the Father and the Son. The *sedro* of the third service beautifully summarizes the doctrine of the Holy Spirit, and indirectly provides the reason for addressing the prayers to him:

> O God, the Comforter, the Sanctifier of the Churches, the Perfector of all the divine ministries, the Giver of priesthood, the Performer of baptism, the Consecrator of the Sacraments (*roze*), and the Absolver of sins. The Holy Spirit, . . . who declares but cannot be expressed in words; the Sanctfier who needs no sanctification, the Deifying, Who has no need to be deified. The Spirit who moves of His own accord; the Spirit Who possess His own authority and power; the Spirit who is glorified in His own glory; the Spirit Who is exalted in His supreme state of dignity; the Spirit, Who is light and the giver of light . . . The beneficent Spirit, the omnipotent Spirit, the Spirit by Whom the Father is known, the Spirit by Whom the Son is believed, the Spirit Who alone is worshipped with the Father and the Son, the Spirit Who possesses all the Father's attributes except the fatherhood, the Spirit Who owns all the Son's qualities other than birth and incarnation . . . We pray to You, O God, the comforter Spirit, by this sweet incense, beseeching the abundance of Your incomprehensible richness, that even now You be pleased to renew unto us Your divine gifts, and to rest upon us as You did upon the holy disciples in the Upper Room, divide among us the heavenly presents, fill us with Your divine wisdom and with the doctrine of Your divine mysteries (*roze*), make us temples for the dwelling of Your glory, . . . grant to us that we live to You and yield ourselves to You that we may, in purity and holiness, worship You, O God, the Comforter Spirit. Through You and by You we worship the hidden Father, from whom You proceed, and the Son of Whom You take, now and forever.[24]

---

21 See Archbishop Basil Krivocheine, *In the Light of Christ: St Simeon the New Theologian. Life, Spirituality, Doctrine*, St Vladimir Seminary Press, New York, 1986, p. 273.

22 *Ma'de'dono*, pp. 351–52.

23 The Order of the Feast of Pentecost consists of three parts: the first is addressed to the Father, the second to the Son and the third to the Holy Spirit.

24 *Ma'de'dono*, pp. 351–53.

2   The Spirit enlightens our minds to understand the depths of the divine wisdom. In
     other words, he grants us faith and leads us to communion with the triune God,
     which consists of a life of praise and adoration. The third service of the liturgy of
     Pentecost begins with a prayer for the gift of the enlightened mind:

> O Comforter, Holy Spirit, who, in the likeness of fiery tongues, descended
> upon the holy apostles in the Upper Room and enlightened their minds with
> divine understanding; we beseech you to enlighten us with the brightness of
> Your blissful gifts, that now and at all times we may glorify You and the
> Father from Whom You proceed, and the Son from Whom You take, now and
> forever.[25]

3   By His dwelling, the Spirit makes us holy temples, that is, places of incessant
     worship, offered to the Trinity:

> Make us worthy, by Your loving-kindness and Your grace, to become pure
> shrines for Your ministry and holy temples for the dwelling of Your glory, so
> that we are proven to be clean and undefiled in Your presence, we may raise
> up glory and thanksgiving and offer prostrate adoration to You, O Spirit
> Comforter and the Sanctifier of our souls, and to Your Father, from Whom
> You proceed, and to the Son from Whose own You take, now and forever.[26]

3. Meaning and Function of the Epiclesis in the Saint James Liturgy

As we have seen in the last chapter, the essence of the anamnesis is to recall 'the great
and unspeakable love of Christ towards mankind'. The memorial of the loving-kindness
of God is completed with the epiclesis, addressed to the Father 'to send the Holy
Spirit upon the faithful and their offerings'. For the convenience of our analysis we
shall give the text of the epiclesis of Saint James in the Greek, Syriac, Georgian,
Ethiopic and Armenian versions.

St James: Greek (PO 26, 204–5)

St James: Syriac (AS II-2, 150–52)

Have mercy on us, Lord God the Father
almighty; have mercy on us, O God,
according to your great mercy, and send
out (*exaposteilon*) upon us and upon these
holy gifts set before you, your all-Holy
Spirit, (<u>the priest bows</u>) the Lord and
Life-giver who is equal to you in throne
and in kingdom, God the Father and to

Have mercy upon us, O God, almighty
Father, and send (*shadar*) upon us and
upon these offerings that are placed,
your Holy Spirit, the Lord and Life-
giver, who is equal to you in throne, God
the Father and to the Son and equal in
kingdom, consubstantial and co-eternal,
who spoke in the Law and the Prophets,

---

25 Ibid., p. 349.
26 Ibid., p. 365.

your only begotten Son, consubstantial and co-eternal who spoke in the Law and the Prophets and in your New Covenant, who descended in the likeness of a dove upon Our Lord Jesus Christ in the river Jordan and rested upon Him, who descended upon your holy apostles in the likeness of fiery tongues in the upper room of the holy and glorious Zion on the day of the holy Pentecost. (He stands up and says in a low voice): Send down (*katapempson*) Master, your all-Holy Spirit himself upon us and upon these holy gifts set before you (aloud) that he may descend (*epiphoitesan*) upon them and by his holy and good and glorious coming (*parousia*) he may sanctify (*hagiase*) and make (*poiese*) this bread the holy body of Christ (People: Amen), and this cup the precious blood of Christ (People: Amen). (*The priest stands up and says in a low voice*) That they may become to all who partake of them for forgiveness of sins and for eternal life, for sanctification of souls and bodies, for bringing forth good works, for strengthening your holy, catholic and apostolic Church, which you founded on the rock of faith that gates of hell should not prevail against it, rescuing it from every heresy, and from the stumbling blocks of those who work lawlessness, and for the enemies who rose up until the consummation of the age . . .

and in your New Covenant, who descended (*nheth*) in the likeness of a dove upon Our Lord Jesus Christ in the river Jordan, who descended (*nheth*) upon your holy apostles in the likeness of fiery tongues (and he raises his voice). So that overshadowing (*kad magen*) he may make (*ne'bed*) this bread, the life-giving body, the redeeming body, the heavenly body, the body which frees our souls and bodies, the body of Our Lord and Saviour Jesus Christ, for the remission of sins and eternal life for those who receive (People: Amen).

And the mixture which is in this cup, he may make (*ne'bed*) the blood of the New Covenant, the redeeming blood, the life-giving blood, the heavenly blood, the blood which frees our souls and bodies, the blood of our Lord and God and Saviour Jesus Christ for the remission of sins and eternal life for those who receive, that they may be to all who partake of them the sanctification of the souls and bodies, the bearing of fruits of good works, for the confirmation of Your holy Church which you had founded upon the rock of faith and the gates of hell shall not overcome against it, delivering her from all heresy and from the stumbling blocks of them that work lawlessness, even unto the end of the world: both now and at all times and to the ages of ages. Amen.

SJ. Georgian (ROC.18, pp. 406–7)

Have mercy on us, O God, of thy grace . . . and send upon us and on this awful sacrifice of these holy oblations here offered, thy Holy Spirit (*encomium of the Spirit*) . . . To the end that now also his gracious and glorious advent may bless and hallow and make this bread the

SJ. Ethiopian (OC.4, pp. 9–11)

Barmherziger, allmächtiger Gott, sende herab auf uns und auf diese Opfergabe, die wir dir darbringen, dem hl. Geist (*encomium*) . . . und nicht ist es daß wir dieses Brot trennen vom Leibe Christi. Amen . . .

precious flesh of Christ: Amen. And this cup into the true blood of Christ.

Und auch den Kelch zu seinem Blute [mache].

SJ. Armenian (OC.7–8, p. 18)

Mitte in nos et in propositum panem hunc sanctum Spiritum . . . ut faciat panem hunc corpus (*adjectives*) . . . corpus et calicem hunc sanguinem (*adjectives*). Amen.

Cyril of Jerusalem (MC.V, 7)

We beseech God to send forth (*exaposteilai*) the Holy Spirit upon the (gifts) set before him, that he may make (*poiese*) the bread the body of Christ . . .

The Syriac text uses a series of adjectives for the body and blood, apparently to emphasize their sacramental character. We shall examine the vocabulary used to describe the action of the Holy Spirit.

A. 'Send your Holy Spirit'

The epiclesis is addressed to the Father 'to send' (*exapostello*) the Holy Spirit, a general feature universally attested since the end of the fourth century.[27] Cyril of Jerusalem uses this word when speaking of the epiclesis. It is rendered in Syriac by *shadar* (from *sdr* = to send).[28] The Syriac verb *sdr* henceforth became a keyword in the West Syrian epicleses to denote the movement of the Spirit in the sacraments.

The Greek text repeats the demand to 'send down' (*katapempo*) the Holy Spirit. Since the second demand is absent in other versions, we can rightly assume that it was added later, probably at Antioch.[29]

In Saint John's Gospel the advent of the Spirit is described mainly by two verbs: 'come' (*erkhomai*: John 16:7; 13) and 'send' (*pempo*: 14:26; 15:26; 16:7). In the variant reading of the Lord's Prayer in Saint Luke (11:2) we find: 'Your Holy Spirit come (*elthato*) upon us and cleanse us.' Various forms (often imperative) of the verbs 'come'

---

[27] On the meaning of the term 'epiclesis' see M. Jugie, *De forma eucharististiae de epiklesibus eucharististicis* (Rome, 1943), pp. 13–14; see also S. Salaville, 'Epiclèse eucharistique', *DTC* 5, 194–300. On the epiclesis is various Christian traditions, see John H. Mckenna, *Eucharist and Holy Spirit: The Eucharistic Epiklesis in 20ᵗʰ century Theology*, Alcuin Club Collections No.57 (London, 1957).

[28] For an analysis of the epiclesis of St James, see B.D. Spinks, 'The Consecratory Epiklesis of the Anaphora of Saint James', *SL* 11 (1976), 19–38. On the use of the verb *exapostello* in other anaphoras, ibid., pp. 31–32.

[29] On the origin and use of this verb, see Spinks, pp. 32–33.

or 'send' have been fairly regularly used in all known texts of the epiclesis. Recent scholarship has demonstrated that the imperative form of 'come' (*elthe* in Greek and *tho* in Syriac) is used in the earliest form of the epiclesis.[30] This pattern gives the Spirit a direct role in the action and conforms to an early Christian liturgical practice of invoking Christ. The petitions '*Marana tha* or Our Lord come!' (1 Cor. 16:22; Rev. 22:20; *Didache* 10:6) might be examples of it.

However, an epiclesis addressed to Christ, asking him to 'come' is attested in a baptismal account of the *Acts of Thomas* (third century):[31] 'Yea Lord, come and abide on this oil, as you abided on the tree' (ch. 157). In another text, which probably represents an archaic liturgical tradition, the 'Holy Name of Christ' and the 'power' of Christ are invoked and are identified with the Holy Spirit: 'Come, Holy Name of the Messiah; Come power of grace; Come revealer of hidden mysteries . . . Come Spirit of Holiness and purify their reins and hearts' (ch. 27). Both the Greek and Syriac versions of the *Acts* identify the 'Name of Christ' with the Holy Spirit. Here we can find an early stage in the transition to an epiclesis addressed to the Holy Spirit.

In an account of the Eucharist in the *Acts of Thomas* (ch. 50), an epiclesis addressed to Christ is followed by that to the Spirit:

> Jesus, who has deemed us worthy to draw nigh unto your holy Body and to partake of your life-giving Blood; and because of our reliance upon you we are bold and draw nigh, and invoke Your holy Name which has been proclaimed by the Prophets as your Godhead willed; . . . We beg that you may come and communicate with us for help and for life, and for the conversion of your servants unto you . . . [And the Apostle Thomas began to say]: Come, gift of the Exalted; come perfect mercy; come Holy Spirit; come, revealer of the mysteries of the Chosen among the Prophets; come, proclaimer by His Apostles of the combats of our victorious Athlete; come treasure of majesty; come beloved of the mercy of the Most High; come, (thou) silent (one), revealer of the mysteries of the Exalted; come, utterer of hidden things, and shewer of the works of our God; come giver of life in secret, and manifest in your deeds; come giver of joy and rest to all who cleave unto you; come power of the Father and wisdom of the Son, for You are one in all; come and communicate with us in this Eucharist which we celebrate, and in this offering which we offer, and in this commemoration which we make.[32]

Here also the 'Name' is identified with the Holy Spirit. We cannot simply dismiss the epiclesis directly addressed to the Spirit as a Gnostic practice. This type of epiclesis belongs to a theological tradition which emphasized the distinctiveness of the operation of the Holy Spirit. In fact Origen refers to the prayer addressed to the Holy Spirit: 'Let

---

30 See S. Brock, 'The Epiklesis in the Antiochene Baptismal ordines', in *Symposium Syriacum-1972*, *OCA* 197 (Rome, 1974), 183–215 (esp. pp. 199–200; 213); G. Winkler, 'Nochmals zu den Anfängen der Epiklese und des Sanctus im Eucharistischen Hochgebet', *Theologische Quartelschrift* 174 (1994), 214–31.

31 For a study of the baptism in the *Acts of Thomas*, see B. Varghese, *Les onctions baptismales dans la tradition syrienne*, CSCO 512, Subsidia 82 (Louvain, 1989), 1–10.

32 W. Wright, *Apocryphal Acts of the Apostles*, Vol.II (reprint: Philo Press, Amsterdam, 1968), pp.189–90. Chapter 158 gives a Eucharistic account without an epiclesis in the strict sense.

us pray to the Lord; let us pray to the Holy Spirit, so that he might drive away all the clouds, all the darkness, which darkens our vision because of our sins.'[33]

Following this ancient tradition, the early Syriac baptismal epiclesis was more or less regularly addressed to the Holy Spirit, with the demand 'come and sanctify' the baptismal water.[34] But in the case of the Eucharistic epiclesis, the form of address has been modified, apparently under the influence of the developed Trinitarian theology of the fourth century. Thus, while retaining the verb 'come', the demand is directed to the Father. The East Syrian anaphoras of Addai and Mari, Theodore of Mopsuestia and Nestorius, and the Maronite Peter Sharar, as well as a few West Syrian anaphoras, follow this pattern.[35] (West Syrian anaphoras attributed to Jacob of Serugh, Cyril of Jerusalem/Alexandria, Basil, Gregory Yohannan, Eusthathius and Dioscorus of Gazarta are examples.) The Byzantine anaphora of Saint Basil also belongs to this group ('We pray and beseech . . . that Your all-Holy Spirit may come upon us and upon these gifts set forth').

The pattern 'may your Holy Spirit come' might be a revised form of the epiclesis originally addressed to the Spirit.[36] Here the specificity of the person and work of the Spirit is maintained and is presented within the Trinitarian framework. This expression might be used to relate to the coming of the Spirit, in the economy of salvation with his eternal procession from the Father. Thus the dynamic relationship between the Father and the Son and the distinction in hypostases are apparently emphasized. On the other hand, the personal role of the Spirit in the Incarnation and his operation in the redemption of man, continued through the sacraments, are also underlined.

The two verbs used by the Greek Saint James (*exapostello* and *katapempo*) obviously reflect a further developed pneumatology. The idea of being 'sent' corresponds to the pneumatology of Gregory of Nazianzus. Gregory describes the characteristics of each of the three divine hypostases and says that that of the Spirit is 'being sent' (*ekpempsis*).[37] In fact there is no opposition between the 'sending' and 'coming' of the Spirit. Both ideas are rooted in the Johannine pneumatology and are related to the procession of the Spirit from the Father.

---

[33] Hom. 1 in *Lev.*1, *SC* 286 (Paris, 1981), 71.

[34] S. Brock, *Holy Spirit in the Syrian Baptismal Tradition*, The Syrian Churches Series 9 (Kottayam, 1979), 70–115.

[35] Cf. Brock, *Holy Spirit*, pp.119–21; I.H. Dalmais, 'L'Esprit Saint et le mystère de salut dans les épiclèses eucharistiques syriennes', *EL* 90 (1976), 262–71; Spinks, 'Consecratory Epiklesis', pp. 25–27.

[36] We cannot exclude the possibility that the invocation of the Logos in the Egyptian anaphora of Serapion ('O God, may your Holy Logos come – *epidemesato* – upon this bread . . .') had been derived from a tradition in which the Logos was directly invoked. The 'Come' form is also found in some of the Ethiopic anaphoras: see S.A.B. Mercer, 'The Epiklesis in the Ethiopic Liturgy', *Oriental Studies to Paul Haupt* (Baltimore and Leipzig, 1926), 446–453.

[37] See Gregory of Nazianzus, *Sermon* 31:8. *SC* 250 (1978), 291. Also Gregory of Nyssa, *On the Holy Spirit*, against the Macedonians the pneumatomachi, 2, *PG* 45, 1301ff. For a summary of the pneumatology of the two Gregorys, see Franco Bolgiani, 'La théologie de l'Esprit Saint de la fin du 1er siècle après Jésus Christ au concile de Constantinople (381)', *Les quatre fleuves* 9 (1979), 33–72 (see 66–69).

Greek Saint James uses a third verb, *epiphoitao*, a word frequently used of the Spirit's activity in liturgical and patristic texts: 'descending (*epiphoitesan*) upon them'. In Syriac it has been rendered as 'overshadow(ing) [*kad magen*]'.[38]

Epiphoitao is not found in the Bible. In the Syriac (*Peshitta*) New Testament, *agen* has been used to render two key Greek verbs: *episkaiazein* (Luke 1:35 – overshadow) and *skenoo* (John 1:14 – tabernacled).[39] Throughout the Syriac version of Saint James, the word *agen* has entered the West Syrian epikleses.[40] Later West Syrian anaphoras modelled on Saint James use *rahef* (= to hover: derived from Gen. 1:2; Deut. 32:11) or its derivative nouns to describe the descent of the Spirit in the epiclesis. In its Old Testament use, *rahef* (hovering; brooding over; overshadowing; indwelling; tabernacling) implies the life-giving presence of the Spirit. In fact *rahef* seems to have been more influential in the history of the West Syrian liturgy than *agen*. Thus after the twelfth century, the use of the verb *rahef* gave rise to a symbolic waving of the hands over the Eucharistic elements during the epiclesis. This waving has been extended to the epikleses in the consecration of the baptismal water, consecration of Myron and the Ordination. Gradually a threefold waving of the hands followed by three signs of the crosses became the essential part of the blessings of the objects (for example blessing of the wedding ring, or water for the benediction of a house). Thus the particular meaning of the Syrian verbs *agen* or *rahef* got its permanent ritual expression in the West Syrian tradition.

Agen or *rahef* signifies the transforming presence of the Spirit who descends upon the Eucharistic elements as well as upon the community. This is related to the verb *shro* (= to dwell, to rest; to abide).[41] In the Syriac *Acts of Thomas*, the verb *shro* is regularly used (chs 121 and 157).

The Greek Saint James further emphasizes the idea of the descent: 'and by his holy and good and glorious coming (*parousia*)'. This expression might go back to the earliest textual tradition, as it is attested in the Georgian version (though absent in Syriac, Armenian and Ethiopic texts). In the New Testament, Parousia is generally associated with the glorious coming of Christ. For Saint Paul, the Eucharist is a proclamation both of Christ's death and of the faith in his Parousia (1 Cor. 11:26). The liturgical invocation *Marana tha* (1 Cor. 16:22) is in fact a request for the Parousia of Christ. In the New Testament, the Parousia of Christ is called revelation (*apokalypsis*)[42] and appearance or manifestation (*epiphaneia*).[43] The meaning of the word *Parousia*

---

38 *Magen* is the present participle of *agen* (Aphel form of *gn*).

39 Also used in Acts 10:44 and 11:15 to render *epipipto* and in Acts 5:15 and 2 Cor. 1:9 for *episkenoo*. For the use of the verb *agen* see Brock, *Holy Spirit*, pp. 6–7.

40 See S. Brock, 'The Background to some terms in the Syriac Eucharistic Epikleses', *The Harp* XI–XII (1998–99), 1–12 (here 8–10).

41 In the Peshitta Old Testament *shro* is always associated with the operation of the Spirit: see Num. 11:26; 2 Kgs 2:15; 2 Chr. 15:1; 20:14; Isa. 11:2 (rest and reside upon). In all these texts the Spirit (in the feminine) is the subject.

42 1 Cor. 1:7; 2 Thess. 1:7; 1 Pet. 1:7; 13; 4:13.

43 1 Tim. 6:14; 2 Tim. 4:1; 8; Titus 2:13.

(of the Spirit) agrees with the nuances of the Syriac verbs *agen, rahef* and *shro*. It is very possible that the expression 'holy and glorious coming (of the Spirit)' was introduced in Syria in a bilingual Syriac-Greek-speaking area. The Syriac tradition, which has a variety of terms to designate the coming of the Spirit, might have influenced the epiclesis of Greek Saint James.

The West Syrian understanding of the descent of the Spirit as a dynamic presence is attested in the deacon's exhortation that accompanies the epiclesis:

> How awful is this hour and how perturbed this time, my beloved ones, wherein the Holy Spirit from the topmost heights takes wings and descends and broods and rests (*mrahef wshare*) upon this Eucharist here present and hallows it. In calm and in awe were you, standing and praying.

The expression 'descent from above' is not to be understood in a spatial sense but rather as a 'manifestation of the sanctifying presence' of the Spirit, in the liturgical celebration of the Church, the Body of Christ.

B. 'Sanctify and make'

After having recalled the advent of the Spirit using different terms, the epiclesis demands the sanctification of the elements: 'may [he] sanctify (*hagiase*) them and make (*poiese*) this bread the holy body of Christ'. Here the Georgian version follows the Greek, against Cyril's Mystagogical Catechetical homilies (V,5), Syriac, Armenian and the Ethiopic versions which omit 'sanctify'. However, the idea is very well implied in the use of the verb 'make' (*'bd*). However, several West Syrian anaphoras use both verbs.

The Byzantine Saint Basil uses three verbs: 'Your Holy Spirit may come upon us and upon these gifts set forth, and bless (*eulogesai*) them, and sanctify (*hagiasai*) and make (*anadeixai*) this bread the precious body . . .'.[44] The Coptic fragment of Basil omits 'bless'.[45] Since the Syriac agrees with the Mystagogical Catechesis (V,5), we can assume that 'make' (*poieo*) was the original verb and that other terms were borrowed from the Byzantine anaphoras to emphasize the 'transformation'. The Apostolic Constitutions use *apophaino*, a verb that has a similar connotation: 'send

---

[44] On the use of the verb *anadeiknymi* in the anaphora of Basil and other sources, see Bobrinskoy, 'Liturgie et ecclésiologie trinitaire de Saint Basile', in B. Botte et al. (eds), *Eucharistie d'Orient et d'Occident* (Lex Orandi 47, Paris, 1970), pp. 214–17. Saint James uses it in the Institution Narrative: 'he looked unto heaven and showed it (*anadeixas*) to you' (used for both bread and wine). It has been rendered into Syriac with *hawi* (= showed) (only in the case of the bread).

[45] 'may he sanctify and make (*hagiasai kai anadeixai*)'; see J. Doresse and E. Lanne, *Un témoin archaique de la liturgie copte de Saint Basile*; en annexe: Les liturgies 'basiliennes' et Saint Basile par D.B. Capelle, Bibliothèque du Muséon 47 (Louvain, 1960), p. 21. *Anadeiknymi* is also used by Basil himself when he speaks of the epiclesis: 'Which of the saints has left us in writing the words of the invocation at the displaying (*epi te anadeixei*) of the bread of the Eucharist and the cup of the blessing', *On the Holy Spirit* 27:66; *SC* 17bis (1968), 480.

down (*katapempses*) upon this sacrifice your Holy Spirit . . . that he may manifest (*apophene*) the bread the body of your Christ'.[46] In the liturgical use, the verbs *poieo*, *anadeiknymi* and *apophaino* are synonymous. Their meaning is not merely 'to make', but rather 'to display, to manifest or to elevate'. These verbs describe the dynamic presence of the Spirit in the consecration of the Eucharistic elements. By his abiding presence, the Spirit manifests ('makes') the bread and wine as the body and blood of Christ and the worshipping community as the Church, the Body of Christ.

In the West Syrian anaphoras (and in baptismal epicleses), this idea has been rendered using two verbs: *'bd* (= to make) and *hawi* (= to show forth; to manifest; to elevate). The latter is the exact rendering of *apophaino* and *anadeiknymi* and is theologically richer than the former.

By the presence of the Spirit, the Eucharist is manifested as the feast of the Kingdom of God. The eschatological nature of the Eucharistic celebration, as 'the gathering before the throne of God', is manifested. In the New Testament, the descent of the Spirit is the sign of the presence of the eschaton (Acts 2:17–20; Joel 2:28–32), and the manifestation of the Kingdom of God (Rom. 14:17). As we have already noted, in an ancient variant of Luke's version of the Lord's Prayer, the Kingdom is identified with the Holy Spirit (Luke 11:2).[47]

By the sanctifying presence of the Spirit, the bread and wine are 'pneumatized' and become the body and blood of Christ that pneumatize and deify those who partake of it. The epiclesis of the Apostolic Constitutions asks God that those who partake of the body and blood of Christ 'may be filled with the Holy Spirit and [be] worthy of your Christ'.[48] The sanctification or 'making' of the Eucharistic elements as the body and blood of Christ is not an end in itself. They become a means of 'deifying pneumatization' of the communicants. They are associated with the 'fullness of life' in Christ and are 'Christified'. This is implied in the second part of the epiclesis. Their association with the life of Christ grants them 'the forgiveness of sins, eternal life, sanctification of the souls and bodies', and makes them capable of producing good works. This will ultimately result in the strengthening of the Church 'until the consummation of the age'.

C. The Encomium of the Spirit

The epiclesis of Saint James (both in Greek and Syriac) gives a long encomium of the Holy Spirit, which probably belongs to the original form.[49] The encomium (see the texts quoted elsewhere) gives a summary of the pneumatology as it developed

---

[46] *AC* VIII,12,39, *SC* 336 (Paris, 1987), 198–200.

[47] Gregory of Nyssa (also Marcion and Maximus) knew this reading: 'May the Holy Spirit come upon us and cleanse us'. See R. Leaney, 'The Lucan Text of the Lord's Prayer (in Gregory of Nyssa)', *Novum Testamentum* 1 (1956), 103–11.

[48] *AC* VIII,12,39; *SC* 336, 198–200.

[49] See the reconstruction by A. Tarby, *La prière eucharistique*, pp. 65–66.

after the Council of Constantinople (381). In fact Saint Basil and the Nicean–Constantinopolitan Creed do not use the term 'consubstantial' to describe the equality of the Spirit with the Father and the Holy Spirit. However, the idea is strongly implied in the adjective 'worshipped and glorified with the Father and the Son' (*sumproskunoumenon kai sundoxazomenon*).[50] The first part of the encomium underlines the divinity of the Spirit and his consubstantiality with the Father and the Son. Surprisingly, the encomium does not articulate themes such as the procession of the Spirit from the Father and his indwelling in the Son. The expression 'Your Holy Spirit' could be an allusion to the procession of the Spirit from the Father. The encomium is concerned with the distinctiveness of the Spirit as God, rather than his unity with the Father and the Son. This should be understood in the context of the pneumatological controversies of the late fourth and early fifth centuries.

In the second part of the encomium, the personal role of the Spirit in the economy of salvation has been described vividly. The Spirit who spoke through the Law and the Prophets descended on Christ in his baptism 'in the form of a dove', and upon the apostles 'in the form of fiery tongues'. There are striking resemblances between this part and the Baptismal Catecheses of Cyril of Jerusalem.[51] It is likely that Cyril would have played a role in the redaction of the anaphora of Saint James, or at least parts of it, including the epiclesis.[52]

The unity and diversity between the two covenants is emphasized in the epiclesis. This is also one of the favorite themes of Cyril.[53] The reference to the descent of the Spirit in the baptism of Christ and upon the apostles is of great theological significance. Thus the Eucharist, especially the descent of the Spirit, is related to the baptism of Christ and the Pentecost. In the baptism of Christ, the role of the Spirit was precisely to bear witness to Christ as the Son of God. The same Spirit constituted the apostolic community as the Church, the body of Christ. This theological vision is further emphasized in the epiclesis with the demand: 'send out upon us and upon these holy gifts . . . Your Holy Spirit . . . [so that] he may . . . sanctify and make the bread the body of Christ . . .'. The apostles received 'power' by the descent of the Spirit (Acts 1:8). Similarly the epiclesis demands 'the strengthening of the holy Church'.

The structure of the epiclesis is similar to that of the account of the economy of salvation given in the first part of the anaphora (Post-Sanctus followed by Institution/Anamnesis). The Post-Sanctus gives an encomium of the Father: 'Holy, almighty, omnipotent, awesome, good and compassionate'. This is followed by an account of the loving-kindness of God that includes the creation of man in the image of God, his Fall, God's chastisement as a kind father, his guidance through the prophets and finally the Incarnation 'to renew the image of God'.

---

50 Saint Basil uses the term *homotion*.

51 See Tarby, *La prière eucharistique*, pp. 166–71.

52 On the role of Cyril in the evolution of the liturgy of Jerusalem, see A. Paulin, *Saint Cyrille de Jérusalem, Catéchète* (Lex Orandi 29, Paris, 1959), p. 40ff.

53 Tarby, *La prière eucharistique*, pp. 166–71.

In its structure and meaning, epiclesis is inseparably linked to the anamnesis.[54] The whole Eucharistic prayer that concludes with the epiclesis is an 'anamnesis' of the loving-kindness of God towards humanity. In its structure, the Eucharistic prayer was originally a single unit. The 'anamnesis' of the economy of the Son is continued and concluded with the epiclesis.[55] Having commemorated the death, resurrection, the glorious ascension and position at the right hand of God, the Second Coming, the Last Judgement and the reward in the kingdom, the priest supplicates:

> Do not reward us according to our faults . . . but according to your gentleness and your love for man, blot out [our sins] . . . for your people and your inheritance pray to you . . . *People*: Have mercy upon us, Father Almighty. *Priest*: Have mercy upon us (*the Epiclesis follows*).

In the Greek and Georgian versions, the concluding supplication of the anamnesis is addressed to the Father,[56] whereas in the Syriac and the Ethiopian (but not in the Armenian) versions, it is addressed to the Son. In Greek the supplication agrees with the orientation of the anaphora in which all the prayers (except the final thanksgiving prayer) are addressed to the Father. Although the Syriac also follows this pattern, the supplication in the anamnesis has been addressed to the Son and the epiclesis is presented as a demand to the Father through the Son. Thus the following petition has been added to the concluding part of the anamnesis: 'For Your people and Your inheritance pray to You, and through You and with You to Your Father saying: (*People*): Have mercy upon us O God almighty . . . (*Priest says the Epiclesis*).'

Originally the supplication might have been addressed to the Father as a prelude to the epiclesis. But the West Syrians might have modified the anamnesis for reasons that are not very clear. In the early Edessan (or Mesopotamian) anaphoras the anamnesis was probably addressed to the Son. The Maronite anaphora of Peter Sharar and the East Syrian Addai and Mari (only partly) have retained this feature. Therefore we cannot exclude the possibility that the anamnesis of Saint James was modified, probably to suit the Edessan pattern. Christological reasons also cannot be excluded. Some of the early West Syrian anaphoras have a rather long anamnesis summarizing the non-Chalcedonian Christology.[57] The anaphoras attributed to Timothy of Alexandria and to the Patriarch John I are examples.[58] Thus the old Syriac version of Saint James, attested by a group of manuscripts (all fragments), has a long

---

[54] Y. Congar, *Je crois en l'Esprit-Saint*, III (Paris, 1980), pp. 294–304.

[55] According to Louis Bouyer, the anamnesis was the core of the primitive Christian Eucharist and the epiclesis was merely a development of the anamnesis. L. Bouyer, *Eucharist* (Notre Dame and London, 1968), p. 278.

[56] Also in Apostolic Constitutions VIII,12,38; *SC* 336, p. 199.

[57] On this long anamnesis, see O. Heiming, *Anaphora syriaca sancti Jacobi fratris Domini*, *AS* II-2 (1953), 124–25.

[58] See A. Rücker, *Anaphora syriaca Timothei Alexandrini*, *AS* I-1 (1939), 3–47; H. Fuchs, *Die Anaphora des monophysitischen Patriarche Johannan I*, Münster, Westfalen, 1926.

anamnesis, which was abridged in the 'new recension', allegedly made by Jacob of
Edessa (+708).[59]

What is the rationale behind the confession of the attributes of the Spirit in the
epiclesis? To confess the attributes of the Spirit is to confess his divinity and
consubstantiality with the Father and the Son. When his divine attributes are confessed,
the Spirit's sovereignty and absolute freedom *vis-à-vis* the Church and the faithful are
proclaimed. To confess the presence and action of the Spirit in the history of salvation
is to acknowledge his role in the preparation of the Incarnation and in the
accomplishment of the redemption.

4. The Presence of the Spirit in the Eucharist

By the descent of the Spirit, the bread and wine are 'sanctified and made' the body
and blood of Christ. However, this does not mean that in the anaphora of Saint James,
epiclesis is 'the moment of consecration'. Although the Eastern tradition always insists
on the reality of the change of the bread and wine after the consecration, it has almost
never attempted to specify the moment and manner of change. The anaphora as a
whole is a 'moment', a single liturgical rite, in which the worshipping community
experiences the presence of the triune God and enters into communion with him. The
presence is gradually unfolded through a series of prayers and symbolic gestures, and
each of them is an inseparable part of that liturgical 'moment'.

In the epiclesis the reality of the change is emphasized using a series of adjectives
for the body and blood. It is not easy to decide on the origin of these adjectives. They
might have been borrowed from the early West Syrian anaphoras.

The change of the Eucharistic elements cannot be understood with reference to the
Son or to the Holy Spirit alone. It is a Trinitarian action, for salvation is always
Trinitarian. Dionysius Bar Salibi writes: 'Although it is the body of the Son, it is
given to us by the Father, through the Holy Spirit'.[60] The meaning of the Eucharist is
ultimately grounded in Trinitarian theology, because as St Athanasius says, 'The Father
does all things by the Word in the Holy Spirit'.[61]

The epiclesis does not imply that the Spirit is added to the consecrated gifts. The
aim of the consecration itself is to make the bread and wine the pneumatized body
and blood of Christ. The Syro-Antiochene tradition has always insisted on the presence
of the Spirit in the Eucharistic elements. This tradition has left its traces of influence
on the institution narrative found in *Vaticanus graecus* 2282, a ninth-century text of
Saint James, which says that Christ filled the cup with the Holy Spirit.[62] In *Testamentum*

---

[59] See A. Rücker, *Die syrische Jacobusanaphora nach der Rezension des Jaqob(h) von Edessa* (LF,4),
Münster, Westfalen, 1913.

[60] Bar Ṣalibi, *Commentary on the Eucharist*, ch.13:3, p. 70.

[61] *Athanase d'Alexandrie: Lettres à Sérapion*, I,28: *SC* 15 (1947), 133–35.

[62] See Tarby, *La prière eucharistique*, p. 178.

Domini, another document that originated in this tradition, the Holy Communion is given with the words: 'The body of Jesus Christ, Holy Spirit, for healing of soul and body.'[63]

We can give several quotations from the works of the Syriac fathers, namely Saint Ephrem, Issac of Antioch (fifth century) and Jacob of Serugh (+521) who insist on the pneumatic dimension of Eucharist.[64] Issac of Antioch exhorts the faithful: 'Come and drink! Taste the savour of the Spirit, so that your names shall be inscribed with the spiritual powers'.[65]

The last part of the epiclesis of Saint James should be understood in the light of this tradition: 'that they may become to all those who partake of them for forgiveness of sins and for eternal life, for the sanctification of souls and bodies, for bringing forth good works . . .'. These are the results of communion with Christ, in the Spirit. The Spirit comes not for the well-being of the faithful and the Church, but to the very being of the Church. The Spirit sanctifies the faithful, and thus confirms the Church, and protects it from all divisions and heresies. In fact this is the result of our life in Christ that the Spirit grants us.

5. Meaning of Consecration

Consecration implies that the sanctifying action of the Holy Spirit is extended by the Church over the whole of nature. The destiny of nature is allied to that of man. Corrupted because of man, she awaits with him for healing (cf. Rom. 8:19–23).[66] In Christ everything has been restored and sanctified. There is nothing in all creation (outside of evil and sin) that remains foreign to his humanity. By the act of sanctification, the Church incorporates everything into its mission in the world. Thus it brings back to God the elemental principles of the material world. Consecration makes a thing or a place a symbol, a means and a place of manifestation of the divine presence in space and time.

Consecration is an act of restoration to the pre-lapsarian condition. It is an act of liberation. The Church proclaims something to be free from the bondage of sin, evil and corruption. For example, in the consecration of water, it has been restored to its primordial condition. By the epiclesis, the Spirit of God broods over it and makes it life-giving. The water becomes a 'symbol' of divine presence and operation. Thus in

---

63 *TD* II,10; Grant Sperry-White, *The Testamentum Domini: A Text for students*, Alcuin/GROW Liturgical Study 19 (Nottingham, 1191), p. 30.

64 See Brock, *Holy Spirit*, pp. 116–28; E.P. Siman, 'La dimension pneumatique de l'Eucharistie d'après la tradition syrienne d'Antioche', in *L'Expérience de l'Esprit: Mélanges Schilleebeeckx: Le point théologique* 18 (1976), 97–114; also E.P. Siman, *L'Expérience de l'Esprit par l'église d'après la tradition syrienne d'Antioche*, Théologie Historique 15 (Paris, 1971).

65 G. Bickell, *Issac Antiochini, Doctoris Syrorum I* (Giesen, 1873), pp. 32; 8.

66 Cf. S. Bulgakov, *The Orthodox Church*, SVS Press, New York, 1988, pp. 136–37.

the Syrian Orthodox baptismal liturgy, during the consecration of the water, the priest recites the following prayer:

> Almighty God, make (*hawo*) these waters, waters of refreshment, waters of happiness and rejoicing, waters which symbolize (*metarzin*) the death and resurrection of Your Only-Begotten Son, waters of consecration, ... For the purification of the defilements of the body and soul, for the loosening of bonds, for the remission of sins, for enlightenment of the souls and bodies ... for the washing of regeneration, for the gift of adoption, for the robe of incorruptibility, for the renewal of the Holy Spirit. The waters that wash away the defilements of the soul and body; and to You we offer glory now and for ever.[67]

It is not a magical invocation and the changing of a profane object into a divine one. As the Body of Christ, the Church participates in the eternal 'epiclesis' of Christ addressed to the Father to send the Holy Spirit.

In a sense, the prayer of consecration is a request to open our eyes to see the material elements as symbols (*roze*), as a manifestation of God's glory, as well as a source of life and communion with God. It is significant that the verb 'show' (*hawo*) is used in the epiclesis over the baptismal water (also in a few of the West Syrian anaphoras). It is a request for the opening of the eyes of the world to see the object or a place as a *rozo*, of divine presence and operation. The Spirit unveils our eyes, as we turn to Christ – because 'only through Christ is the veil taken away' (2 Cor. 3:14).

Similarly, the Spirit who descends upon the offerings 'makes' them a 'sacrifice', a means of encounter, bond of communion, around which men gather together in Christ. The same Spirit manifests the Eucharistic assembly as the Body of Christ, as the community redeemed in Christ, and as the eschatological gathering ('the festal gathering'). The Spirit opens the eyes of the faithful to realize that they are the manifestation of the Church, the festal gathering.

In the Eastern tradition, Christology and pneumatology are united in one synthesis both liturgically and theologically regardless of the priority of the one aspect over the other. This theological vision provides the key to understanding the meaning of the epiclesis in the anaphora. The epiclesis is the fulfilment of the Eucharistic action as Pentecost is the fulfilment of the economy of salvation.[68] The place of the epiclesis after the anamnesis does not imply any chronological sequence in the works of the Son and those of the Spirit. The liturgy is from beginning to end an epiclesis, an invocation of the Holy Spirit. The Church invokes the Spirit by uniting to the permanent epiclesis of Jesus the Eternal High Priest (John 14:16). The role of the Holy Spirit in the sacraments transcends the limits of a specific formula. The epiclesis shows that the Spirit is a gift of the Father given to the Church, the Body of Christ, that is, to a community that lives in Christ. The Spirit as the gift of the Father is received in a liturgical attitude, in a life of prayer and adoration that unites us with Christ and

---

[67] S. Athanasius (ed.), *The Sacrament of Holy Baptism* (1974), pp. 62–64.

[68] J. Meyendorff, *Byzantine Theology* (New York, 1974), p. 207.

through him with the Father. Spirit is a gift as well as the giver of gifts who comes to complete the works of Christ, that is, to fulfil the will of the triune God for our sanctification and our communion with him. The epiclesis implies that the Holy Spirit, the source of our life and the perfecter of our salvation, is invoked and received in a liturgical context.

CHAPTER 7

The Festal Gathering: The Church and the Communion of Saints

Liturgy is the 'common action' of the Church, in which the head and the body are involved. This is the main task of the Church and goal of its very existence. The nature and vocation of the Church find their best expression in a liturgical celebration.

The Syrian Orthodox ecclesiology, which has not yet been the subject of any major study, is essentially the same as the Syro-Antiochene ecclesiology, as developed by the Byzantines. Following the New Testament understanding of *ecclesia*, the Syrians and the Byzantines saw the Church primarily as a liturgical gathering. In the Pauline Epistles, the word *ecclesia* denotes the community of believers gathered together in a particular place or house for worship. In the First Epistle to the Corinthians, the expressions 'come together' (11:17), 'assemble as a Church' (11:18), 'meet together (to celebrate the Lord's Supper)' (11:20) are somewhat synonymous. Thus the 'assembly', 'Church' and 'the Lord's Supper' are inseparable.[1] The New Testament images of the Church, such as the Body of Christ, the Bride of Christ, New Israel, and Temple of God, reflect the liturgical experience of the first Christians and thus various aspects of the interconnectedness of 'assembly, Church and liturgy'.

This rediscovery of the Eucharistic dimension of the ecclesiology, which is deeply embedded in the biblical and the early patristic traditions, is perhaps one of the most significant contributions of Orthodox theology in recent years.[2]

This relationship between the Eucharist and the assembly was perhaps in the mind of Moses Bar Kepha when he listed the names of the Eucharist. Thus in the opening words of his commentary, he writes:

> It is called 'Assembly' (*knushyo*), 'Communion', 'Access' (*qurobo*), 'Oblation' (*qurbono*), 'Mysteries', 'Perfection of Perfections'. It is called 'Assembly', because it assembles the scattered faculties that are in us into the unity of one God . . .[3]

The West Syrian liturgical texts present the Church as a liturgical assembly, a community that prays. The *shehimo* often speaks of the Church: 'Behold she sings praise.' The theme has been further developed in the offices of the Consecration of the Church and the Renewal of the Church, the first two Sundays of the liturgical year. As we shall see, the liturgical year gradually unfolds the vocation of the Church:

---

[1] Pierre Grelot, 'Liturgie et Vie spirituelle', *DS* 9 (1975), 879–80.

[2] See Jean de Pergame (Métropolite), *L'Eucharistie, l'évêque et l'église durant les trois premiers siècles*, Paris, 1994; Nicholas Afanassieff, *L'Eglise du Saint-Esprit*, Paris, 1975; Paul McPartlan, *The Eucharist Makes the Church*, Edinburgh, 1993 (with bibliography).

[3] Bar Kepha, *Eucharist*, p. 24.

to sanctify and dedicate it for the glory of God and to wait for the Second Coming of Christ. The *Lilyo* of the *Renewal of the Church* speaks of the praying Church in vivid terms: 'The assemblies of the Church are like doves cooing, with the mouth they sing praise, and with the tongue they offer thanksgiving.'[4]

In a *Sedro* of *Lilyo*, the feast of the Renewal of the Church is qualified as the marriage feast. Having referred to the Old Testament types of the Church, the *Sedro* continues:

> And as she stands at the right hand side of the Bridegroom, her Lord, who is there who will not desire her beauty! Therefore, rejoice O Bride of the heavenly King . . . This is the banquet of his praises, this is the marriage feast of the bride and these are her songs of delight.[5]

Psalm 45:10 ('The princess stood in glory, and the queen at your right hand side') is often repeated in the liturgical texts. The princess/queen of whom the Psalm speaks is understood as a prophecy concerning the Mother of God or the Church. The *Ramsho* of the *Qudosh Edto* (Consecration of the Church) contains a beautiful *Sedro,* which gives an exposition of the Psalm (45:10–11). Thus the liturgical texts present the Church as a bride, standing in a liturgical attitude, at the right-hand side of Christ:

> It is of her that David sang when he said that the daughter of the king is adorned with all spiritual beauty within, not like the tabernacle of the Law which Moses raised as a shadow of that which was to come, but with the glorious royal robe of faith and with the holy mystery of baptism and the radiance of the Holy Spirit, with the spiritual and heavenly table of the blood of the Lamb without stain or blemish, and with the Sun of righteousness Christ her Bridegroom, and with the brightness of the doctors inspired by the Holy Spirit . . . David sang of her when he said: Leave your people and your father's house for the King of kings has desired your beauty.[6]

It is in the liturgy that the Church experiences the presence of her heavenly Bridegroom. Liturgy is her life with and in him. The goal of worship is precisely to be with God always.

1. The Spirit and the Bride say 'Come' (Rev. 22:17)

The Church has been saved from error by the living blood of Christ, and has been betrothed to Christ.[7] She is living in a condition of paradox. The fiancé is at the same time present and absent. The liturgy is the expression of her love for the bridegroom who is with her, and is to come. Her attitude, her love, and eagerness to meet the

---

4 *Lilyo,* Third *Qaumo, Crown* I, p. 31.

5 *Lilyo, Renewal of the Church,* Second *Qaumo, Crown* I, p. 29.

6 *Ramsho, Sedro, Crown* I, p. 3.

7 Cf. *Qudosh Edto, Ramsho, Enyono:* 'Blessed are you O Church, the fiancé of Christ, for you have been saved from error by his living blood', *Penkitho* (Pampakuda), I,1.

heavenly beloved are expressed in her worship. Thus the *Ramsho* of the *Qudosh Edto* exhorts the Church to sing praises:

> O Church, sing praise to the heavenly king, for you have become his bride. He has written the marriage contract with his blood. Sing [praise] to him, for he dwells within you and his cross protects you. Faithful Church, sing praise to him, to the bridegroom who has betrothed you and adorned you with glorious gifts. Behold the high priests and pious priests, and all your children who are in you offer praises.[8]

In a liturgical celebration, the Church realizes her identity as the Bride of Christ. She becomes aware of her calling and mission. In and through the liturgical gathering, she manifests herself as the beloved of Christ, and she proclaims his Good News:

> Rejoice, thrill with joy, Church of true believers.
> Raise your voice in song and chant the praise of the Beloved Son
> who suffered for you and delivered your children from death,
> and translated them into the dwellings of life.
> He has placed in you his body and his blood
> that you may be purified from your sins, that you may enter the bridal chamber,
> that you may take your pleasure with him in the heavens and inherit eternal life
> in the mysterious dwelling place where death has no power.
> O Church, stand on the high mountains
> Sing praise to your Bridegroom who has taken away from you
> the evil of the darkness of error, and made the true light to shine upon your face,
> that it may spread on earth and dissipate the darkness.[9]

Liturgy is her self-affirmation, the manifestation of her very being. She says to the nations: 'I stand and will not be shaken.' Her hymns and prayers are the proclamations of the mystery of the Incarnation:

> Say to the nations: I stand and I will not be shaken.
> Confess without ceasing how great is the fruit within you.
> he who is sacrificed by you for the remission of sins
> instead of lambs and other victims.[10]

She offers true worship and invites the whole of humanity to be united with her to worship the triune God. Thus in the *Promiun* of the third hour of *Qudosh Edto* we find: 'The holy Church teaches to worship the Father and You, the only incarnate Son, and Your Holy Spirit, the Trinity who is equal in essence, glory and worship . . .'.[11]

The Bride of Christ, the Church, never stands without the Spirit.[12] Worship is the sign of her permanent possession of the Spirit. In the Spirit, she eagerly waits for the glorious coming of Christ, with the invocation 'Come Lord' (Rev. 22:16).

---

[8] Ibid.

[9] *Qudosh Edto, Ramsho, Crown* I, pp. 4–5.

[10] Ibid., p. 5.

[11] Pampakuda, MS 13, p. 18 (Mal. tr. p. 17).

[12] Paulose Mar Gregorios (= Paul Varghese), *The Joy of Freedom. Eastern Worship and Modern Man*, CLS, Madras, 1986, p. 11.

2. The Great Cloud of Witnesses: Liturgy and the Communion of Saints

The West Syrian tradition gives great importance to the commemoration of the Mother of God, prophets, apostles, saints, doctors and martyrs. The Church honours or venerates them and seeks their intercession. This is based on the vision of the dynamic unity of all believers in Christ. The bond of mutual love and prayer that unites all – saints and sinners alike – with Christ makes this intercession possible.

The veneration of the Mother of God and saints has its theological basis in the organic unity of all in Christ, the most striking aspect of the New Testament ecclesiology. The various New Testament images of the Church underline the fact that Christians are united not only among themselves, but they are one in Christ. They are united with Christ for ever. This oneness in Christ is realized in Baptism and maintained through the Eucharist. Christians are 'baptized into one body by one Spirit' (1 Cor. 12:12. cf. Rom. 6:3; Gal. 3:27–28). Through our participation in one bread 'we who are many are one body' (1 Cor. 10:17).

As George Florovsky says, 'The Christian Church is a sacramental community, *communio in sacris*, a fellowship in holy things, that is in the Holy Spirit or *communio sanctorum*.'[13] It is this sacramental communion in Christ by the Holy Spirit which makes the communion of men, both living and departed, possible. Their bond of unity is so solid and dynamic that, as Paul says, 'nothing, even death, can dissolve it' (Rom. 8: 38–39).

The whole of liturgical life is a deepening and realization of our Eucharistic union with Christ, which implies the company of all the living and the departed, all who are eternally united with Christ. All are united in Christ in a bond of brotherhood, in a filial relationship with God the Father, which is maintained in an act of prayer and praise. As Nicholas Arseniev writes:

> The Spirit of communion here [that is, in the Eucharist] finds its expression, the bond of brotherhood, organically uniting in an act of prayer and praise, all the faithful, both the living and the departed, and the whole Church, heavenly and earthly, and – what is more – the whole of creation gathered around 'the head of the body, the Church'.[14]

The Church in the New Testament is above all a liturgical gathering: 'The Church of the first-born whose names are enrolled in heaven' (Heb. 12:33) is also engaged in continuous prayer. According to the Book of Revelation, the martyrs who have 'washed their robes and made them white in the blood of the Lamb' are 'worshipping him day and night within his temple' (7:14–15). St John adds that 'their prayers ascend before God with the smoke of incense' (8:4). These images imply that our unity in Christ, our liturgical existence, is not dissolved by death. The Spirit of God, who is the Spirit

---

13 George Florovsky, *Bible, Church, Tradition: An Eastern Orthodox View*, Vol.I (Massachusetts, 1972), p. 61.

14 N. Arseniev, *Mysticism and the Eastern Church* (SVSP, New York, 1979), p. 147.

of communion, perpetuates our oneness in Christ even after the end of our earthly life. It is through prayer that we live in communion with our Lord, because the Spirit never ceases to intercede for us (Rom. 8:26). The Spirit of God, which each believer receives in Baptism and Chrismation, unites him with the body of Christ, the communion of saints. His prayer, even if it is feeble, is joined to the prayers of the saints, which ascend to the presence of God (cf. Rom. 8:26–27; Rev. 8:14). He has become a member of a praying community, in which all are 'one body in Christ' (Rom. 12:5), 'members of one another' (Eph. 4:25), called to 'bear another's burdens' (Gal. 6:2). The bond that unites the community is that of love, which finds its expression in mutual prayer. As Bishop Kallistos Ware rightly says, 'The communion of Saints is especially a communion of prayer; we pray with each other and for each other.'[15]

The saints, who were the best examples of true prayer, never cease to pray even after the end of their earthly sojourn (cf. Rev. 6:9–10; 7:9–12 etc.). As members of the Body of Christ, they pray for all, not merely for their individual spiritual growth, but for the coming of God's Kingdom for all and in all.

In each of the major canonical hours, *Ramsho, Lilyo* and *Sapro*, a section has been set apart for the commemoration and intercession of the saints. In the *Lilyo*, the theme of the first *qaumo* (= watch) is 'the Mother of God' (from Easter to the feast of the Cross). Similarly, Wednesday has been dedicated to her memory. The theme of the second *qaumo* is always 'the Saints and Martyrs', whereas that of Thursday is 'Apostles and Martyrs'.

The *Quqliun* sung at the close of a liturgical celebration begins with the memory of the Mother of God and the Saints. The feast of St Peter and St Paul (29 June) and the Ascension of the Mother of God (15 August) are preceded by Lents, and are reckoned as 'Dominical feasts'. In the Holy Eucharist, several prayers of the preparation rites, as well as the fourth and the fifth Diptychs, commemorate the Mother of God and the saints. The general prayer of the preparation rites strongly reflects the West Syrian attitude towards the issue. The priest holds the paten and the chalice in his hands crosswise and commemorates briefly the events of the Incarnation from Annunciation to Ascension. Then he continues:

> We like wise commemorate at this time, upon this Eucharist that is set before us, particularly our father Adam and our mother Eve and the Holy Mother of God, Mary, and the prophets and apostles, preachers and evangelists and martyrs and confessors, righteous men and priests and holy fathers and true shepherds and orthodox doctors, hermits and cenobites and those who are standing and praying with us with all those who, since the world began, have been pleasing unto Thee from our father Adam even unto this day.[16]

In the Eucharistic celebration, the whole Church is present in its oneness and catholicity. It is out of this awareness that this prayer speaks of the saints as 'those who are

---

[15] Kallistos Ware, 'One Body in Christ: Death and the Communion of saints', *Sobornost* 3–2 (1981), 188–89.

[16] Athanasius, *Anaphora*, p. 12.

standing and praying with us'. The idea that the saints 'pray with and for us' appears regularly. Thus in the *Ramsho* of Wednesday, the *eqbo* addresses the Mother of God:

> We beseech you, Mother of God, that with us and for us you may be our intercessor with the king of kings, that he may make his peace and calm to dwell in all the world, and to make to pass the scourge of wrath from all the world in his mercy.[17]

3. The Mother of God

Among the saints, the most exalted position has been given to the Blessed Virgin Mary. She is both the personification of the Church and the role model for each Christian, because she is the one who is 'full of grace' (Luke 1:28, *Peshitta*), and the 'Holy Spirit had dwelt in her' (Luke 1:35). The fourth Diptych qualifies her as '[the one] who is worthy to be blessed and glorified of all the generations of the earth, the holy, the exalted, the glorious and Ever-virgin Mary, Mother of God'.[18] The hymns of the breviary have lavished various titles on Mary and used imageries that are rooted in the Old Testament.

> In the law and in prophecy Moses, the head of the prophets, represented the figure of the blessed mother by the ark of the law and the pot of manna and by the staff of Aaron which budded within the holy of holies (Heb. 9:4), and by the dew and the fleece of Gideon (Judg. 6:37), and by the new jar of Elisha (2 Kgs. 2:20) and by the light cloud of the glorious Isaiah (Isa. 19:1).[19]

> The just of the old gave fair and lovely names to Mary, the daughter of David, the holy virgin: Ezekiel, the exile, called her the closed door (Ezek. 44:2); Solomon, the garden enclosed and the sealed fountain (Songs 4:12); David named her a city (Ps. 48:2) and Christ is the blade which shot up within it without seed; he has become the food of the nations and he has exalted her memory in heaven and earth.[20]

In the Eastern and in the Latin traditions, she is venerated or honoured, but not worshipped.[21] We ask her to be our 'intercessor', or to pray for us so that 'your Son may have mercy on us'. This petition stems from a continued meditation that the person whom Mary brought forth was truly God.[22] The amazing paradox that God became man has been expressed in poetic terms. Thus in the offices of Nativity we can find a series of hymns on Mary, which are in fact the glorifications of 'the Great One who became small for our sake':

---

17 *Shehimo*, p. 121.
18 Athanasius, *Eucharist*, p. 45.
19 Wednesday, *Ramsho, Shehimo*, p. 130.
20 Wednesday, *Lilyo, Shehimo*, p. 137.
21 Ware, *The Orthodox Church*, pp. 261–62.
22 Bede Griffiths, Introduction to *Shehimo*, p. ix.

> The Virgin has begotten the Wonderful (Isa. 9:6), let us go and behold Him, who is older than time, wrapped in swaddling clothes, the Old One, the Ancient of Days, who was born of the Virgin; the Almighty who weighs the mountains was carried on the maiden's arms; He who gives food to the hungry, was sucking milk like a babe, the Son who is without beginning, wished to have a beginning, He came to be born, whereas He is eternal.[23]

Mary is the embodiment of humanity. Therefore God honoured her by dwelling in her and taking flesh from her. Through the humiliation and the 'sufferings' that she had endured (cf. Luke 2:35), Mary had participated in the cross of Christ and, consequently, she was glorified and made blessed among women. She is the prototype of our participation in the cross of Christ and the consequent deification and exaltation:

> In whom indeed shall I dwell, but in the gentle and humble? He looked upon her and dwelt in her who was humble among the children of men; for no one was ever so humble as Mary, and it is manifest that none was ever so exalted as she was.[24]

Mary is also a model for prayer. Thus according to one of the prayers of *Shehimo*, the angel appeared to her 'while Mary was standing in prayer and making supplication before God'.[25]

The reason for attributing the highest position to Mary among the saints is that 'she brought forth us in her virginity Christ the King, the Saviour of the whole creation'.[26] 'She was able to bear the hidden power which bears heaven and earth.'[27]

In Eastern Christian spirituality, Mary is a model for saintly life, absolute trust and hope in God, in spite of the 'sword that pierce through the soul'. She is the unique example of simplicity, poverty and crucified life and the life resurrected in Christ.

4. Those who have Pleased God

The horizons of the Church are not limited to the new dispensation. Thus the memory of the prophets and the Old Testament saints are regularly evoked along with the apostles and the martyrs, for they are 'the builders of faith and pillars of the holy Church'.[28] They have confessed the mystery of Christ and laboured for the Kingdom of God: 'The prophets sowed in suffering, the apostles reaped in joy, and the doctors gathered a harvest full of joy.'

---

[23] *Ma'de'dono*, p. 11; also *Shehimo*, p. 136.

[24] Wednesday, third hour, *Shehimo*, p. 163.

[25] Wednesday, *Sapro*, *Shehimo*, p. 153; Wednesday, *Lilyo*, First *Qaumo*, *Shehimo*, p. 137.

[26] Monday, *Ramsho*, *Shehimo*, p. 33.

[27] Ibid., p. 32.

[28] Thursday, *Ramsho*, *Shehimo*, pp. 170–71. In Revelation also the Prophets are mentioned along with the Apostles (Rev. ch.4).

The first men on earth also are members of the mystical body of Christ. Thus a *Qolo* poetically expounds the parable of the hired labourers and underlines the unity of the two testaments:

> Come, my brothers, let us consider who were the labourers, whom the Son of the King hired for the vineyard of his Father. In the morning of the day he hired Abel and Seth; at the third hour Abraham, Isaac and Jacob; at the sixth hour, he hired the prophets, at the ninth hour again he chose apostles; at the eleventh hour the thief; may their prayer assist us.[29]

Thus the great cloud of witnesses includes all the saints who have pleased God since Adam. The same Son of the heavenly Father called and appointed the saints of the Old and the New Testaments for his work of tending the vineyard. All are united in Christ by an eternal bond of love and prayer. That bond is not ephemeral, but it is dynamically continued in the coming world, for everything united to Christ exists for ever.

In the Church, 'the first-born whose names are inscribed in heaven', 'those who have washed their robes and made them white in the blood of the Lamb', stand before God and 'serve him day and night within his temple' (Rev. 7:14–15). Worship is their eternal vocation. The worship in the present world is an image and foretaste of the 'eternal worship' in the coming world.

The life of the saints, both of the old and the new dispensations, is a guarantee of God's promises and the transfiguration of humanity. The awareness of their company assures us that we share in the faith and company of all who have pleased God.

The intercessions addressed to the Mother of God or the saints underline the fact that we worship in the Church as members of the mystical body of Christ. We pray in Christ, and our prayers are joined to his prayers in which the saints also join. Thus our prayers ascend towards God as a single offering in Christ, as a sweet incense that rises before God. In the case of the saints, the bond of prayer that unites them with Christ is never interrupted (Rev. 7:15–17). This is implied in the concluding words of the *Martyrdom of Polycarp*: 'This is the story of blessed Polycarp. Now he is with the Apostles and the entire just; Joyfully glorifying God the Father almighty and blessing our Lord Jesus Christ.'[30]

The whole life of a saint is one of continuous prayer.[31] We are called to achieve this blessed state. The intercession of the saints implies that we join a praying community, a community that intercedes for the whole world, and that intercession is the most perfect form of Christian prayer. By their intercessions, the saints join the high priestly

---

[29] Tuesday, *Lilyo*, Second *Qaumo*, *Shehimo*, p. 94. Cf. Thursday *Sapro*: 'In the morning the Son of the King went forth to hire labourers for the vineyard of his Father's house; he hired first the prophets and the apostles, and at the eleventh hour the thief, and he gave him the key and sent him to Paradise.' *Shehimo*, p. 198.

[30] Agnes Cunningham, *Prayer. Personal and Liturgical*, p. 42.

[31] Cf. Origen, *On Prayer*, quoted by Cunningham, *Prayer*, p. 13.

prayer of Christ, which is nothing but an offering of the whole world before God. Through their intercessions, the saints, 'the living stones of the spiritual house of God, offer spiritual sacrifices acceptable to God through Jesus Christ' (1 Pet. 2:4). Thus, in a sense, the communion of saints reveals the true goal of prayer, which is the salvation of all. It means that true Christian prayer is the prayer with all and for all. It gives a key to understanding the meaning of our existence as Christians. We are members of a community consisting of the living and the departed, gathered together in Christ. We are saved not as individuals, but as members of the Body of Christ. As members of the Body of Christ, our prayers presuppose the prayers of the whole Church. Similarly, our intercessions presuppose the intercession of the whole Church.

5. Place of the Diptychs

In the Syro-Antiochene tradition, the Diptychs have been placed after the epiclesis, as part of the Eucharistic prayer.[32] This arrangement has been attested in the Mystagogical Catechesis of Cyril of Jerusalem, the Apostolic Constitutions, the Testament of Our Lord, the anaphora of St James as well as in the Byzantine anaphoras. In the Syrian Orthodox Church, at least until the tenth century, there existed the custom of reading 'the Book of Life' at the beginning of the anaphora. Pseudo-Dionysius the Areopagite (c. 500)[33] and George, Bishop of the Arabs (d. 724)[34] knew this practice.

During the time of Moses Bar Kepha (d. 903), the Book of Life was still read between the Kiss of Peace and the washing of the hands. However, Bar Kepha says that the sixfold commemorations were made after the epiclesis. The original custom of Mosul and its neighbourhood was to read the Book of Life at the beginning of the anaphora. However, under the influence of the anaphora of St James, the reading of the Book of Life became obsolete. Thus in the twelfth century, Dionysius Bar Salibi writes: 'Nowadays, its reading has disappeared every where'.[35]

Tradition has attributed the same significance to both the Book of Life and the Diptychs. The commemoration of the names of the living and the departed, in both cases, is an act of communion. Thus Bar Kepha writes on the reading of the Book of Life:

> The Book of Life is read upon the altar for these reasons. First: because it proclaims before us those who have piously and holily arrived at a holy end. Secondly: that it may show that they are living and not dead. And this is evident from the fact that they are proclaimed with Jesus, according to that: 'The souls of the righteous are in the hands of God' (Wisd. 3:1). Thirdly: because in their life they cleaved to the holy things, it is right that after their death also they should be proclaimed

---

[32] For a study of the Diptychs, see R.F. Taft, *The Diptychs*, OCA 238, Rome, 1991.

[33] *EH*, III-ii 425D. In the *Ecclesiastical Hierarchy*, the order of the rites is Creed, Kiss of Peace, Book of Life/Diptychs, washing of the hands.

[34] George, *Commentary*, p. 20.

[35] Bar Salibi, *Eucharist*, 8:3, p. 47.

over the holy things. Fourthly: again, whereas they are read upon the altar, which represents Jesus, [this] makes known that they are with Jesus always, according to that: 'Where I am, there shall my minister also be' (John 12:26), and according to that: ['May they be one in us' – John 17:21]. Fifthly: it shows also that there is a holy remembrance of them. Sixthly: by proclaiming them he urges us to imitate their holy conversation, and also their right faith, that we too may be worthy of their blessed end, and after our decease be proclaimed upon the altar, as they are proclaimed.[36]

Although the public reading of the Book of Life has been discontinued, some of its elements were incorporated into the general commemorations in the preparation rites and in the pre-anaphora. Thus the present Syrian Orthodox order of the Eucharist celebration includes 'the reading of the names' on two occasions: (i) in the preparation rites, after having put on the liturgical vestments, and prepared the bread and wine, the priest holds the paten and the chalice in the hands crosswise and remembers the names of the living and the departed; (ii) in the pre-anaphora, after the Creed and the washing of the hands, the priest kneels down before the altar and says an inaudible prayer. When he has concluded it, the priest remembers whomever he may wish to pray for, living or departed, making the sign of the cross with his thumb on the altar. These two 'commemorations' were introduced after the disappearance of the reading of the Book of Life, and are more of a 'parochial style'. Usually, the names of the parish members are remembered. Their communion with Christ is invoked and sealed when the celebrant silently reads their names. The Diptychs that follow the epiclesis are 'official and hierarchical'. We shall deal with them, as they are part of the anaphora.

6. Anamnesis and the Commemorations

Commemoration is a basic and essential element of the anaphora. We commemorate in one way or another events as well as names. In the Eucharist, the Church commemorates the whole economy of salvation and realizes its integration into it. The Church thus confesses its identity as the community redeemed in Christ ('Your people and Your inheritance').[37] This is implied in the anamnesis of Syriac St James:

> Remembering therefore, O Lord, your death and your resurrection on the third day from among the dead, and your ascension into heaven and your position at the right hand of God, and your terrible and glorious second coming wherein you are about to judge the world in righteousness and reward every one according to his deeds: we offer you this fearful and bloodless sacrifice, that you would not deal with us according to our sins, nor reward us according to our iniquities, but according to your mildness and love for mankind, blot out our sins, your suppliants. For your people and your inheritance beseech you, and through you to your Father, saying. (*People*): Have mercy upon us, O God, Father Almighty.[38]

---

36 Bar Kepha, *Eucharist*, pp. 41–42.

37 See the last phrase of the anamnesis in St James.

38 *AS* II-I, 148. Cf. Athanasius, *Anaphora*, p. 40.

The anamnesis evokes the death, resurrection, ascension, the Second Coming and the Last Judgement. Thus the past events and those to take place are commemorated. Here the commemoration implies our participation (or communion) in the sacrifice of Christ and also the foretaste of the world to come. Anamnesis is the 'actualization' or 'representation' of the things that have taken place, and that will take place. As Theodore of Mopsuestia says, 'We perform, therefore, this ineffable mystery (*rozo*) which contains the incomprehensible signs of the economy of Christ our Lord, as we believe that the things implied in it will happen to us'.[39]

The commemoration is an act of the Church, the Body of Christ. It is a proclamation of its communion in the events that have been evoked.

The meaning of the commemoration of the names of the living and the departed should be understood in relation to the theological significance of anamnesis (that is, the commemoration of the events). The Eucharistic celebration as a whole is a 'commemoration'.[40] The Diptychs are an extension of the anamnesis. In Christ, in the Spirit of God who brings all things into memory, we commemorate the whole Body of Christ. The Diptychs that follow the epiclesis integrate the intercession into the Eucharistic action. The Diptychs are the confession of our communion, our oneness in Christ, realized by our 'commemoration of the events' (anamnesis) and the coming of the Spirit. The place of the Diptychs is in harmony with the Trinitarian orientation of the anaphora. The Church, the living and the departed are integrated into the economy of salvation effected by the Trinitarian community. The Diptychs imply that the community of the redeemed has been integrated into the Trinitarian communion.

7. Epiclesis and the Commemorations

In the thought of Cyril of Jerusalem, the commemoration of the names is apparently related to the epiclesis:

> Then after the spiritual sacrifice, the bloodless sacrifice has been perfected, we beseech God over that sacrifice of propitiation, for the common peace of all churches, for the stability of the world, for emperors, for armies and auxiliaries, for the sick, for the oppressed; and praying in general for all who need help, we all offer this sacrifice.[41]

In the anaphora, the prayer *par excellence* of the Church, all classes of men are remembered, because this brings 'help' for all who are in need. For Cyril, this is true in the case of the departed as well. So he adds:

---

[39] *Hom. on Baptism* (ed. Mingana), p. 20.

[40] This is the theological approach of Cyril of Jerusalem (*Myst. Cat.* V). Cf. Schmemann, *Eucharist*, ch.X (= *Sacrament of Remembrance*), pp. 191–211.

[41] *Myst. Cat.* V:8.

Then we commemorate also those who have fallen asleep before us . . . for we believe that it will be the greatest profit to the souls for whom supplication is offered in the presence of the holy and most awful sacrifice.[42]

For Cyril, 'the help' is open to all who have departed this world with sin or without sin:

In the same way offering our prayers for those who have fallen asleep, even though they were sinners . . . we offer Christ slain for our sins, propitiating God, the lover of man, for them and for ourselves.

In the anamnesis, the worshipping community has identified itself as 'Christ's people and inheritance', that is, as the Body of Christ. The Holy Spirit has been invoked upon this mystical body as well as upon its offering ('upon us and upon these offerings'). The Holy Spirit, who transformed the offering into the body and blood of Christ, manifests the community as the mystical body of Christ. This has been alluded to in the prayer that follows the epiclesis, which is in fact a prayer for the Church and serves as the introduction to the Diptychs:

We pray You, O Lord, that these [Holy Mysteries] may sanctify the souls and the bodies of all those who partake of them; that they may bear the fruits of good deeds; for the confirmation of Your Holy Church which is firmly established on the rock of faith and is invincible to the gates of hell. Deliver her, O Lord, from all heretical scandals to the end of time, that she may offer up glory and thanks to You and to Your Only-begotten Son and Your Holy Spirit . . .[43]

Then, as a continuation of the epiclesis, the Church commemorates its members, both the living and the departed, with the demand: 'Remember, O Lord!' The epiclesis, the most ardent prayer of the Church, 'manifests' the bread and wine as the body and blood of Christ. The Spirit dwells upon (or pneumatizes) the offerings as well as the mystical body of Christ. The Spirit manifests the assembly as the *Ecclesia*, the Body of Christ in its catholicity and oneness. In the Spirit, the Church commemorates the whole of its ranks, the living and the departed. In the Spirit, the Bride of Christ asks: 'Remember, O Lord' (cf. Ps. 132:1). It is a plea for the salvation and unity of all in Christ. This theological link between the epiclesis and the commemoration is implied in the anaphora of St James, in the prayer that follows the epiclesis, quoted above.

The Spirit, who brings the Word into the memory of the faithful, 'brings' the Last Supper and the Table of the Kingdom into the 'memory' of the Church. The same Spirit 'brings' the whole Body of Christ, both the living and the departed, into the 'memory' of the Eucharistic community, and enables it to intercede: 'Remember, O Lord'. In the Spirit, the Church offers them to God or, rather, unites their memory

---

[42] Ibid., V:9.

[43] Athanasius, *Anaphora*, p. 42. In the Syriac anaphora of the Twelve Apostles, the Diptychs are the continuation of the epiclesis. See Jasper and Cuming, p. 127.

with the eternal sacrifice of Christ. The whole of humanity has been offered to God the Father 'in the eternal Spirit'.

The epiclesis is the earnest plea that the Spirit may descend upon the ecclesial assembly and make known the mysteries of the Kingdom.[44] The mystery consists of the unity and salvation of all in Christ. The place of the Diptychs after the epiclesis implies that the real purpose of the coming of the Spirit is the building up of the Body of Christ, the bringing together of all in Christ.

Those who are commemorated are placed before God for an eternal memorial. We pray that the person will live on in the memory of God. When God 'remembers' something or someone, he is not operating psychologically, but affirming that particular being, that is, that he has been given eternal life.[45] Therefore the 'help' that the Eucharist brings to a person is of ontological significance. Thus the goal of the Diptychs is the salvation of all. It is a prayer for the grace to stand without blemish before God. Thus, having concluded the Diptychs, the priest continues: 'Keep us, O Lord, without sin until the end of our life, and gather us at the feet of Your elect ones.[46]

The Diptychs are an expression of oneness in Christ and a request for its eternal continuation ('Remember, O Lord!'). It is a confession of the communion, the 'being together' of Christians in Christ. The Church's essential role is to realize the 'oneness' and to lead the way to its eschatological fulfilment in the *Pleroma* of Christ.

The West Syrian Diptychs in their actual form consist of eighteen prayers, arranged in six 'canons'. Each canon consists of three prayers: (i) a prayer (or a proclamation) by the deacon that begins: 'We commemorate'; (ii) during the deacon's prayer, the priest says an inaudible prayer on the same theme; (iii) an ekphonesis by the celebrant follows it.[47]

Among the six canons, the first three commemorate the living and the last three the departed. The arrangement is as follows: (i) Orthodox prelates; (ii) living brethren; (iii) kings and rulers; (iv) saints; (v) doctors of the Church; (vi) the faithful departed. The canons that the deacon reads aloud are not fixed and final. In the Syrian Orthodox Church, different collections of canons have existed, many of which are no longer in use.

The first canon commemorates the Patriarch, the Catholicos of the East,[48] and the diocesan Metropolitan, 'with the rest of all Orthodox Bishops'. In his inaudible prayer, the priest prays for all the priestly orders and the faithful. In the same prayer he says: 'Wherefore we offer unto you, O Lord, this bloodless sacrifice for the Holy Zion the mother of all Churches and for Your Holy Church throughout the whole world; that You may grant her the gifts of Your Holy Spirit.'[49]

---

[44] Dalmais, *The Church at Prayer*, I, p. 261.

[45] See Metropolitan John of Pergamon (Zizioulas), 'The Eucharist and the Kingdom of God', *Sourozh* 58 (Nov. 1994), 1–12; 59 (Feb. 1995), 22–38; 60 (May 1995), 32–46.

[46] Athanasius, *Anaphora*, p. 48.

[47] On the History of the West Syrian Diptychs see B.Varghese, *The Syriac Version of the Liturgy of St James*, pp. 38–39.

[48] The name of the Catholicos is omitted in the Syrian Orthodox Church of Antioch.

[49] First Canon: The inaudible prayer by the priest: Athanasius, *Anaphora*, p. 43.

This prayer shows that what is asked in the Diptychs is inseparable from the epiclesis. The coming of the Spirit enables the worshipping community to see that it offers the Eucharist in union with all the faithful and the departed. It expresses the unity of the whole Body of Christ 'throughout the whole world' by commemorating all the members of the Church. Thus the reading of the Diptychs is an 'anamnesis' of the oneness and catholicity of the Church, a manifestation of the communion, the bond of love that unites each and everyone with the Body of Christ. In the Spirit, the worshipping community places each and every one in the memory of God with the proclamation: 'We remember', or with the plea: 'Remember, O Lord!'

Since the third century, we have evidence that the Church considered the reading of the Diptychs as an act of communion.[50] During the doctrinal controversies of the fourth, fifth and the sixth centuries, the excommunication of heretics and schismatics found its expression in the Diptychs. Thus Diptychs became a test of orthodoxy. 'Diptychs revealed who was considered orthodox and who was in communion with whom'.[51]

Originally the Diptychs included the names of a large number of churches and their prelates. In some churches, the 'Book of Life' that was read before the anaphora served this purpose. But for practical reasons, the scope of the Diptychs was limited. One can suppose that the reading of a large number of names was rather a boring affair, and thus it was reduced to the minimum and gradually became fixed.

However, the commemoration implies two things. First, the Eucharist is celebrated in communion with the local bishop and through him with the Catholic Church throughout the world. In the Spirit of God, the worshipping community confesses the bond of love and prayer that unites it with other communities throughout the world and throughout history. Second, we are all in need of the prayers of others and should pray for others. The Eucharist perpetuates that bond of love and prayer, primarily among those who have assembled around the Table of the Lord and then among other communities throughout the world. All are incorporated into it, so that the Eucharist is manifested as the Church, the Body of Christ.

The last three canons, as we have noted, commemorate the departed. They begin with the Mother of God, then the prophets and the apostles, the preachers and the evangelists, the martyrs and the confessors, St John the Baptist, St Stephen the first martyr, St Peter, St Paul and 'all the faithful departed Saints, both men and women'.[52]

The commemoration of all the departed implies that the Eucharist is offered by the Church and on behalf of the Church. The fact that the whole company of the saints is commemorated demonstrates that all the saints stand in need of the Eucharist and have to be incorporated into it. Although the saints are the privileged members of the Church, they are not outside the Body of Christ. They have lived and attained holiness as members of the Body of Christ. They have been saved only as members of the

---

50 Gregory Dix, *The Shape of the Liturgy* (London, 1982: reprint), pp. 498–511.

51 Hugh Wybrew, *The Orthodox Liturgy* (SVSP, New York, 1990), p. 58.

52 Fourth Canon (by the deacon), Athanasius, *Anaphora*, p. 45.

Body of Christ. In fact, saintliness means a communion in the prayers of the Church and thus in the prayers of Christ. Saintliness is a relation of prayer with God and the world. The saints continue to be the members of the Church and they continue to pray for us. Thus in the fourth canon we pray:

> We beseech You. O Lord Almighty, unite us with the multitude of the First-born whose names are written in heaven. We remember them, that they may also remember us in Your presence and partake with us of this spiritual sacrifice.[53]

The saints' life is a continuous prayer; it is a life in Christ and with Christ. Our prayer for them is an act of love that unites us with their company. The Spirit who abundantly abides in them unites our petitions with theirs, and with the great and eternal intercession of Christ. It is for our salvation, our union with Christ, that we 'remember' them.

The commemoration of the three Ecumenical Councils and the names of the fathers and doctors (in the fifth canon) imply that the Eucharist is celebrated in communion with them and in unity with the faith as handed down by them. As in the case of the Creed, it is implied that unity of faith is the primary condition for the Eucharistic communion.

---

[53] Fourth Canon (Priest's inaudible prayer), ibid., p. 46.

CHAPTER 8

Witness to the Last Things

The specificity of Christian worship consists in its eschatological character.[1] The Syrian Orthodox liturgical texts point out that the 'Last Days' have already begun with the Incarnation: 'The Father begot him without beginning, and at the end of time, he came forth from Mary.'[2] However, as in the New Testament, the liturgical texts reflect the tension between 'already' and the 'not yet', as Christ is the one 'who came and is to come'.[3] This tension has been found throughout the Christian liturgy.

Eschatology, in the Eastern patristic tradition, is not merely the Last Judgement. Its meaning and content cannot be grasped merely in juridical and apocalyptical terminologies. It announces hope and salvation. A hymn of the *Shehimo* neatly summarizes the Syrian Orthodox eschatology:

> O you who died in Christ, do not be grieved, for, behold, the resurrection has come and the day of retribution; you shall rise from your graves without corruption and go forth with speed to meet the Son of the King; you shall be clothed in a garment of glory and shall sing praise before him; O resurrection of the sons of Adam, have pity and mercy upon us.[4]

As in the case of his 'first coming', Christ's Second Coming announces hope and life to all. The Church exhorts its members to trust in God's mercy and to beseech forgiveness of sins and life. This idea is often repeated in the daily offices.

1. Eschatology and Pneumatology

The eschatological dimension of the liturgy has its foundation in the pneumatology. In fact the Church prays in the Spirit for the Parousia of Christ ('The Spirit and the Bride say, "Come"': Rev. 22:17). The Spirit himself yearns and 'intercedes' for the eschatological fulfilment of the economy of salvation (Rom. 8:18–27). As we have

---

[1] A. Schmemann, 'Liturgical Theology: Remarks on Method', in Thomas Fisch (ed.), *Liturgy and Tradition: Theological Reflections of Alexander Schmemann* (SVSP, New York, 1990), pp. 137–44. Here p. 143.

[2] Wednesday, *Sapro, Qolo, Shehimo*, 154. Again: 'Gabriel at the end of time gave you the greeting of peace'. Tuesday, *Lilyo, Shehimo*, 91; this is obviously based on Heb. 1:2 ('in the last days he has spoken to us by a son').

[3] See the Sanctus of the St James Liturgy. 'Who came and is to come' (cf. Matt. 21:1) might be a combination of the Curetonian and the Peshitta version (and perhaps the Harklean version also). Thus the Syriac text of Matt. 21:1 reads: 'he who came (*d-eto*)' [Curetonian and Harklean]; 'He who is coming (*d-ote*)' [Peshitta]. Cf. Rev. 4:8: 'who was, and is and is to come (w-ote)'.

[4] Tuesday, ninth hour, *Shehimo*, 119.

seen, the essential function of the Spirit is to manifest Christ. The Spirit manifests the glory of Christ's reign (that is, the Kingdom of God) in the liturgy. As J.D. Zizioulas says, 'the Spirit brings into history the last days, the *eschaton*'.[5] The Spirit makes the liturgical assembly the manifestation of the Church, the eschatological gathering of humanity in Christ.

The liturgy has been founded on the 'first coming' of Christ in body, and it is the anticipation of the second glorious coming. Eschatology means the ultimate unity of all in Christ, which was inaugurated in the Incarnation, with the death and the resurrection of Christ. It will be fulfilled in the Second Coming of Christ, with the glorious manifestation of the Kingdom of God. This unity is gradually achieved and manifested in and through Baptism and the Eucharist. It is manifested in every liturgical celebration. If the unity of all in Christ is the essence of eschatology, liturgy precisely aims at it.

This fundamental aspect of the liturgy finds its earliest expression in St Paul: 'Because there is one bread, we who are many are one body, for we partake of the one bread' (1 Cor. 10:17). And again: 'For by one Spirit we were all baptized into one body . . . And all were made to drink of one Spirit' (1 Cor. 12:13).

Didache (ch. 9) envisages it as an eschatological unity: 'As this broken bread, once dispersed over the hills, was brought together and became one loaf, so may your Church be brought together from the ends of the earth into your kingdom.' The relationship between the Eucharist and the Kingdom is indicated in the Syriac *Didascalia*. Thus the third-century document directs: 'offer an acceptable Eucharist in the likeness of the body of the kingdom of Christ' (or 'likeness of the body, the kingdom of Christ' – according to older recension).[6]

The eschaton, the manifestation of the Kingdom, the ingathering of all in Christ, has already begun and is being celebrated here in the Church. In its liturgical celebration, the Church witnesses to the Last Things, the unity of all in Christ. The liturgy anticipates and prepares for the Parousia, and offers a foretaste.

The sacraments are the token of the Last Days. They anticipate the fulfilment of the promises in the coming world.[7] The Eucharist, 'the sacrament of the sacraments', is the realization of the Church as the foretaste of the Kingdom. It is the revelation of the Church as the Epiphany of the Kingdom of God. The liturgical *ordo* presents the Church's knowledge of God and the things to come.

---

5 'The Spirit is beyond history, and when he acts in history he does so in order to bring into history the last days, the *eschaton* (Acts 2:17). Hence the first fundamental particularity of Pneumatology is its eschatological character. The Spirit makes of Christ an eschatological being, the "last Adam".' J.D. Zizioulas, *Being as Communion* (SVSP, New York, 1985), p. 130.

6 *Didascalia*, ch.6:22. S. Brock, *The Liturgical portions of the Didascalia*, GLS 29 (1982), 33; A. Vööbus, *The Didascalia Apostolorum in Syriac*, Vol.II, *CSCO* 408, (Louvain, 1979), p. 243, n. 219. Cf. *AC* VI, 30, 2 ('antitype of the royal body of Christ').

7 See the anamnesis of St James: 'Your death, O Lord, we commemorate. Your resurrection we confess, and Your second coming we look for.' (Athanasius, *Anaphora*, p. 40.)

2. Orientation Towards the East

The eschatological dimension of the liturgy is permanently marked in the *ordo*, in the prayer towards the East, a custom that goes back to the beginning of the second century.[8] The early Christian interest in the East was surely inspired by Jewish traditions and solar symbolism.[9] Among the Orthodox Jews, orientation towards Jerusalem had an eschatological significance. It symbolized their messianic hopes, the coming of the Messiah to Jerusalem at the end of time.[10] A number of Jewish sects, like the Essenes and the Therapeutae – both characterized by their eschatological consciousness – had the custom of prayer towards the East.[11]

The eastward direction developed in the Christian tradition naturally claims a strong biblical basis. In the biblical story of creation, 'God planted a garden in Eden, in the East' (Gen. 2:8). Following this tradition, certain Judeo-Christian apocalyptic literature says that Paradise or Heaven is located in the East.[12] The Fall resulted in the expulsion of our first parents from the 'East'. Since the time of the expulsion, all children of Adam and Eve look back to their former home, the Paradise in the East, with a deep sense of spiritual nostalgia. We turn to the East in order to remind ourselves that we have to turn to God our Creator and to return to the joyful communion with God and with the entire creation as experienced by Adam and Eve before their Fall. The eastward orientation is an act of repentance. It stands for hope and homecoming.

On the basis of Matt. 24:27, a popular belief developed that in the Second Coming, Christ would come from the East. This is further supported by Mal. 4:2 ('But for you who fear my name, the sun of righteousness shall rise with healing in its wings'), Rev. 22:16 (Christ as 'the bright morning star') and John 8:12: 'I am the light of the world'). So looking to the East stands for our earnest waiting for the coming of Christ, the true light, the healer and saviour of the world. Following Zech. 6:12 ('Orient is His name': LXX and Peshitta), the East has been often understood as a symbol of Christ himself. However, the emphasis is on the eschatological manifestation of Christ. The eastward orientation symbolizes our hope in the Second Coming of Christ as well as our desire to return to Paradise.[13] It stands for our spiritual wakefulness to receive Christ when he comes for the Last Judgement and our readiness to give account of our life and our hope in the transfiguration of all in Christ. This is a 'sacramental'

---

8 C. Vogel, 'L'orientation vers l'Est du célébrant et des fidèles pendant la célébration eucharistique', *OS* 9 (1964), 3–38 (with bibliography).

9 Louis Bouyer, *Le rite et l'homme* (Paris, 1962), pp. 209–58.

10 Paul F. Bradshaw, *Daily Prayer in the Early Church* (London, 1981), p. 11.

11 Probably following the indications given in Ezek. 8:16 and 11:1. Bradshaw, *Daily Prayer*, p. 11.

12 See *Testament of Abraham*, XI: 'When Abraham was very old, God sent Michael to bring him to heaven. Michael brought Abraham to the East, to the first gate of heaven'. *ANF* X (5th edn, 1969), p. 192. *Apocalypse of Peter*, 6: 'And when we prayed, suddenly there appeared two men standing before the Lord towards the east'. *ANF* V, p. 145

13 Both are combined in *Apostolic Constitutions* II,57,14.

posture in remembrance of all that God grants us from the time of our creation in Paradise to the fulfilment of all in the Second Coming of Christ.[14]

3. For Ever and Ever

The eschatological dimension of the liturgy is emphasized in almost every concluding doxology: 'We offer glory . . . For ever and ever.' As the mystery of the new creation and the mystery of the Kingdom, the Church prays and glorifies 'for ever and ever'. Since the Kingdom is yet to come, the Church, the eschatological gathering, looks beyond history and prays for the grace to worship in the eternal world. In the daily offices as well as in other celebrations, the prayers and the hymns are interposed with the Trinitarian glorification followed by the people's response: 'Glory be to the Father, Son and the Holy Spirit. From age to age and for ever.'[15] The doxology and the response were probably introduced to emphasize the eternal dimension of liturgy.

Eschatology is not a reference to or an indication of future reward. It is a 'personal waiting', an affirmation of a 'personal hope'.[16] It is the manifestation, a 'showing forth' of the world to come, where human beings as well as the entire cosmos will be transformed into a temple of God, a dwelling-place of the Holy Spirit. Matter, sound, words, music, culture and art will be permeated with the radiant and life-giving light of the triune God. Everything will become a symbol, a *rozo*, an epiphany of God's glory.

The most striking characteristic of Christian eschatology is the fullness of the dynamic presence of God, which is the very essence of Christian worship. The regular allusions to the angels, the heavenly liturgy and the divine throne have been inspired by this awareness.

Liturgy is an act of vigilance and an expectation of the glorious coming of Christ. To meet Christ with praises is a blessing that has been asked for:

> Give us wings of the Spirit that we may fly and meet you when you come and sing hymns of praise to you and your Father and your Holy Spirit, now and always and forever.[17]

The spirit of expectation pervades all that the Church does. The wise virgins (Matt. 25:1–13) are always a model of the ardent waiting for the Second Coming. Thus in the dramatic celebration known as 'The Order of the Entrance in the Heaven' (celebrated on Monday night of the Holy Week) we find:

---

14 K.M. George, 'Why turn to the East for prayer?', in *Sahayatra* (Nagpore, June 2002), 26–28.

15 The people's response in Syriac is a combination of Ps. 90:2b and 89:53b (Peshitta): *men 'olam wa'damo l'olam 'olmin wamin* (from age to age and forever).

16 Schmemann, 'Liturgy and Eschatology', in *Liturgy and Tradition*, p. 95.

17 Eighth Sunday after Epiphany, Opening Prayer, *Crown* I, 238.

Grant that, on your second glorious coming with the wise virgins, we too may come out to greet you with radiant lamps that are filled with the oil of righteousness . . . Exalt the horn of your Holy Church all over the world, by your glories, and enrich her with the songs of the Holy Spirit, and instead of the lamps which she is carrying in her hands, may she and her children come to meet you at your Second Coming with spiritual lamps and with garments that are fit for your banquets.[18]

Every liturgical celebration is a foretaste of our participation in the heavenly liturgy. Thus Palm Sunday is presented as the foretaste of our singing of Hosanna in the coming world:

Grant, O Lord, that with the immortal branches of the spiritual Paradise, we may be worthy to celebrate this eternal festival with the congregation of your saints and to offer glory and thanksgiving to You and to Your Father and to Your Holy Spirit.[19]

The reality of the eschaton of the Kingdom consists of the life in Christ, and through him with the Father and the Holy Spirit. This implies a transformed relationship with God, man and the world. The sacraments and the liturgical life enable us to live this new relationship 'already', although it has 'not yet' been fully realized. Yet the Church, as the new creation and the new humanity, manifests this new relationship in space and time. The future life is indeed a life with 'great multitude, which no man could number' (Rev. 7:9). Their oneness in Christ is manifested by their praise and worship (Rev. 7:10–12). The whole Christian life aims at achieving this unity of all in Christ, which is 'already' available in the Church. In other words, the new life or the eternal life for which we are looking is a life in Christ with 'all those who have pleased God'. The Eucharist evokes this new life (for example in commemorations); that is, it 'shows forth'. The whole mystagogical tradition attempts to demonstrate how this true and eternal life can be appropriated. Our life on earth is a preparation for, rather a prefiguration of, that new life to which we have been called.

4. Repentance: the Sign of the Last Days and the New Life

The essence of the Last Days and the Kingdom of God is the change of heart and consequently new life and a new relationship between God and man. Thus St John the Baptist and our Lord began their ministries with the exhortation: 'Repent; for the

---

[18] *Sedro, Ma'de'dono*, p. 159. 'The Order of the Entrance in the Haven, commonly called the Parable of the Ten Virgins', is a service held as part of the *Lilyo* of Monday of Passion Week. Text in *Ma'de'dono*, pp. 151–71. See B. Varghese, 'Holy Week celebrations in the West Syrian Church', pp. 171–76 (with bibliography).

[19] Concluding prayer (*Hutomo*), *Ma'de'dono*, p. 133. 'Make us worthy, O Lord God, to be adorned with the incorruptible garments and to hold glorious and spiritual [olive] branches and to celebrate joyful and exalted feasts with the multitude of your elected and to offer glory and praise to You, and to Your Father and to Your Living Holy Spirit . . .'. *Hutomo, Ma'de'dono*, Pampakuda, 1984, p. 304.

Kingdom of heaven is at hand' (Matt. 3:1; 4:17). Repentance includes a renewal of human relationships (Luke 3:10–14). The mission of the Holy Spirit includes leading men to repentance (John 16:8–9). In other words, repentance is the very sign of the Kingdom.

In its worship the Church continues to exhort its members to repent, the very condition of entering the Kingdom. Thus repentance is a principal theme of the West Syrian offices, especially that of the daily offices, festal breviary, Lenten breviary, most of the *Sedre*, and the Anointing of the Sick. In the daily offices, the theme of *Sutoro* is always 'repentance'. Several *qole* of the *Ramsho, Lilyo* and *Sapro* are dedicated to it.

It is significant that the prayers use the first person singular ('I') only with reference to sin. For example, the *Ramsho* of Monday begins with the following *eqbo*:

> I have sinned against heaven and in your sight and I am not worthy to be called your son. Take me as a hired servant and let me be a servant in your house, because I have sinned.[20]

The prayers usually refer to the biblical figures that have set an example of true repentance and thus encourage the sinner to approach the merciful Lord:

> I have remembered you on my bed, O lover of men, and by night I have meditated on you, because you are greatly to be feared; I see my stains and my defilement and I am ashamed to call on you; but the thief, the publican and the sinful woman encourage me, and the Canaanite woman and the woman that was afflicted and the Samaritan woman at the well of water; they say to me: approach and receive mercy, because your Lord is full of mercy.[21]

Thus repentance is the acknowledgement of the loving-kindness of God, his infinite mercy and willingness to save us. In fact the experience of the Kingdom of God includes our awareness of God's philanthropy and our openness to receive forgiveness of sins and eternal life. The meaning of repentance and that of worship is not different.

As Basil Krivocheine says, repentance is the 'beginning of the Christian life and the permanent foundation of all our efforts toward God'.[22] It is a constant yearning for God's mercy, trust that the Lord is seeking for us and that he will find us:

> Do not fear, sinner, to tread the way of repentance; for your Lord is gone in search of you and greatly will he rejoice if he finds you; he will forgive you your sins like the sinful woman; he will open the door of paradise to you, as to the thief, and will rejoice in you and receive you better that those who remain; he will bear you on his shoulders and carry you in honour, halleluiah, and he will embrace you.[23]

---

[20] *Shehimo*, p. 35. Cf. Luke 15:18–19. This text, which is a combination of the Peshitta text and a paraphrase, very well illustrates the West Syrian use of the Bible in the liturgical texts.

[21] Tuesday, *Lilyo*, Third *Qaumo, Shehimo*, pp. 96–97.

[22] Archbishop, Basil Krivocheine, *In the Light of Christ: St Simeon the New Theologian. Life – Spirituality – Doctrine* (SVSP, New York, 1986), p. 87.

[23] Tuesday, *Sutoro, Shehimo*, p. 86.

Redemption implies the sharing of the cross and the victory over sin and death. It is a life-long struggle, in which repentance is an essential element. We imitate the sufferings of Christ through repentance. Repentance repeats existentially in us the death of Christ.[24] By humbling ourselves before the all-merciful Lord, we share in his cross. The old, sinful man is crucified with him and dies away. This leads us to share in his glorified life. As Nicholas Arseniev writes, 'The first step, along this path, all-pervading keynote, the starting point and, at the same time, the deepest foundation is a feeling of unqualified contrition.'[25]

Deep sorrow makes the prayer a cry to the unfathomable depths of God's mercy:

> Look, Lord, upon my weakness because I have sinned much and have angered you and I do not know in whom I may find refuge. I approached the physicians and they spent their medicines on me and the abscess remains infected and there is none to bind it up. I heard of you, good physician, that you had many medicines and that, he receives help who approaches you. By the love of the Father who begot you and by the prayer of her who bore you, halleluiah, pardon me my offences.[26]

Scriptural passages are rendered into verse, along with a brief exhortation or word of consolation: 'Not for the sake of the just did I come, said Our Lord, but for the sinners, that they may repent. Behold the door of the Lord is open; sinners, repent and live, for I desire not your death, said God.'[27]

Thus repentance is, above all, absolute trust in Christ, the heavenly physician who came to heal our infirmities. It means stretching out our hands towards the merciful Lord, the fundamental meaning of Christian prayer. Thus repentance is an expression of the very nature of the Kingdom of God and the articulation of one of the fundamental principles of prayer. A prayer or a simple phrase like Glory be to God is a turning towards God, a confession of our attachment to God, as well as a denial of Satan, sin and death. It is indeed an act of repentance. The theme of repentance is in harmony with the spirit of the Psalms, the model for all Christian prayers. The Jesus prayer ('Jesus, Son of God, have mercy on me a sinner'), that inspiring and transfiguring formula, which has largely shaped Byzantine spirituality, is primarily a prayer of repentance.

As we have noted, in the Christian East, sin and death are seen in terms of an illness, for which the heavenly physician, in his loving-kindness, has brought medicine and healing. Most probably, it is in this sense that Ignatius of Antioch refers to the Eucharist as the 'Medicine of immortality' (*Pharmakon athanasias*: Eph. 20:2). This idea appears regularly in the West Syrian prayers.

---

[24] Nikos A. Nissiotis, 'The Importance of the doctrine of the Trinity for Church life and Theology', in A.J. Philippou (ed.), *The Orthodox Ethos. Studies in Orthodoxy*, Vol.I (Oxford, 1964), pp. 32–69 (here p. 59).

[25] Nicholas Arseniev, *Mysticism and the Eastern Church* (SVSP, New York, 1979), p. 45.

[26] Monday, *Sutoro, Shehimo*, p. 40.

[27] Monday, *Sapro, Shehimo*, p. 64.

> I confess the sins and offences, of my being before you, and I do not hide the multitude of my faults, O lover of men; I said: I will not hide my evil deeds; I will confess my iniquity to the Lord, in his mercy he will heal me; Physician of our souls, I beg you, have mercy upon me.[28]

Thus repentance is the confession of our illness to the heavenly physician as well as a remedy for our ailments.

Repentance is also a second baptism that cleanses us and makes us beloved of Christ. Tears of repentance are a bath that radically renews a man. It is a precious offering to the Lord:

> The sinner is loved when his face is bathed in tears and his mouth is cleansed by sorrowful mourning full of pain; precious gems are not so much loved as the drops which flow from the eyes of him who repents.[29]

Again:

> Lord, let me not die in my sins; now I offer you the tears of my eyes, a bribe that you love; I do not offer oxen or lambs or goats or doves or young pigeons, but two tears of my eyes like the sinful woman in the house of Simon; accept them and have pity upon me . . .[30]

One of the questions that has been often asked even by Christians is the following: is it necessary to give such an emphasis to human sinfulness and the need to repent? The Syriac poet–theologians had anticipated this question. Thus in a *B'outo* of Mar Jacob of Serugh we find the question and its answer:

> Perhaps you will say, why do you demand mourning from me? Hear from our Lord when he said, blessed are those who mourn; great indeed is the reason for mourning with him who has discernment; if a man did not look and see his faults, he would not mourn.[31]

Repentance is not merely contrition. It must be total and should embrace the whole person. It implies a state of vigilance; a permanent preparedness for the coming of Christ. Thus a *qolo* of Tuesday evening exhorts: 'Repent, repent, sinners, said our Lord; that when the bridegroom appears you may enter the marriage-chamber with him.'[32]

---

28 Thursday, *Ramsho, Shehimo*, p. 169. Again: 'Merciful Lord, have compassion on me on the thief; not that I am worthy but because of your grace, by which you descended to the race of men, that you might save it from its oppressors, death and sin; Physician of our souls, I beg you, have mercy on us.' Tuesday, *Ramsho, Shehimo*, p. 172.

29 Tuesday, *Sutoro, Shehimo*, p. 87.

30 Monday, *Sutoro, Shehimo*, p. 41.

31 Tuesday, *Sutoro, Shehimo*, p. 87.

32 *Shehimo*, p. 77.

Repentance is presented as the mark of a true Christian. The *Sedro* of Monday evening asks God to 'make us true penitents'.[33] Repentance must always be a permanent disposition of the soul, so that one should not fall again. It implies an alertness as well as ardent prayer that we may not be deprived of the garment of glory and incorruptibility. Thus we find: 'clothe our bodies in incorruptibility and make us all resplendent in the garments of glory, that we may behold you, our true Bridegroom, in light'.[34] Repentance is an effort to live in the baptismal grace, and to preserve the gifts of baptism. It is a daily experience of our life in Christ.

5. Genuflection

The importance of the penitential dimension of a daily office is underscored with genuflections, one of the regular and most striking features of the daily offices in the East. In an ordinary weekday office, the Trisagion as well as the section of the Creed that narrates the passion and death of Christ are accompanied by threefold genuflections. However, Sundays, feast days and the fifty days between Easter and Pentecost are exempted. The general rule is that the genuflection is observed on a fasting day. Thus we can note that there is a link between genuflection and fasting; both are expressions of repentance. The Eucharistic celebration, the preparation rites and the pre-anaphora include genuflections, also symbolizing penitence. Similarly, in the ordination rites as well as in the monastic consecration, the normal posture of the candidate is to kneel, also a symbol of his repentance and humility. In the Syrian Orthodox Church, in some places there was the custom of bowing down during the epiclesis, attested by a few ancient manuscripts of the St James Liturgy.[35] However, it was abandoned under the influence of the Patriarchate of Antioch, and the other Eastern Churches, which always emphasized the festal character of the Eucharist.

6. Meaning of Fasting

The meaning of fasting, an integral part of the Eastern liturgical tradition, should be understood in relation to repentance, a dominant theme of several of its offices. As we have already seen, fasting is never observed on Sundays, feast-days and the days between Easter and Pentecost. The Eucharistic fast is an act of preparedness and its meaning is in a sense inseparable from penitence. Thus strict fasting is a precondition to receiving the Holy Communion. However, it may be relaxed in the case of infants, the sick, the aged and pregnant women. Thus in principle, Sunday, the 'Weekly

---

33 *Shehimo*, p. 37: 'And now, O Lord, be reconciled, be converted, have pity, have mercy, forgive and pardon us your servants, who in the sorrow of repentance pray before you; cleanse and purify us, hallow and keep us, make us true penitents, make us perfect guardians of your law.'

34 Thursday, *Sutoro, Sedro, Shehimo*, p. 180.

35 See Varghese, *The Syriac Version of the Liturgy of St James*, p. 36.

Passover', is preceded by fasting. Besides all Wednesdays and Fridays (except those that come between Easter and Pentecost), there are five canonical fasts.[36]

1 The Advent Lent: originally lasted for forty days (15 November to 25 December), but for twenty-five days (1–25 December) since the last decade of the nineteenth century.
2 The Nineveh Lent (three days): begins on the third Monday before the Great Lent. Formerly, in some places, it was observed for five days.
3 The Great Lent: for seven weeks before Easter.
4 Fast of the Apostles: formerly started one week after the feast of Pentecost and ended with the feast of the apostles St Peter and St Paul (29 June). Since the 1890s it has lasted for thirteen days (16–29 June).
5 The Assumption Fast (1–15 August).

The Christians of the West seem to have ignored the liturgical dimension of fasting and have included it among the monastic/ascetic disciplines. In the East, on the other hand, liturgical life is regarded as incomplete without fasting.

In the Old Testament, as an act of repentance, fasting accompanies ardent prayers.[37] In the words of our Lord, '[Evil] cannot be driven out by anything but *fasting and prayer*'.[38] In the apostolic Church also, important decisions or appointments for a ministry were accompanied by 'prayer and fasting'.[39]

In the liturgical context, fasting has two meanings: it is an act of repentance and an act of preparation. The two are intertwined. Repentance prepares us for receiving the grace of God and purifies us to be the dwelling place of the triune God. This may perhaps explain the origin of the pre-baptismal fasting, from which the Great Lent seems to have developed.

7. Fasting as an Act of Repentance

Repentance, as we have seen, is the beginning and the condition for Christian life. In the biblical tradition, repentance was always accompanied by bodily gestures such as fasting or genuflection. In the Christian tradition, fasting is regarded as the best expression of repentance. In the Syriac *Didascalia of the Apostles* (third century), we find one of the earliest references to fasting as a condition for the reconciliation of a penitent. Thus the *Didascalia* directs a bishop: 'And if he [the penitent] is worthy to be received into the Church, appoint him days of fasting according to his transgression,

---

36 For a study on the historical development of the canonical fasts, see B.Varghese, 'Canonical fasts in the West Syrian Tradition', *The Harp* VII (1994), 89–108.
37 See Lev. 23:27; Zech. 7:5; Joel 1:4; 2:12; 2 Sam. 1:12; 12:16; Ps. 35:13; Esther 4:16; Ezra 8:23; Neh. 9:1–2; Dan. 9:3; 20.
38 Mark 9:29 (Peshitta).
39 Acts 13:2; 14:23.

two weeks, or three, or five, or seven.'[40] The reconciliation was, of course, a liturgical ceremony and was preceded by fasting, whose meaning is inseparable from the liturgical life.

Repentance includes visible actions expressing our sorrow, humility and change of heart. Food is, in a sense, the symbol of our dependence on the 'material world' for the continuation of life. Fasting reminds us that 'man does not live by bread alone'. 'The primary aim of fasting is to make us conscious of our dependence upon God.'[41] It is the first step toward self-control, because food can serve as a source of temptation and alienation from God. In the story of the Fall, food (or fruit) became the very cause of sin and death, because the temptation to eat prevailed over trust in God's words. The parable of the rich fool shows that food and riches might even lead to spiritual indolence and forgetfulness (Luke 12:15–21; 33–34; 45). Fasting is the voluntary experience of physical hunger in order to make us aware of our true spiritual hunger, our poverty of spirit.[42] Fasting is not in order to destroy the body, but to save it. That is, fasting awakens us from spiritual slothfulness and helps us to concentrate on our spiritual growth.

Fasting does not imply that food in itself is evil. The fasting pleasing to God is that which is followed by a complete change of heart. A hymn of the Great Lent speaks of this aspect:

> The bread and water which the Lord has given for the sustenance of the body are not [the sources] of sin or righteousness. Keep away from evil and do good. For this is the fasting that pleases the Lord. Give us Our Saviour [the grace] to fast as it is pleasing to you.[43]

Fasting becomes meaningful when it is followed by repentance. Thus the prayers of Lent present repentance as the main theme of the whole season:

> My Lord, I am the lost sheep that went astray from the path of life. I have run after vanity. O Good Shepherd, go out in search of me. Do not forsake me to be lost completely. But number me in your sheepfold with the publican, the sinful woman and with those [five] wise [virgins] and make me worthy to enter your bridal chamber. Absolve my debts, O God, and forgive all my iniquities, for I have sinned and I have angered you. Like the sinful woman, I call upon you. Be gracious to me, O Lover of man, so that I may sing glory to your grace, with the company of the saints when you come in glory. Like the prodigal Son I call upon you with groaning. Be gracious to me and have mercy upon me, O my Father. I have sinned against heaven and before you. Receive me like a hired servant in your home. Forgive me all that I have sinned against you [for] you are merciful God. O Lord, I was afraid when I heard that there is no remembrance of you in death and who will praise you in Hades and therefore, with my whole heart, I call upon you. I

---

40 *Didascalia* ch.6, *CSCO* 402, pp. 64–65.

41 Mother Mary and Kallistos Timothy Ware (tr.), *The Lenten Triodion* (London, 1978), p. 16.

42 Clark Carlton, *The Faith. Understanding Orthodox Christianity. An Orthodox Catechism* (Regina Orthodox Press, Salisbury, MA, 1997), p. 224.

43 Tuesday morning, *Qolo*, A. Konat (ed.), *Ktobo d-Sluto d-saumo* (5th edn. Pampakuda, 1967), p. 62.

will glorify the Lord in my life and I will sing to him while I exist, for he is the One
who saves me from judgment. My Lord, hear the prayers of your servants, for,
behold we knock at your door. Look at our groaning. We offer repentance. Do not
turn your attention away from us, because of the ungodly gentiles, who have turned
up against us. But save us with your mighty hand and have mercy upon us.[44]

The long text that we have quoted provides an example of the content and spirit of the
prayers of the Great Lent. It is a season for repentance, a time to turn to God, and to be
renewed by Easter. Every fast is, in fact, an occasion for renewal, because a fast is a
preparation for a feast, whose meaning is inseparable from that of Easter. In this
sense, the weekly fasts of Wednesday and Friday are a preparation for Sunday, the
'Weekly Easter'. In fact, in the Syriac patristic tradition the meaning of these two
days is explained in relation to the passion and death of our Lord.[45]

8. Fasting and the Way of Salvation

Fasting is an inseparable part of our journey towards the Kingdom of God. The Syriac
tradition even speaks of an institution of fasting by Christ himself, who 'taught us to
fast and thus to fight against Satan'. Thus in the first prayer of the Lenten cycle we find:

> Christ humbled himself for our salvation and consented to fast and to be tempted
> by the enemy and he taught the Church to conquer Satan who fights against her
> with proper fasting and pure prayer.[46]

By his fasting, Our Lord has taught us the way of life which leads to the Father: 'Our
Saviour had fasted and prepared for us the way of life, so that we may walk in it to his
Sender without stumbling.'[47] Again: 'As man, Christ the God of all fasted for us and
prepared for us the way so that we may walk in it without stumbling and we may
inherit eternal life.'[48]

Thus the fasting of Christ is an integral part of the mystery of the Incarnation,
inseparable from his birth, baptism, victory over Satan, public ministry, passion, death,
resurrection and ascension. By his fasting, our Lord won victory over Satan, which is
in fact the anticipation of his victory on the cross.

> Our Redeemer had completed his economy [*lit.* way] by his fasting, passion,
> humiliation. By his fasting, he raised our fall, and healed [*lit.* straightened] our
> bending. By his passion, he repaid our debts. Blessed is his humiliation for us;
> glory to him who endured all these things for our mortal race.[49]

---

[44] Great Lent, Tuesday morning, Konat, *Ktobo*, pp. 57–59.

[45] *Didascalia* ch.3:8 (Commandments from the writings of Addai the Apostle, 3–4), *CSCO* 402, p. 37.

[46] Great Lent, Monday evening, *Ktobo*, p. 4.

[47] Monday morning, ibid., p. 38.

[48] Ibid., p. 36.

[49] Great Lent, Thursday morning, ibid., p. 101.

The fasting of Christ illustrates his humility and thus anticipates his true humiliation on the cross. Thus the meaning of the fasting is inseparable from that of the cross. Our fasting is in a sense a participation in the cross of Christ, who was thirsty and deprived for our sake.

The prayers of the Great Lent repeatedly refer to the fasting of Christ as the basis and model for our fasting: 'If the merciful incarnate Lord fasted the holy fast for our salvation, how much more is it meet that we may fast and seek mercy?' asks a *qolo* of Wednesday, third hour.[50]

According to Severus of Antioch (d. 536), we are obliged to fast because of the transgression of Adam: 'If Adam had fasted at the time when it was necessary by abstaining from the fruit of that tree, there would not be need for us to fast.'[51] A *qolo* of the Great Lent presents it in a slightly different way:

> As Adam was overcome by gluttony and had eaten the fruit in Paradise, because of food, he was expelled in shame from the Garden of Eden. Our Lord descended and overpowered gluttony by pure fast. Blessed is the One who, by his mercies, had pity on his servant who ate, and defeated the evil one who had deceived him.[52]

As we have already seen, in the Syriac tradition, salvation is presented in terms of healing and restoration. Fasting is a means of healing for humanity, which became sick because of food. Severus of Antioch made use of this imagery and his arguments can be summarized as follows: 'An efficient physician asks the patient who became sick because of aliments, to fast and thus to regain health. Similarly, fasting has been prescribed for us as a medicine to regain the former glorious condition.'[53]

The therapeutic meaning of fasting is emphasized in the Gospel readings of the Great Lent. Thus on the Sundays of the Lent, the healing miracles of Christ are read.[54] Fasting is a means of healing as well as of purification. Christ 'instituted' fasting as a means to cleanse the image of God, which had been obscured, and thus to restore the former glory of creation.[55]

When Christ was hungry, Satan approached and tempted him, as in the case of Adam. But Christ conquered him and showed us an example of how to overcome the evil one.[56] Those who fast participate in that victory and thus imitate Christ:

---

50 Ibid., p. 84.

51 Hom. 39, *PO* 36, p. 513.

52 Friday, *Lilyo*, Fourth *Qaumo*, p. 118.

53 Hom. 39, *PO* 36, 513; Hom. 15, *PO* 38, p. 421.

54 The Lectionary, published from Pampakuda, has the following arrangement: first Sunday – Miracle of Cana; second Sunday – Healing of the Leper (Luke 5:12–17); third Sunday – Healing of the Paralytic (Mark 2:1–12); fourth Sunday – Healing of the Canaanite woman's daughter (Matt. 15:21–32); fifth Sunday – Healing of the woman who was bent over (Luke 13:10–17); sixth Sunday – Healing of the Blind (John 9:1–41). On the variations in different lectionaries of the West Syrians, see Jean Tomajean, 'Les dimanches du carême dans le rite syro-antiochien', *OS* 7 (1962), 357–64.

55 Severus, Hom. 15, *PO* 38, p. 419ff.

56 Cf. Aphrahat, *Demonstrations* 3:16: 'He fasted indeed for us and conquered our adversary, and commanded us that we should fast and keep vigil always (Matt. 26:41) so that we will come to his rest through the power of pure fasting' (tr. K. Valavanolickal, p. 63).

> My brethren, let us fight with the weapon of fasting. The abstainers [*lit:* those
> who fast] who have been perfected in Christ win victory by it. By it, our Lord
> fought against the evil one; by it, Moses became glorious on the mountain; by it
> Elijah was lifted up in a chariot; by it the righteous are exalted and the martyrs are
> crowned. Blessed is He who gave it to us.[57]

The fasting of Christ was the declaration of warfare against Satan. He himself said to
his disciples: 'This kind cannot be driven out by anything but fasting and prayer'
(Mark 9:29 Peshitta). By its fasting, the Church takes up that warfare. Like the
athletes who engage in combat with their adversaries, those who fast are anointed
with the Holy Spirit, says Severus of Antioch.[58] (The association of the gift of the
Spirit with fasting seems to be have been inspired by St Luke's account of Christ's
baptism – 4:1–2; 18–19.[59]) Fasting confers on them the strength for that combat.
Here we can find a similarity between the interpretation of the baptismal rites and
that of fasting,[60] which seems to imply the sacramental/liturgical character of
fasting.

By fasting we imitate the life of the angels, who do not eat any material or perishable
food. They do not need food for survival, because the grace of God sustains them.[61]
Thus a hymn of the Great Lent says:

> The deeds of he who fasts with purity are mingled with those of the angels. He
> becomes a friend of the glorious ones who became triumphant with their fasts.
> The evil one will not be able to approach him as the Lord himself is his protector.[62]

It is a means to regain our former inheritance that we have lost. The experience of
Elijah is a guarantee of our hope:

> How pleasant is the odour that breathes from the fast and Elijah who was lifted up
> to heaven witnesses to it. Therefore our Redeemer has given it as an instrument
> [*lit.* weapon] through which we will be lifted up to our former inheritance.[63]

Thus as a liturgical act, fasting has eschatological implications. It announces and
anticipates the life in the Kingdom of God, and provides a foretaste of the glorious
condition to which we look forward. The East Syrian monastic writer Martyrius
(Sahdona) says: 'The fast designs [in the body] by its beauty an image of the eternal

---

[57] Great Lent, Tuesday morning, Konat, *Ktobo*, pp. 60–61.

[58] Hom. 39, *PO* 36, p. 515.

[59] The association of the gift of the Spirit with fasting is also implied in the pre-ordination fasts (Acts
13:2–3) and perhaps in the pre-baptismal fasts as well.

[60] See St John Chrysostom, *Baptismal Catechesis* 3:27 (= pre-baptismal anointing of the body) in
E.C. Whitaker, *Documents of the Baptismal Liturgy* (SPCK, London, 1970), p. 37.

[61] We can find this idea in *De Virginitate*, attributed to St Athanasius (*De Vir.* 7). Cf. Art. 'Jeune', in
Catholicisme Vi, 831.

[62] Tuesday morning, Konat, *Ktobo*, p. 65.

[63] Monday evening, ibid., pp. 4–5.

life, a character which suggests the condition of the new age, and it tells us what kind of spiritual food we will receive at the resurrection.'[64]

Fasting is not an end in itself. Prayer, psalmody and the reading of the Scriptures should accompany it. Severus of Antioch instructs those who fast to spend the day in the church to attend worship.[65] If prayer and fasting are the expressions of our love for God, these should be made perfect with the love for our brethren. Thus the Syriac tradition always insists on charity, without which fasting has no reward. 'When the fast lacks charity', says Severus, 'it appears to be something empty and vain.'[66]

The hymns of the Great Lent point out that fasting and prayer devoid of love are unacceptable to God:

> Fasting is good and if anybody fasts without love, his abstinence is without any profit. Prayer is being loved [by God]; and if love does not strengthen its wings, it does not [ascend and] see the heights [where God abides].[67]

Thus we can note that the Syriac writers have not ignored the ethical dimension of fasting or liturgical life. Their approach is not merely otherworldly. Sometimes our social responsibility is presented in clear terms. A hymn of Thursday, ninth hour of the Great Lent, reminds the one who fasts of his responsibility towards his brethren:

> O the one who fasts, call the poor and give him bread. Not just when he comes [to you], but go after him and fill his stomach. The fields do not go after the farmers. But they bring the seeds and go to [the fields] to sow. When the poor knocks [at your door] do not say to him that the Lord will provide [for him]. That word is futile and without profit to him who says it. [But] give him the gift and say this word; it will not be odious to you for he knows better than you who does provide for him.[68]

Fasting thus has a social dimension. We are provided with an opportunity to identify with those who 'fast' because of poverty. The prayers of the Great Lent exhort us to give the money or food that has been saved to the needy.

In the liturgical life, prayer and fasting are inseparable. Their aim is to bring us closer to God and thus to have communion with him, or rather to make us partakers of the divine nature. In his fortieth cathedral homily, Severus of Antioch writes:

> All the things that are accomplished and done in the churches of God are aimed at only one goal: to correct us and to bring us nearer to what is the best and to make us to progress towards the heights [of perfection], whether it is the observation of fasting or something of this kind.[69]

---

64 *Livre de la Perfection* II,7, *CSCO* 215, p. 85.

65 Hom. 87, *PO* 23, pp. 86–87; Hom. 39, *PO* 39, p. 521.

66 Hom. 87, *PO* 23, p. 88.

67 Great Lent, Monday morning, Konat, *Ktobo*, p. 39.

68 Ibid., p. 108.

69 Hom. 40, *PO* 36, p. 9.

CHAPTER 9

Mystery of the Time

The characteristic of the time of the Church is the permanent presence of the risen Lord, and consequently that of the Father and the Holy Spirit.[1] Time is sanctified by the presence of the Holy Trinity. In fact, it is not the time, but our vision that has been sanctified and transfigured to behold the presence of the triune God. When the Church gathers together for worship, the time transforms into a 'now', 'today', a 'moment' of Christophany. It is precisely this presence of Christ that makes the liturgy an eschatological event. The liturgical time is the anticipation of the 'fullness of time' in which Christ will 'unite all things in him, things in heaven and things on earth' (Eph. 1:10).

The 'decisive time' of history was the resurrection of Christ. In a liturgical gathering, where the risen Christ is present in the Spirit, 'the hour of his glorification has been re-presented. For a Christian every moment of the day, week, and the year is centered on that "hour of glorification". It is significant that in the early Church, each canonical hour was associated with the passion, death and resurrection of Christ.'[2]

Following Jewish liturgical tradition, Christian liturgical time is centred on the hour, the day, the week and the year. As in Judaism, the month has little significance in the liturgical year, and has been replaced with liturgical seasons that follow or precede great feasts. The threefold division of liturgical time into a daily, weekly and yearly cycle implies that the mystery of Christ permeates the whole of cosmic time.

1. The Weekly Cycle

According to the story of creation, the week is the fundamental unit of the liturgical cycle. The week is rooted in creation and redemption, the two acts that constituted the covenant. The Sabbath commemorates the creation of the world by God in seven days (Exod. 20:11), as well as the liberation of God's people from bondage (Deut. 5:15), which itself is a prefiguration of the final and full salvation in the Messianic age.[3] In the rabbinic and apocalyptic literature, the weekly Sabbath rest points to the final consummation Sabbath.[4] Sabbath means that the divine ordering of time has a

---

[1] Andre Feuillet, 'Le temps de l'Eglise d'après le quatrième évangile et l'Apocalypse', *LMD* 65 (1961), 60–79; Louis M. Dewailly, 'Le temps et la fin du temps selon Saint Paul', ibid., pp. 133–43.

[2] *AC* VIII, 14, 1–7, *GLS* 61, p. 53; *TD* II, 24, *GLS* 66, p. 38; Cyprian, *De. Dom Orat.* 3–4, quoted by Bradshaw, *Daily Prayer*, p. 52; Hippolytus, *Ap. Trad.* ch.41, Bradshaw, pp. 53–54.

[3] W. Rordorf, 'Sunday: The fullness of Christian Liturgical Time', *SL* 14 (1982), 90–96.

[4] A.T. Lincoln, 'Sabbath, Rest and Eschatology in the New Testament', in D.A. Carson (ed.), *From Sabbath to Lord's Day. A Biblical, Historical and Theological Investigation* (Zondervan, Grand Rapids, MI, 1982), pp. 197–220, here p. 199.

goal, a consummation, which is to be celebrated, anticipated and prayed for in community. The liturgical gathering on the Sabbath anticipates the eschatological gathering on the day of Yahweh.

Thus Sabbath was seen as the goal of history and the framework of the movement from creation to consummation. Following the Jewish tradition, the week became the 'axial element' in Christian liturgical time.

Although Christianity has inherited the Sabbatical structure of liturgical time, Sabbath was replaced with the 'first day of the week', in which Christ rose from the dead. Every Sunday was regarded as a miniature Pascha, called 'Lord's Day' in the early Christian documents (Rev. 1:10; *Didache* 14). In the Jewish apocalyptic literature, the seven days of the creation story were given a millenarian interpretation, and eventually there arose the idea of an eternity of the 'eighth day'. Thus in the second century, Sunday was also called the eighth day, the 'day' beyond the time cycle.[5] This early Christian theology of Sunday has left traces of influence on the Syriac tradition.[6]

In the West Syrian tradition, Sunday is called 'first day of the week' (*had bshabo*).[7] It is also called *qyomto* (= resurrection). The whole liturgical year is centred on '*Qyomto*, the weekly celebration of the resurrection. On Sundays, the themes of creation (the first day), new creation as well as the end of time (eighth day) are evoked, along with that of resurrection. The significance of Sunday has been further emphasized by qualifying it as the 'first-born' (*bukro*) of the days. Sunday is the 'first-born' of the days of the week as well as the entire phenomenon of time. It is the day on which the 'first-born' of the Father rose from the dead. Thus Sunday has become the 'first-born' of the new age. A hymn of Sunday, third hour puts it:

> On the first day of the week, which is the first-born of days, he rose from the grave, the first-born from on high, and raised up with him Adam, who is the first-born of all mankind and made him ascend to his Father; you sons of Adam, give praise to the Lord of Adam, who came and delivered you.[8]

The great event that took place on Sunday provides the reason for glorifying God 'all the moments of our life'. On Sunday hope dawned for humanity and life sprang up from the tomb:

> On this day of Sunday hope and encouragement came to us, because the living rose from the house of the dead and put to shame those who had crucified him. On Sunday, the great day, the living one rose from within the grave and ascended and sat down on high at the right hand of him who sent him.[9]

---

5   Jean Danielou, *Bible et liturgie* (Lex Orandi 11, Paris, 1958), 355–87; R.J.Bauckham, 'Sabbath and Sunday in the Post-Apostolic Church', in Carson (ed.), *From Sabbath to Lord's Day*, pp. 251–98.

6   See P. Sherwood (Syr. & tr.), 'Mimro de Serge de Reshaina sur la vie spirituelle', *OS* 5 (1960), 457.

7   Following the Jewish tradition, the Semitic languages, including Syriac, named the days of the week in relation to the Sabbath. See Rordorf, 'Sunday . . .', *SL* 14 (1982), 91, n.7.

8   *Shehimo*, pp. 348–49.

9   *Bo'uto* of Mar Ephrem, ibid., p. 349.

On Sunday, Christ sat down at the right hand of the Father and raised up with him Adam, and made him ascend to his Father. The new age, the eternal life, begins with our ascension with and in Christ.

This Sunday, on which we worship, is transitory. It is the image and foretaste of the 'great Sunday' that never passes:

> On this passing Sunday you gave me your body and blood to eat, Son of God; on that Sunday which does not pass, make us all worthy to exult at your right hand, and to behold your compassion.[10]

This liturgical text follows an early Syriac tradition attested by St Ephrem. Commenting on Luke 17:30–33, Ephrem says that at the end of time, Christ will come on a Sunday from the East:

> And our Lord said this because we should always be watchful, waiting and hoping for those who are sent for us, in order to take us away from him, every day and every night [for] that Sunday on which he enters. Whether we shall be on the roof or somewhere outside, we shall be ready; and if we shall be with great precaution, let us also raise our eyes to the East to the high heavens, in order to look for the sign of the cross every day and every night, for our Lord is to be revealed. And let us persevere, and have ourselves ready with great precaution every day and every night, for that Sunday in which he enters.[11]

The identification of Sunday as a symbol of the day of Parousia underscores the eschatological nature of worship and its settings. All our prayers, whether hourly or daily, are the preparation for the 'great and eternal Sunday'. Here we can find a key to the meaning of the daily offices. Their meaning is inseparable from that of Sunday. The weekly cycle is oriented towards Sunday, the day of resurrection and the symbol of eternal rest. Similarly, the whole Christian life is oriented towards the 'Great Sunday', the eighth day, the eternity. The week is the symbol of the duration between the new creation and the consummation in the Kingdom of God. It is a period of vigilance and expectation for the coming of Christ. The daily offices express the attitude of wakefulness and expectation.

2. Mystery of the Day

God's first creation was light (Gen. 1:3–5). The separation of light from darkness marked the creation of the day. It was for the sake of man, the crown of creation, that

---

10 Monday, *Ramsho, Shehimo*, p. 34.

11 George A. Egan (tr.), *Saint Ephrem. An Exposition of the Gospel*, CSCO 292, Scriptores Armeniaci 6 (Louvain, 1968), no. 118, p. 86. Elsewhere Ephrem writes, 'and when the last day approaches, in which there shall be one night for the Sunday to dawn'. No. 120, p. 88. This tradition is attested in the Syriac *Didascalia* (III,8), *CSCO* 402, p. 37.

the day and the night were established. A *Sedro* of Tuesday comments on the mystery of the day, the basic unit to measure the span of life:

> Lord God, who in your everlasting wisdom divided our earthly life into days and nights for the sake of labour in good works and rest from toil; we beg of you, that as you protected the Hebrews by a cloud and pillar of fire from being harmed by heat and from stumbling in the darkness, so this night give us the light of your knowledge and bestow on us pure thoughts which are pleasing to you . . . make us worthy to shine before you in spiritual conduct and to thank and praise and exalt and worship your majesty.[12]

A day is the miniature form of our life span as well as that of the entire phenomenon of time. The sevenfold division of the day corresponds to 'the Sabbatical structure of time'.[13] It means that the whole day and the earthly life should be centred on God.

The Creator of the day and night in his loving-kindness protects us. It is indeed our spiritual conduct and worship of God that makes our life meaningful.

3. Meaning of the Evening and the Darkness

In the Syriac tradition, as in Judaism, the day begins with the evening ('And there was evening and there was morning, one day' – Gen. 1:25). Dionysius Bar Salibi discusses the reasons for beginning the day with the evening:

> Other doctors, however, assert that [Moses] refers by the word 'evening' to the night, and by the word 'morning' to the day, and thus what they say (Gen. 1:25) means: 'And the night and the day constituted the first day'. These doctors assert that the night precedes the day.[14]

Thus the day begins with *Ramsho*, the evening prayer. In a sense, prayer is the first act of the 'new day'. The evening prayer is a symbol of 'ceaseless praise and uninterrupted thanksgiving' that we are called to offer in our lives. The common introductory prayer of *Ramsho* asks God for the grace of living a life of praise and thanksgiving:

> Grant us, Lord God, that while our bodies rest from the labours of the day and our souls are released from worldly thoughts, we may stand in your presence with tranquility at this time of evening and that we may offer you ceaseless praise and uninterrupted thanksgiving; that we may acknowledge your loving kindness by which you direct and rule our lives and protect and save our souls; to you we offer praise and thanksgiving, now and always and forever.[15]

---

[12] Tuesday, *Sutoro, Sedro, Shehimo*, p. 85.

[13] The sevenfold division of the daily office was probably based on Ps. 119:164 ('Seven times a day I praise thee . . .').

[14] A. Mingana (tr.), *The Work of Dionysius Bar Salibi against the Armenians* (Woodbrooke Studies IV, Cambridge, 1931), p. 66.

[15] *Shehimo*, pp. 4–5.

In the evening we rest and refresh ourselves from our labours, symbolizing the end of our life and eternal rest. This is recalled in the common introductory prayer of *Sutoro*:

> Grant us to know and to consider that the evening which has called us to rest and refreshment from labour, is a figure of the end of this present life; that we may be diligent in good actions which are pleasing to your will . . .[16]

Evening or morning is the time of transition from light to darkness or darkness to light. Both therefore symbolize the transitory nature of human life. Darkness is, in a sense, the symbol of 'the shadows of doubt that get hold of our hearts',[17] and also of 'the evil one and his powers'.[18] Divine protection is sought against the darkness:

> In the evening Abraham called upon you on the mountain-top and you answered him, O lover of man; and in the evening we call upon you, come to our help, O God, full of mercy, and have mercy upon us.
> In the evening Hezekiah called upon you and you delivered him from the power of the Assyrian; and in the evening we call upon you, deliver us, Lord, from the evil one and his powers, who fights against us.[19]

Evening and darkness also symbolize ignorance. But the Word of God serves as a light to our path. Thus commenting on Ps. 119:105 (one of the Psalms of *Ramsho*), the *B'outo* of Mar Jacob asks:

> In the evening when the light of the sun sets upon earth, may I be enlightened, Lord, to praise your creation; may your word be a lamp to my feet, Son of God, and in place of the sun, may it give light to me, and I will walk by it.[20]

When we pray in the evening, we follow the example of the Old Israel. Following the Law, Moses and the priests of the old dispensation offered sacrifices in the evening. But, instead of sacrifices, the New Israel offers pure prayer and praises:

> At the time of evening the priests sang in praise; and the sacrifices of Moses were offered in the evening; evening and morning the law prescribed that sacrifices should be offered, and the priests were moved to offer praise to your Godhead in the evening. In the time of evening instead of all sacrifices give thanks, and instead of holocausts offer pure prayer in love; and he who has mouth and word and tongue ought to give thanks for the creatures which are silent.[21]

---

[16] Ibid., p. 7.

[17] See *Revelation of Joseph, Ramsho, Enyono*: 'Be gracious to us, O God, be gracious as we turn to you at this evening hour, when the shadows of doubt get hold of our hearts, as they seized Joseph, and you sent your word to him . . .'. *Crown* I, 92.

[18] See Monday, *Ramsho, Shehimo*, pp. 37–38: 'Be to us, Lord, a day which this passing evening shall not overtake and may your cross be a wall to protect us against the evil one and his powers, who fights against us.'

[19] Monday, *Ramsho, Shehimo*, p.37.

[20] Ibid., p. 38.

[21] Ibid.

In the evening the Church glorifies the Lord, for he was sacrificed as an offering 'in the evening', that is, he gave his body and blood in the evening:

> Praise to you at this time of evening from your flock, for which you were sacrificed as an offering in the evening; she sings praise to you who gave her your blood to drink on the cross and she takes pleasure in your flesh and blood, glory be to you.[22]

Thus the prayers enumerate the reasons for Vespers. Vespers is part of God's plan concerning our salvation. It was in the evening that the Old Testament sacrifices were offered and the Lord's Supper was instituted. The evening marks the beginning of a 'new day' as well as 'the end of time'. Absence of light symbolizes the absence of divine knowledge, which can be overcome only by the 'light' of the Word of God, which drives away the 'shadows of doubt' and the darkness of ignorance. Darkness also symbolizes the 'absence of good' or the power of evil over our life. Here also God is our refuge and help to fight against the powers of darkness.

4. 'Be Vigilant!': The Meaning of *Lilyo*

Following the Greco-Roman usage, in the West Syrian tradition, night has been divided into four *qaume* or watches.[23] The *Lilyo* presents sleep as the symbol of sin and death that overpowers man. Slumber symbolizes spiritual inaction and indifference to God's living and loving presence. Vigilance, on the other hand, is spiritual alertness.[24] Wakefulness is the very nature of God, who never 'sleeps'. It is a 'Paschal' or an eschatological attitude. It anticipates the light of the eighth day, the new age already present in the liturgy. Thus *Lilyo* indicates awakening from sin and death. The common introductory prayer of *Lilyo* summarizes the meaning of this liturgical hour:

> Awaken us, Lord, from our sleep in the sloth of sin that we may praise your watchfulness, you who watch and do not sleep; give life to our death in the sleep of death and corruption, that we may adore your compassion, you who live and do not die; grant us in the glorious company of the angels who praise you in heaven, to praise you and bless you in holiness, because you are praised and blessed in heaven and on earth, Father, Son and Holy Spirit, now and always and for ever.[25]

Wakefulness is a paschal attitude as well as a sign of eschatological preparedness. It anticipates the life of the new age, already present in the Church. In the age to come, slumber has no place, where we will be vigilant like the angels.

---

22 Ibid.

23 This is followed in Matt. 14:25 and Mark 6:48. In Jewish usage, night was divided into three watches. See Bradshaw, *Daily Prayer*, p. 6.

24 See Olivier Clément, *Le Chant des larmes. Essai sur le Repentir* (Paris, 1982), p. 88.

25 *Shehimo*, p. 11.

Sometimes the opening *enyono* exhorts the faithful to awake and worship: 'How long will you be engrossed in pleasures that do not profit? Awake now and rise and sing praise. Lord of all, to you the praise.'[26]

In our night vigil, we join 'the glorious company of the angels' who never sleep and who worship God ceaselessly. This is repeatedly evoked in the *Lilyo*:

> It is good to rise early to praise you, Our Creator, and with the angels to make a joyful noise, singing the threefold hallowing: 'Holy, holy, holy are you, O God . . . As the angels keep vigil and never cease to praise, awaken us also, earthly-ones, to praise you with them.[27]

In the Spirit, our songs are mingled with those of the angels. The Spirit also grants unity to the ecclesial body and unites our prayers with those of the celestial choir. Our praises become part of the one, eternal and ceaseless glorification of the triune God:

> Mingle, Lord, by your grace, our songs with the songs of the angels without flesh above this world, that with one accord, with the voice of the Spirit we may cry and cry: 'Blessed be the glory of the Lord in his place forever and ever.' (Ezek. 3:12)[28]

This theme is further developed in the common introductory prayer of the Third *Qaumo*: 'Sincere and grateful praises with sweet and pleasant voices does the Church with her children raise to the Father, the Son and the Holy Spirit at all times, together with the four-faced Cherubim and six-winged Seraphim and with the angels who cry and say: Blessed is the glory of the Lord in his place for ever.'[29]

The five wise virgins set a model for wakefulness and the reward that they received gives us hope. Watchfulness marks our love for the heavenly Bridegroom, who expects us to be vigilant against the slumber of sin and spiritual laziness:

> By night let those below praise you, watching with those above, and let them raise the voice of their praise to the Watcher who never sleeps.
> Grant us the watchfulness of the wise virgins, that, when you come in the middle of the night, with them we may enter the bridal chamber.
> Let us not be drowned in sin as in sleep, my beloved; let us watch at the door of the bridegroom, that with him we may enter the bridal chamber.[30]

Thus *Lilyo* indicates our watching for the coming of the Lord. It is the expression of our eschatological readiness to meet him, even if 'he comes in the second or in the

---

[26] *Dedication of the Church, Lilyo, Crown* I, 25; first Sunday after the Nativity, *Lilyo, Crown* I, 128.

[27] First Sunday after Epiphany, *Lilyo, Enyono, Crown* I, 158; also third Sunday after Epiphany, *Crown* I, 185.

[28] Common introductory prayer, *Lilyo, Second Qaumo, Shehimo*, p. 13. In the *Lilyo*, instead of Trisagion, Ezek. 3:12 is repeated at the end of the first and the second *Qaume*.

[29] *Shehimo*, p. 13.

[30] Tuesday, *Lilyo*, Fourth *Qaumo, Bo'uto* of Mar Ephrem, *Shehimo*, p. 99.

third watch' (Luke 12:38). Those who have pleased the Lord are in a watchful state and they will enter the heavenly bridal chamber with him:

> By night let us rise and give thanks to the Son of God; for by night there will be a cry, the Lord is coming; the just and righteous, prophets, apostles and holy martyrs will go forth to meet him, and enter with him the marriage-chamber, full of joy; they will inherit life and the kingdom and sing praise to the Lord of glory.[31]

In the Bible, some of the most significant events take place in the night. This provides an additional reason to keep awake and pray:

> At night Simon Peter went forth from prison and at night the chains fell from the hands of Paul, and at night do you cut off from us the fetters and bonds of sin.
> By night our Lord walked upon the Sea of Galilee and by night the disciples cried: Lord, help us, and like them we call upon you, God, come to our help.
> At night a star appeared to Jacob in the open country, and at night a pillar of light stood over Israel, and at night let your light shine in the hearts of your worshippers.
> At night God called to Samuel, the chosen, and made him head over Israel to admonish and correct; and at night do you admonish and correct the hearts of your worshippers.[32]

David, who is a perfect example of prayer pleasing to God, prayed at night. The prayer in the night opened his eyes to behold the wonders of the creation and enabled him to give thanks to God:

> In the middle of the night David arose to give praise for the wonders of the Godhead and the judgments of the most High; he looked on the heaven and saw the firmament, the stars and the beauty of their courses; he saw the peace and calm of the creation and his soul was filled with wonder, and he gave thanks to you, Lord, because he saw its marvels.[33]

These hymns provide an example of the Syriac poetical genius, which always presented the meaning of each and everything in terms of the Bible.

5. The Dawn Announces God's Victory

Morning symbolizes the beginning of creation with the light. It evokes the resurrection of Christ, with which life and light dawned over the creation. It also points to the 'great morning', the day of Christ's Second Coming when his Light will overpower darkness, sin and death.[34]

---

31 Monday, *Lilyo*, Third *Qaumo*, *Qolo*, *Shehimo*, p. 51.

32 Thursday, *Lilyo*, Third *Qaumo*, *Qolo*, *Shehimo*, p. 191.

33 Monday, *Lilyo*, Third *Qaumo*, *Qolo*, *Shehimo*, pp. 51–52.

34 See I.H. Dalmais, 'Le thème de la lumière dans l'office du matin des Eglises syrienne orientales', in *Noël, Epiphanie, retour du Christ* (Lex Orandi 40, Paris, 1967), pp. 257–76.

God the Creator, who drove away darkness and created light, renews creation by giving light, life and joy. The common introductory prayer of *Sapro* puts it:

> Creator of the morning, who drives out the darkness and brings light and joy to the creation, create in us habits of virtue and drive from us all the darkness of sin; give us light and joy by the glorious rays of your grace, Lord our God, forever.[35]

Every morning is, in a sense, the image of the morning on which Christ rose from the dead, and therefore of His victory over darkness, Satan and death:

> All the time of morning praise to you from those above and those below, O Son who sits at the right hand, by whose command darkness and death and Satan were destroyed and your light has reigned over the world.[36]

Each morning is the foretaste of the great morning of the Second Coming. On 'both mornings' we are called to sing praise to 'the Lord of the two worlds':

> From morning to morning I have sought your salvation, O lover of man; on your great morning when you come, make us to stand at your right hand.
> On this morning, I will sing praise to you, and on that which is to come, I will magnify you; on both mornings glory to you, Lord of the two worlds.[37]

This 'passing morning' will prepare us for 'that morning which does not pass':

> On this passing morning we worship you, who give light to creation; on that morning, which does not pass, grant that we may all exult at your right hand, O living Lamb, who redeemed us by your cross.[38]

On that great morning we will surely see Christ face to face. He will welcome us and reward us:

> In the morning let us hasten to prayer like Abraham to the sacrifice; that on the great morning which is to come we may see Christ and he may say to us: Come in peace, good and trusty servants; come and enter and inherit the kingdom and life which does not pass away.[39]

Morning is the time to begin labour. 'The morning of the Lord' is not very distant. It will come suddenly and the diligent will be rewarded. Prayer is the sign of diligence and labour:

---

[35] *Shehimo*, p. 22.

[36] Tuesday, *Sapro, Qolo, Shehimo*, p. 107.

[37] Tuesday, *Sapro, Bo'uto* of Mar Ephrem, *Shehimo*, p. 113.

[38] Thursday, *Sapro, Qolo, Shehimo*, p. 197.

[39] Monday, *Sapro, Qolo, Shehimo*, p. 61.

The morning of our Lord will come and suddenly salvation shall appear; he will give to the just their reward; blessed is he who has been diligent and has laboured in the vineyard of Christ; because he shall receive reward in full.[40]

6. Themes of the Liturgical Hours

The West Syrians have associated a particular theme with some of the liturgical hours.[41] The third, sixth and ninth hours are associated with our Fall and salvation. They are decisive moments in the history of salvation. Thus we find in a hymn of the *Shehimo*:

> At the third hour Adam ate the fruit of death in Eden from the tree, and at the sixth hour the Lord of the worlds ascended the cross for the sake of his servant who had sinned; at the ninth hour he wrote the deed of his deliverance on the cross and restored him to Eden, his inheritance.[42]

As we will see below, this hymn retains the themes traditionally associated with these hours.

In the Syro-Antiochene tradition, the *Didascalia* may be the first document that attributes a theme to each of the liturgical hours. Thus in a canon attributed to St Paul we find the following instruction:

> Perform prayer in the morning and at the third hour and in the evening and when you go to sleep, and at compline (*Sutoro*) and at the cock crow. In the morning namely, having made the night to pass and brought the day; at the third hour because at it our Lord received the judgment from Pilate. In that of the sixth hour because in it Christ was crucified, all creatures were shaken, trembling at the audacity which the wicked Jews did: he was pierced in his side by a spear, and shed forth blood and water; in that of the ninth hour because when our Lord was crucified the sun was darkened in the midst of the noon, and the dead arose from their graves . . . in that of the evening, however, thanking God, who gave us the night for rest from the toils of the day; but in that of compline while you now slumber the sleep of rest from work; but pray that in sleep and in rest you may not leave this world, and if that should happen, the prayer which you have prayed will help you in the way that is everlasting; and at cock crow, because that is the hour which announces to us the coming of the day, and for the service of the works of light.[43]

---

[40] Tuesday, *Sapro*, *Qolo*, *Shehimo*, p. 107.

[41] On the West Syrian daily offices, see J. Mateos, 'Les matines chaldéenes, maronites et syriens', *OCP* 26 (1960), 51–73; 'Une collection syrienne de "prières entre les marmyata"', *OCP* 31 (1965), 53–75; 305–35; 'Prières initiales fixes des offices syriens, Maronites et byzantins', *OS* 11 (1966), 489–98. 'Les strophes de la nuit dans l'invitatoire du nocturne syrien', in F. Graffin (ed.), *Mémorial Mgr Gabriel Khouri-Sarkis* (1898–1968) (Louvain, 1969), pp. 71–81. A. Cody, 'L'Office divin chez les syriens jacobites. Leurs eucharisties épiscopales et leur rite de pénitence', *POC* 19 (1969), 293–319.

[42] Friday, third hour, *Qolo*, *Shehimo*, p. 260.

[43] *Didascalia* III, 7, *CSCO* 402, p. 36. Cf. *Apostolic Constitutions* VIII, 34, 1–7; *Testamentum Domini* II, 24; *Synodicon* I, p. 63.

According to the *Testament of our Lord*, the canonical hours are not merely for the clergy or the monks or for individual piety. The lay people are exhorted to pray seven times a day. A canonical hour is the gathering of the Church:

> At early dawn let the bishop gather the people together, so that the service is finished at the rising of the sun. As the bishop says the first hymns of praise of dawn, with the presbyters and deacons and the others (the faithful also) [standing] nearby, let him say thus . . .[44]

Then follows the hymn of praise and a series of prayers with the people's responses. The catechumens also attended the offices, and they were dismissed after the reading of the scriptures and sermon.[45] After their dismissal, the bishop or the presbyter explained the mysteries of faith, 'so that the people know whom they approach and who is their God and Father'.[46]

According to the *Testament of our Lord*, the canonical hour has a place in God's plan for our salvation. Thus after the dawn hymn of praise and the people's response ('We praise you, we bless you, we give you thanks, we beseech you our God'), the bishop says: 'We treble this hymn of praise from our mouths to you, as an image of your kingdom, O Son of God who [are] through eternity, who [are] above all, with the Father, whom all creation praises . . .'.[47]

The presbyter's daily hymn of praise concludes with a similar doxology:

> We praise you, we unceasingly depict in ourselves the image of your kingdom for your sake, also [for the sake] of your beloved Son Jesus Christ, through whom to you be praise and might with the Holy Spirit, to the ages of ages, forever and ever Amen.[48]

Thus the meaning and purpose of the daily offices is similar to that of the Eucharist. They provide us with a foretaste of the life in the kingdom, where we will glorify God unceasingly. As we have already noted, the Book of Revelation (the earliest treatise on 'Liturgical Theology') presents the experience of the kingdom of God in terms of an eternal liturgy (4:8–11; 5:6–8; 7:9–13 etc.). This understanding of the eternal life has undoubtedly influenced the Syro-Antiochene tradition. In fact, the New Testament references to the life in the Kingdom are to be understood in relation to the Johannine vision. Thus 'we shall always be with the Lord' (1 Thess. 4:17) and 'we will worship him forever' are the same. Similarly, to stand 'holy and blameless and irreproachable before Christ' (Col. 1:22) would mean 'to worship him ceaselessly' (Rev. 7:9–12).

The gift of sonship or the inheritance of the Kingdom that we have been granted in baptism[49] consists of the privilege to stand before him and to worship him forever.

---

[44] *Testament of Our Lord*, I, 26: Grant Sperry-White, *The Testamentum Domini*, *GLS* 66 (1991), p. 32.

[45] Ibid., II, 27, p. 35.

[46] Ibid., II, 28, p. 35.

[47] Ibid., I, 26, p. 33.

[48] Ibid., I, 32, p. 38.

[49] Seventh Sunday after Epiphany, *Ramsho*, *Crown* I, 230.

Thus in a prayer of incense (*Etro*) of the Epiphany cycle, we find: 'Preserve in us the gift of the inheritance of the sons gained at baptism, that we may praise you and your Father and your Holy Spirit now and forever.'

The 'royal robe of baptism' makes us worthy of participating in the heavenly liturgy along with innumerable saints since Adam:

> Lord, make us worthy to feed in joy on the vision of your glory, to take our delight in the splendour of your face and to attain that bliss which you have prepared for us from the foundation of the world. Help us to make the royal robe of our baptism to shine that we may be worthy to sing songs of joy, in voices of praise with thanksgiving in the dwelling of the just, for the glory of your name, without ceasing, forever. Amen.[50]

7. Themes of the Days and Hours

Each day and hour has a dominating theme. Thus the theme of Sunday is almost always 'the resurrection of Christ'. That of Monday and Tuesday is 'repentance' and Wednesday 'the Mother of God'. On Thursday, the apostles and the doctors are commemorated. The themes of Friday are 'the Cross, Martyrs and the Saints'. Saturday is dedicated to all the departed members of the Church, both clergy and laity.[51]

The theme of *Sutoro* is always 'repentance' and that of the ninth hour is the departed. The sixth hour has general themes. But in the case of the third hour, the themes vary according to the days (for example Wednesday: Mother of God; Friday: the Cross; Saturday: the Departed).

The four *Qaume* (watches) have variable themes. The theme of the First *Qaumo* is always 'the Mother of God' except on Fridays, when 'the cross' is commemorated. That of the Second *Qaumo* is always 'the saints' (on Thursday 'the apostles'). In the case of the Third *Qaumo*, on Monday, Tuesday and Thursday the theme is 'repentance', whereas on Wednesdays and Fridays the 'departed ones' are commemorated. The Fourth *Qaumo* always has general themes.

The reason for dedicating Sunday to 'resurrection', Friday to 'the 'cross' and Saturday to 'the departed' is evident. Often the liturgical hours explain the themes of the day:

---

50 Second Sunday after Epiphany, *Opening Prayer, Crown* I, 166.

51 This is the arrangement of the present *Shimo* used in India. It is more or less the same as the arrangement known to Bar Salibi (twelfth century): 'Sundays are consecrated to the festival of the Resurrection; Mondays and Tuesdays are devoted to prayers for repentance; Wednesdays are to the Mother of God, to the martyrs and the dead. Thursdays to the Apostles and doctors, to the Mother of God, to the martyrs and to the dead. Fridays to the cross; and Saturdays to the Mother of God to the martyrs and dead.' A. Mingana (ed.), *A Treatise of Bar Salibi against the Melchites* (Woodbrooke Studies, Cambridge, 1927), p. 33. Cf. the Byzantine themes of the days: N. Zernov, *The Church of the Eastern Christians*, (SPCK London, 1947), p. 32.

On Friday, which is the sixth day, wicked men set up the cross of the most High, and on Friday again they pierced his side with a lance and there flowed from it for us the blood and water of life, in propitiation for the people, who confessed and believed in him.

Tell me, Friday, why is there great honour to you among all the churches? On me was created Adam, the head of mankind, and on me he entered Paradise and the Watchers bowed down before him, and on me was crucified the first-born, who redeemed the world.[52]

The martyrs confessed the victory of the cross by laying down their lives, and the saints followed the path of the cross. That is why their memory is evoked on Friday, the 'day of the cross'. On Saturday, our Lord 'rested' in the tomb, and brought hope to the departed. Saturday is also the symbol of the 'Last Days' and our 'sleep' in the tomb in the hope of the resurrection.

Wednesday has been associated with the memory of the 'Mother of God', probably on the basis of some traditions attested by the apocryphal literature. Thus in his commentary on the Eucharist, John of Dara (ninth century) says that Saint John the Evangelist baptized Mary on Wednesday after the feast of the Pentecost.[53]

8. Eucharist and the Daily Offices

The meaning of the daily offices is inseparable from that of the Eucharist, the centre of Christian worship. The elaborate cycle of daily offices has been built, in the course of time, around this centre.[54] As in the case of the Eucharist and other sacramental celebrations, there is much serenity and solemnity. As Father Florovsky says, 'the ultimate purpose is to put man before God and to impress upon him all that God has done for him'.[55]

Eucharist is the 'thanksgiving' for all God has done in Christ. In its essence, an office is a *eucharistia* for the *mirabilia dei*, as in the prayers of the offices given in the *Apostolic Constitutions*[56] and the *Testament of our Lord*.[57] In the case of *Lilyo* (or *Laudes*), this has been underscored by the use of the Psalms of glorification (Pss. 148–50). In *Ramsho*, the group of psalms (Pss. 141–42; 119:105–12) concludes with Ps. 117, one of the *Hallel* psalms.

---

[52] Friday, *Sapro, Qolo, Shehimo*, p. 253.

[53] John of Dara, *Eucharist*, Introduction: 4 (tr. B. Varghese, pp. 14–15). But according to the *Book of Life*, edited by Connolly, John baptized Mary on the 'fifth day', that is, on Thursday. Connolly, *Two Jacobite Commentaries*, pp. 120–21.

[54] G. Florovsky, 'The Worshipping Church', in Mother Mary and Kallistos Ware, *The Festal Menaion* (London, 1969), p. 29. See also G. Florovsky, 'Worship and Everyday Life. An Eastern Orthodox View', *SL* 2 (1963), 266–72.

[55] G. Florovsky, '(The elements of liturgy) Orthodox', in P. Edwall et al. (eds), *Ways of Worship* (London, 1951), p. 64.

[56] *Apostolic Constitutions* VII, 47, 1–3 (morning hymn), VII, 48, 1–4 (evening hymn); VIII, 37, 1–3 (evening office); VIII, 38, 3–5 (morning). Texts in *GLS* 61, pp. 52–61.

[57] *Testament of Our Lord* I, 26, *GLS* 66, pp. 31–39.

As we have noted, the mysteries of Christ, of the economy of salvation and of the Church have been extensively contemplated from Monday to Saturday, which leads to the celebration of the Eucharist, the prayer *par excellence* of the Church. The daily offices prepare for the communion, for the gathering together of the Eucharistic assembly as the Church, as the manifestation of the Kingdom. Almost every aspect of the mystery of the Church is commemorated in offices. The relationship between the two is further evident from the fact that, in the East, the celebration of the Eucharist is inconceivable without the completion of the canonical prayers. In other words, the canonical prayers are part of the *ordo* of the Eucharist. This seems to be why the *Apostolic Constitutions* (II, 59, 1–4) and *Testament of the Lord* (I, 26) prescribe the daily offices as obligatory for the clerical orders as well as for the laity.

Signing with the sign of the cross and prostrations are integral to the daily offices. Through them the body shares in the *eucharistia* offered to God. Weekly fasts (Wednesday and Friday) emphasize the penitential dimension of the *ordo* of the canonical hours. Since Wednesdays and Fridays are associated with the betrayal (therefore beginning of the passion) and crucifixion of Christ, the weekly fasts are in a sense a 'miniature lent' that leads to Sunday, the 'weekly passover'. Expressive gestures such as bare feet and outstretched hands manifest awareness of the presence of God. The reading of the Gospel and the use of incense further underscore the sacramental character of the daily office. As in the case of the Eucharist and other sacramental celebrations, in the daily office, there is much serenity and solemnity.

9. The Liturgical Year

The liturgical year aims at the 'anamnesis' of God's work of revelation and redemption in a rhythmical sequence. The church feasts allow the sequence to be kept in sight at all times. As we have already seen, in the West Syrian tradition, the liturgical year is centred on the feast of the Resurrection (*Qyomto*).[58] Each Sunday is in fact called *Qyomto*, for it is a weekly celebration of the resurrection of Christ. The common introductory prayer of an ordinary Sunday presents the theme:

> Grant us, Lord God, that with the heavenly hosts we may exalt this day of your resurrection on the third day in purity and holiness, that we may shine before you in virtuous conduct and may praise you without ceasing, with your Father and your Holy Spirit, now and always and forever.[59]

In the Malankara Orthodox Church (India), the office of the *Qyomto* is used for almost all the Sundays of the year. Thus the theme of the resurrection is evoked practically every week.

---

58 I.H. Dalmais, 'Note sur l'année liturgique dans les Eglises de tradition syriaque', *LMD* 148 (1981), 141–44.

59 *Shehimo*, p. 311.

The liturgical year begins with 'the Sunday of the Consecration of the Church or *Qudosh 'edto* (first Sunday of November, or 30/31 October if it falls on a Sunday), followed by the Sunday of the Renewal of the Church (*Hudosh 'edto*) and the Sundays of Advent. 'The liturgical year can be divided into a cycle of seven periods (each consisting approximately of seven weeks).'[60] However, the length of the cycles varies (with the exception of the Advent, Lenten and Easter cycles). The following are the liturgical cycles as they are found today:

1   *Qudosh 'edto, Hudosh 'edto* (two Sundays).
2   Advent cycle (six Sundays)
3   Nativity–Epiphany cycle (up to seven Sundays, depending upon the date of Easter).
4   'Sundays of the departed clergy and faithful' (two Sundays that precede Lent).
5   Lenten cycle (seven Sundays).
6   Easter cycle (seven Sundays including Easter).
7   Pentecost cycle (up to eleven Sundays, depending upon the date of Easter).
8   Transfiguration–Ascension cycle (up to seven Sundays).
9   Cycle of the feast of the Cross (up to eight Sundays, depending upon the *Qudosh 'edto*).

Generally speaking, each cycle is centred on a principal feast. A cycle begins and ends with Sunday, indicating that each cycle is rooted in the mystery of Easter. The Christmas and Easter cycles begin with the quadragesimal fast. In the West Syrian tradition, formerly the feast of the Apostles (29 June) was also preceded by a similar fast.[61]

The Advent and Lenten cycles are preceded by 'introductory cycles' consisting of two Sundays each. The first is preceded by *Qudosh 'edto* and *Hudosh 'edto*.[62] The offices of the 'two festivals of the Church' do not discuss the doctrine of the Church. The Church remains a mystery. Yet 'she' is a living reality of which the faithful are the members. She is 'the bride whom Christ bought with his precious blood'.[63] In the Old Testament the Church was prefigured and its nature and vocation were alluded to in the prophecies.[64] The *Sedro* of *Qudosh 'edto* (*Ramsho*) gives a beautiful summary of the Old Testament types and images of the Church:

> Praise to you and thanksgiving to you, Jesus Christ, unshakeable Rock of truth on which the holy Church is established, rock of Moses which gave forth twelve

60 See I.H. Dalmais, *Eastern Liturgies* (New York), p. 133.

61 See *Synodicon* II, *CSCO* 376, p. 233. Canons of Mar Hananya (7); Bar Hebraeus speaks of it as a practice of the 'Easterners' (that is, Syrian Orthodox Christians of Tagrit and Mosul), *Nomocanon* 5:2, Bedjan, pp. 56–57. See also my study, 'Canonical fasts', pp. 96–103.

62 On the origin of these Sundays, see B. Botte, 'Les Dimanches de la Dédicaces dans les Eglises Syriennes', *OS* 2 (1957), 65–70.

63 Cf. Pampakuda, *Promioun-Sedra*, MS 13, p. 1; Mal .tr. p. 2.

64 Cf. The Old Testament readings of the two feasts: *Qudosh 'edto*: Exod. 33:5–11; 1 Kgs 6:1–8 ; Jer. 31:10–14; 22–26 ; Ezek. 9:11; 10:5; 18–22. *Hudosh 'edto*: same.

streams to quench the thirst of Israel . . . It is from this Church that in due season, streams of spiritual water flow, her true doctrine to give to drink in joy to all peoples. It is of her that David sang when he said that the daughter of the king is adorned with all spiritual beauty within, not like the tabernacle of the Law which Moses raised as a shadow of that which was to come, but with the glorious royal robe of faith and with the holy mystery of baptism and the radiance of the Holy Spirit, with the spiritual and heavenly table of the blood of the Lamb without stain or blemish, and with the Sun of righteousness, Christ her Bridegroom, and with the brightness of the doctors inspired by the Holy Spirit. It was the Church that Solomon saw, in a vision, in the house, which he built for the Most High. It was for her that Isaiah prophesied when he said: 'Stand and be enlightened because your light has come and the glory of the Lord is rising upon you'. David sang of her when he said: 'Leave your people and your father's house, for the King of kings has desired your beauty'. Of her all wondrous things are spoken: her countenance is bright, her eyes are shining, her garments are resplendent. The Lord of the worlds is her Bridegroom. John is the Bridegroom's friend, the apostles and martyrs the wedding-guests.[65]

The Church is the Bride of Christ and the Temple. She has been called to be with Christ and to be a dwelling place of the triune God. To be with Christ means to love him and to serve him. As we have seen, the West Syrians understood salvation in terms of worship. Christ has redeemed us and made us his worshippers:

And with the blood from your side you brought us from the slavery of the demons, and from the worthless worship of the idols. By your grace, you have called us to the service (*teshmeshto*) of life and the spiritual sheepfold.[66]

Again in the *Promiun* of *Qudosh 'edto* (third hour) we find:

God, you alone have the power for salvation. You came down towards our human race from the divine and incorruptible heights because of your mercy and compassion, while we were sitting in the darkness and shadows of death, and while we were going down like the wheels [of a cart] into [the mud] of sin after [our] fall from the blessed life of Paradise, so that those who were the children of the earth and aliens and sinners and destitute of every righteousness, and of every spiritual and divine company (*baitoyuto*), you made [them] sons of the heavenly Father and at the same time worshippers and singers of praise along with the spiritual and the invisible armies.[67]

Condemnation by God is separation from him (Matt. 25:30; 46), which means deprivation of the very possibility of worshipping. A *Sedro* of *Hudosh 'edto* (morning), implores: 'Do not abandon us to hell, where there is no worship of you'.[68] Worship is

---

65 *Crown* I, 3.
66 *Hudosh 'edto* (= Renewal of the Church), *Lilyo*, First *Qaumo*, *Promiun*, Pampakuda, MS 13, p. 26; Mal. tr. p. 24.
67 Pampakuda MS 13, pp. 16–17; Mal. tr., p. 16.
68 Pampakuda MS 13, p. 35; Mal. tr., p. 32.

the very goal of the Church's existence. This is recalled in the concluding doxology of almost every prayer: 'We will [or 'make us worthy to'] offer praise and thanksgiving, now and always and forever.'

Thus the first two Sundays introduce the goal of the liturgical year: through her worship, the Church realizes her vocation and she proclaims that she has been 'firmly established on Christ, the rock of faith'. It is for this goal that she celebrates the whole economy of salvation, beginning with the Advent cycle (symbol of the Messianic expectation) and concluding with the Feast of the Cross cycle (symbol of the victory of the cross over the powers of evil and death and the ardent expectation of the Second Coming).

In and through the liturgical year, the life of Christ has been 'publicly portrayed' before us. It serves as a means to proclaim the reality of the Incarnation and thus to unite us with him and to grow into his stature. The Church relives the whole life of Christ: Nativity, Baptism, Fasting, Passion, Resurrection, Sending of the Holy Spirit, and finally the Triumph of the Cross. As an Eastern Orthodox monk writes, 'The liturgical year forms Christ in us, from his birth the full stature of the perfect man. According to a Medieval Latin saying, the liturgical year is Christ himself, *annus est Christus.*'[69]

When we commemorate a particular event in the life of Christ, the whole of his life, work and words are implied.[70] Each phase in the earthly life of Christ, whether Nativity, Baptism, Passion or Resurrection, includes and anticipates the whole economy of salvation. The celebration of a particular event manifests the whole economy of salvation, a striking characteristic of Syriac thought, especially that of St Ephrem.[71] Each celebration is set in the context of the whole, for each leads us to life, to the Kingdom of God. Thus in the prayers of a dominical feast, the whole mystery of Christ is often evoked, giving emphasis to his pre-existence, equality with the Father, Incarnation, Resurrection and the Second Coming. Similarly, a feast of the Mother of God or a saint is celebrated as part of the Mystery of Christ, as an example of our glorification in Christ. As the fulfilment of Christ's promise, 'where I am you may be also' (John 14:3), they have been glorified in and through Christ. Their triumph is a witness to the mystery of Christ. Thus each feast and each day of the year contains the fullness of the mystery of Christ.

10. Feasts of the Saints

The liturgical year consists of the dominical feasts as well as the feasts of the Mother of God, the Apostles, the Martyrs, the Saints and a 'great cloud of witnesses'.[72] In

---

69 *The Year of the Grace of the Lord: by a monk of the Eastern Church* (SVSP, New York, 1980), p. 2.

70 Ibid., pp. 245–46.

71 S. Brock, 'The Poet as Theologian', *Sobornost* 7–4 (1977), 246.

72 See I.H. Dalmais, 'Mémoire et vénération des Saints dans les églises de traditions syriennes', in *Saints et Sainteté dans la liturgie: Conférences S. Serge, XXXIII semaine* (ed. A.M. Triacca and A. Pistoia) (*Eph. Lit. Subs.* 40, 1987), 79–91.

other words, in its liturgical calendar the Church commemorates the economy of salvation and the memory of the glorified members of the Body of Christ. A feast, in a sense, is a celebration of a dogma. The Church celebrates the events in the life of Christ and the memory of the saints, who have witnessed to the truth of our doctrines. Saints have 'completed Christ's afflictions for the sake of his body, the Church' (cf. Col. 1:24). They have set an example for imitating Christ. Their sufferings did not deprive them of their joy and trust in God. Their life and death are undeniable proof of the reality of the Kingdom of God. As a hymn of the *Shehimo* puts it:

> I saw the martyrs, my brothers, how their blood is poured out on the earth, and their heart is full of joy and exultation and they say: how sweet it is to die for the sake of God, who gives life as an inheritance to those who believe, halleluiah, make us inherit the kingdom on high, Jesus, Saviour of the world.[73]

To inherit life and Kingdom means to stand before God and to worship him forever. Thus the saints and the martyrs have joined the heavenly choirs, and all those who have pleased God since Adam. The martyrs were convinced of this fact. Thus in the *Ramsho* of Friday the following hymn is placed on their lips: 'The martyrs say to their persecutors: we do not fear the fire or the sharpened sword, and if the body perishes, the soul shall live and sing praise and thanksgiving.'[74]

As we have seen, the members of the Body of Christ pray in Christ and by their prayers they participate in that of Christ. Thus the prayers of the martyrs and the saints are eternally united with that of Christ, and 'ascend to God as a well-pleasing incense' (cf. Rev. 8:3–4). Thus the celebration of the feast of a saint or a humble request for intercession addressed to a saint enables us 'to enter into the relationship of prayer which unites that saint to Christ'.[75] 'It is still more', says the (anonymous) monk of the Eastern Church:

> In the same way that the feasts of our Lord in a mysterious way renew the events of his life, so the feasts of the saints make their lives, their merits and their deaths, mysteriously actual, in as much as they participate in the life, the merits and death of the Lord Jesus. Thus commemorations of the martyrs some how renew the grace of their violent deaths, so that as these were a participation in the passion of Christ, it is this passion, which is relived in remembering the martyrs. The liturgical year has but one and the same object, Jesus Christ; whether we contemplate him directly, or whether we contemplate him through the members of his body.[76]

---

73 Friday, *Sapro, Shehimo*, p. 248.

74 *Shehimo*, p. 216.

75 *The Year of Grace of the Lord*, p. 2.

76 Ibid.

11. The Meaning of Advent

Advent is a time of waiting for the 'coming of the Lord Jesus Christ'. Waiting implies spiritual preparedness, which includes repentance and 'turning to the Lord'. Thus in the East, the whole Advent time is a season of fasting. The Advent Lent formerly began on 15 November (now on 1 December) and ended with the feast of the Nativity. On the Sundays of Advent, the events and the personalities related to the story of the Nativity are commemorated. Thus following are the Sundays of the season:

1   The Annunciation to Zechariah
2   The Annunciation to Mary
3   The visitation of Mary to Elizabeth
4   The birth of John the Baptist
5   The Revelation to Joseph
6   Sunday of the Genealogy ('Sunday before the Nativity').[77]

Unlike the Byzantine Advent, which above all looks to Epiphany, the Syrian Orthodox cycle is a preparation for the Nativity, the guarantee of the Second Coming of Christ. Thus Advent has an important eschatological significance. Christ is the 'one who came and is to come'.[78] The Advent cycle portrays before us the lives of those who were chosen by God to prepare the way of the Lord. Zechariah and Elizabeth, who were 'both righteous before God and were blameless' (Luke 1:6), John the Baptist, who was filled with the Spirit since his mother's womb (Luke 1:15), Joseph, 'a just man' (Matt. 1:19) and above all Mary, 'the blessed among women' and 'the Mother of our Lord' (Luke 1:42–43) are included among them. The coming of Christ had already been prefigured in their personal lives. Their suffering prefigured the Cross of Christ; their glorification in Christ is the guarantee of the future glory that we will be granted in the Second Coming. The 'Sunday of Genealogy' places the Incarnation and the Feast of the Nativity in the wider context of God's redemptive history throughout history.

The festal cycle that begins with the Nativity helps the faithful to relive the mystery of the Incarnation in a series of celebrations. Epiphany, the Presentation in the Temple, Great Lent, Palm Sunday, Passion Week, Maundy Thursday ('Thursday of the mysteries', as it is usually called), Good Friday, Easter and the Ascension celebrate various phases in the economy of the Son. The cycle finds its goal in Easter and its perfection in Pentecost, the outpouring of the Holy Spirit and consequently his permanent dwelling in the Church and humanity. Through the descent of the Holy Spirit, the revelation of the Holy Trinity reached its culmination. In fact the whole economy of salvation was aimed at making us 'christs', the anointed ones and thus the 'sons of the Kingdom'.

---

[77] It is almost a universal custom to read the genealogy according to St Matthew on the Sunday before Christmas.

[78] Cf. the Sanctus of St James; B. Varghese, *The Syriac Version of the Liturgy of St James*, p. 25.

The celebration of each of the feasts picks up all the elements of the Gospel narratives related to the event that has been commemorated. They have been commented upon in relation to the Old Testament and the witness of the apostles. The hymns draw abundantly on the biblical texts and expound the mystery in vivid phrases.

The offices of the day, whether Nativity, Epiphany, Good Friday or Easter, reiterate the expression 'today' or 'on this day'.[79] This shows that the feast makes present the reality that is being celebrated. A feast manifests the reality and the implication of the economy of salvation in our life. It reminds us that its meaning and implication are not limited to the present life and that it provides a 'glimpse' of the eternal life.[80] 'Today' refers to the 'sacramentality' of the liturgical time. Time 'distorts' and makes eternal reality imperfect, multiple and successive. It makes the economy of the salvation an event of the past and its fulfilment a 'remote' experience. Liturgical time transcends duration. In the presence of God, everything becomes present. In God, there is but one moment, in which everything is included.[81]

Some of the elements of the Gospel narratives find their concrete expression in the form of processions, symbolic gestures or special services. Thus the 'Service at the fire-pond' on the feast of Nativity (at the conclusion of the *Lilyo*) accompanied by the reading of the Gospel (Luke 2:1–20) is a dramatization of the experience of the shepherds, to whom the angels announced the Good news.[82]

Similarly, the procession, followed by the blessing of the water on the feast of Epiphany, emphasizes the significance of the feast. Epiphany is the feast of Christ's baptism as well as the celebration of his 'manifestation' to the world as the Son of God. The feast also aims at relating our baptism to that of Christ. According to the Syriac tradition, Christ received baptism in order to 'institute' Christian baptism. Christ sanctified the waters of baptism as the 'first fruits' of our baptism: our baptism is willed and sanctified by the Father, the Son and the Holy Spirit. At Jordan, the Holy Trinity has opened a font of life.[83] The sanctification of water – a key element of material creation – effected in Jordan, was the 'first fruit' of the liberation of the

---

[79] For example 'Today a child was born', *Ma'de'dono*, p. 31; 'Today, the Judge of the world bent His head in the court and was condemned like a servant' (Good Friday), *Ma'de'dono*, pp. 207–208.

[80] See a prayer of Palm Sunday: 'Make us worthy O Lord God, to be adorned with the incorruptible garments and [to hold] glorious and spiritual [olive] branches and to celebrate joyful and exalted feast with the multitude of your elected and to offer glory and praise to You and to Your Living Holy Spirit . . .'. *Ma'de'dono*, Pampakuda, p. 304.

[81] See *The Year of the Grace of the Lord*, p. 245. For the Jews, eternity is a convergence, a synthesis of past, present and future. See Robert Aron, 'Réflexions sur les notions de temps dans la liturgie juive', *LMD* 65 (1961), 127–32, here p. 127.

[82] The *ordo* directs the priest to prepare a fire-pond in the western courtyard of the church. After having completed the third *qaumo*, the procession leaves the church by the northern door and goes in the anticlockwise direction. It stops at the fire-pond. Heb. 1:1–12 A and Luke 2:1–20 are read. When he has finished verse 13, the priest discontinues the Gospel, and lights the fire and chants Luke 2:14, followed by the 'Hymn of the Angels' (*Shimo*, 20–21). The people go around the fire-pond and throw incense into it.

[83] This is stated in a hymn of the Epiphany: 'Baptism, the fount of life has been opened. The Father, the Son and the Holy Spirit sanctified it by His compassion', *Ma'de'dono*, p. 41.

universe from the bondage of evil and corruption. The matter has been restored to its prelapsarian state. By sanctifying the water, Christ has 'drowned the mob of demons and blotted out our sins'.[84] Christ 'healed' the waters from their fallen condition. The 'healing of the bitter water' by Moses (Num. 2:1–11) or by Elijah (2 Kgs 2:19–25) is the type of the permanent healing and the purification of the water, as well as the matter.[85] Water, which was a symbol of chaos and death, has been rendered a key element in the new dispensation and a source of new life. The natural quality of water as an element of refreshment and renewal has a 'sacramental' significance. The baptism of Christ has manifested it as a source of consolation, hope and new life for humanity. The consecration of water is thus a sacramental act. In the Syrian Orthodox Church, the faithful drink the blessed water and keep it in their home. The feast of Epiphany is thus more than a commemoration of the baptism of Christ. It manifests the cosmic dimension of the Incarnation. This is true of most of the celebrations.

If water is blessed on Epiphany, palms are blessed solemnly on Palm Sunday. This constitutes a blessing of all trees and vegetation. Thus the prayer of the blessing says: 'Now bless, Lord, by Your great mercy, these branches and the trees from which they were cut and also all the vegetation that Your Lordship has created. Let them be for the blessing of those who hold them and for the protection of those who bear them.'[86] The Church, as the priestly community, blesses the matter as well as the vegetation and asks God to make them a source of blessing and communion with God. In Christ, the Church asks God to integrate the whole creation with his saving plan and to restore them to their prelapsarian condition. This is an extension of the prayer: 'Your Kingdom come and Your will be done on earth.' A blessing is a prayer for the liberation of the entire creation from the bondage of evil and corruption.

The washing of the feet on Maundy Thursday, the Good Friday procession with the cross, and the order of the veneration of the cross ('The Service of burial') 'publicly portrays' the crucifixion and the burial before our eyes.[87] The reality of the resurrection is emphatically proclaimed and manifested in the 'Service of the Resurrection'.[88]

The last cycle, that of the Cross, has the same significance. It is significant that the liturgical year begins and ends with the cycles having important eschatological overtones. Advent and the cycle of the feast of the Cross are inseparable, as both anticipate the Parousia. Both envisage the coming of Christ into the individual and his growth into the stature of Christ. Both remind us that the glory of the Second Coming must first be prefigured by the coming of Jesus into the individual's life.

---

[84] Ibid., p. 57 (Litany after the Gospel).

[85] Ibid., p. 59. These two OT lessons are read in the service of the blessing of the water.

[86] *Ma'de'dono*, Pampakuda, p. 305.

[87] I.H. Dalmais, 'Une relique de l'antique liturgie de Jérusalem: l'office de l'ensevelissement du Christ', *OS* 6 (1961), 441–54 ; R. Lanchon, 'Le temps pascale dans la liturgie syrienne', *OS* 7 (1962), 337–56; B. Varghese, 'Holy Week', pp. 179–83.

[88] K. Valuparampil, 'An investigation into the theology of the "Resurrection Service" in the Syro-Malankara Church', *Christian Orient* 6 (1985), 137–41; 175–80.

In the celebration of a dominical feast, the cross has a central place. In the procession, a bare cross (symbolizing the resurrection) is carried and the service concludes with the exaltation of the cross toward the four sides.[89] The priest, accompanied by the deacons, stands on the *Bema* (if there is one) or in the sanctuary and exalts the cross three times and blesses the people. As the priest raises the cross he cries out: 'He to Whom the angels minister. He whom the cherubim bless,' etc. To each of his acclamations the people sing a verse of the Trisagion as a response.[90] This is a proclamation to the entire world of the victory of the cross.

The cycle of dominical feasts and the cycle of the feasts of the Blessed Virgin Mary and the Saints are not two strands that run parallel to, or separate from, each other. The Mother of God and the saints are the glorified members of the Body of Christ. They are 'wrapped with the mantle of eternity', our future reward in the Kingdom of God. They are unique witnesses to the power of the cross and the veracity of the resurrection and future glory. Their life and glory are the guarantee for our hope.

It has been said of Judaism that its theology was its calendar.[91] This is true for the Eastern liturgical year as well. The liturgical year is an expression of its liturgical theology. The liturgical year, with Easter as its axial element, celebrates various phases in the life of Christ.[92] The arrangement of the year around the principal feasts of the Lord and of the Saints gradually unfolds the mystery of faith, the foundation of our salvation. It invites and inspires the faithful 'to be rooted in Christ', and to be the 'bearers of the Holy Spirit'. The feasts are often preceded by fasts (for example Nativity, Easter, Apostles' Lent and the Ascension of the Blessed Virgin Mary). This *ordo* is aimed at renewing Christ and the grace of the Holy Spirit in us.

---

89 See A. Rücker, 'Die Adoration Crucis am Karfreitag in den orientalischen Riten', in *Miscellanea L.C. Mohlberg*, Vol.I (Rome, 1948), pp. 383–87.

90 See S. Athanasius, *Ma'de'dono*, pp. 33–35 etc.

91 Robert Aron, 'Réflexions', p. 18.

92 The centrality of the Paschal Mystery is sometimes expressed in vivid phrases. Thus Moses Bar Kepha says that as the important events of the economy of salvation have taken place in the month of Nisan (= April), the Second Coming also will take place in the same month: 'Christ rose from the dead in the month of Nisan. In this month, the creatures were created in the beginning. On the sixth day of this [month] [God] created Adam. The conception [of Christ] was announced in this month. Since he was in this month, he suffered and was crucified and rose in his first coming, the sequence of his second coming is to take place in this month'. Bar Kepha, *Exposition of the feast of the Resurrection*, ch.29, *MS OTS* 5861, fol.140r.

CHAPTER 10

The Meaning of the *Ordo*

In the East, the liturgy is celebrated according to an *ordo*, or an order, a rite established by the Church. By the word *ordo* (*tekso* in Syriac, from the Greek word *taxis*), we mean 'the shape of worship'.[1] The *ordo* consists of liturgical texts, lectionary, gestures, time, music, architecture and symbols. The enumeration of all the elements of an *ordo* is not easy, and is in fact 'problematical'.[2] Everything related to the liturgy (including the ministry of the bishop, presbyter and deacon) comes under the scope of the *ordo*. The content and the function of the *ordo* consist of the arrangement and the enactment of various elements. Their interconnectedness implies a theological vision of the community that adopted them by a process of 'reception'. The structure of the *ordo* has a meaning within the spiritual experience, or within the tradition of the Church that uses it.

In the Syrian Orthodox liturgical tradition, the structure of the sacramental celebrations and that of several other consecrations has been largely inspired by the Eucharist. Similarly, the divine offices have more or less the same structure. This uniform arrangement of the celebrations is not accidental. Obviously, the structure is determined on the basis of certain theological principles, which have not yet been defined. Therefore the elucidation of the meaning of the *ordo* is the primary task of liturgical theology.[3]

Ordo is an ordering of a vision; it expresses the mind of the community. It orders and orients the community, by assigning each member his/her role and function in the celebration. In the Syrian Orthodox liturgy, there is no place for passive participation. Each member 'con-celebrates' with a prayer, hymn, gesture or movement. *Ordo* implies the presence and participation of the people. Thus the meaning of the *ordo* is inseparable from that of the Church. The *ordo* enacts the vocation of the Church as 'a royal priesthood', which offers 'spiritual sacrifices acceptable to God through Jesus Christ' (1 Pet. 2:5; 9).

The goal of the *ordo* is to make the worship the expression of the faith of the Church, or to actualize the Church as the people of God, the worshipping community. Different elements have been arranged as a consistent whole precisely for the self-realization of the Church. *Ordo* is a theologically inspired 'language' by which the Church expresses itself. It actualizes itself as the fulfilment of the 'mystery of God', which was hidden and is finally revealed in Christ. Each element, whether it is time, texts, gestures or symbols, is rooted in and reflects the mystery of God. The West Syrian commentators have pointed out this fundamental principle.

---

[1] A. Schmemann, *Introduction to Liturgical Theology* (New York, 1975), p. 28.
[2] As Schmemann says, the exact scope of the *ordo* is problematical. Ibid.
[3] Ibid.

In the course of liturgical development, the *ordo* has been expanded by incorporating new elements worthy of the mystery of God. The function of the *ordo* is in a sense similar to that of the doctrinal formulations. Their nucleus, or source, is to be found in the person and work of Christ. But the Church has made explicit the meaning and implications of both in the course of time.

In the Old Testament, the liturgical *ordo* was part of God's revelation, and it served as a means of communion with him. Similarly in the Christian tradition, the Church Fathers have explained the meaning of the elements of the *ordo* in terms of the economy of the person and work of Christ, that is, in terms of God's revelation and plan for our salvation. For them, these elements are rooted in the economy of salvation and are means of communion with God. This principle lies behind the typological or allegorical interpretation of the sacraments. Thus for Antiochenes such as Theodore of Mopsuestia, the *ordo* of the Eucharist reveals the successive phases in Christ's earthly life. Thus for him, the *ordo* is a means of representing the mystery of God as revealed in Christ.

1. Elements of the *Ordo*

We need to elaborate on the structure of a few celebrations in order to elucidate the theological meaning of their *ordo*. The content of the *ordo* was fixed after a long process of development. A historical study of the development and fixation of various types of *ordo* is beyond the scope of the present study.

The Structure of the Eucharistic Ordo

1. Preparation rites

1.1   The First Service
1.1.1   The opening prayer
1.1.2   Psalm 51
1.1.3   Entry into the sanctuary (Ps. 43:4)
1.1.4   Kissing and going around the altar (Ps. 118:27–8)
1.1.5   Arrangement of the bread and wine
1.1.6   Service of penitence
1.1.6.1   *Promiun-Sedro*
1.1.6.2   *Qolo*
1.1.6.3   *Etro*
1.1.6.4   *Eqbo*
1.1.6.5   *Hutomo*
1.1.6.6   Our Father

1.2   The Second Service
1.2.1   The opening prayer
1.2.2   Washing of the hands

1.2.3   Vesting
1.2.4   Kneeling before the altar
1.2.5   Spreading of the veil (*annapuro*) over the paten and chalice
1.2.6   General commemoration prayer and commemoration of names
1.2.7   *Promiun-Sedro*
1.2.8   Censing of the paten and chalice
1.2.9   *Hutomo*
1.2.10   *Qaumo* and Creed

2. The pre-anaphora ('public celebration')

2.1   Entrance procession around the altar and the Responsory (*m'anito*) of Mar Severus
2.2   The Trisagion
2.3   The reading of the Epistles
2.4   The reading of the Gospel
2.5   *Promiun-Sedro*
2.6   Blessing of the censer and the censing
2.7   Creed
2.8   Kneeling before the altar
2.9   Silent commemoration of names

3. The anaphora

3.1   Introductory prayers: 'The three prayers'
3.1.1   Prayer of peace
3.1.2   Prayer of the imposition of hands
3.1.3   Prayer over the veil
3.2   The anaphora ('the Eucharistic prayer')
3.2.1   Trinitarian blessing
3.2.2   Introductory dialogue
3.2.3   Prayer of the offering
3.2.4   Sanctus
3.2.5   Post-sanctus
3.2.6   Institution narrative
3.2.7   Anamnesis
3.2.8   Epiclesis
3.3   Intercessions: sixfold canons
3.4   Preparation for the Communion
3.4.1   Rites before the Fraction
3.4.2   Fraction
3.4.3   Lord's Prayer
3.4.4   Rites before *Sancta Sanctis*
3.4.5   Holy Things to the Holy
3.5   Communion and post-Communion

Baptismal Ordo

The First Service
1 *Gloria Patri*
2 Opening prayer
3 Ps. 51
4 *Enyono*
5 *Quqliun* Ps. 29:1; 3; 4
6 Prayer
7 *Eqbo*
8 *Promiun Sedro*
9 *Qolo*
10 *Etro*

11 Epistle
12 Gospel
13 Inaudible/audible prayers (two sets)
14 Signing of the forehead without oil
15 Inaudible/audible prayers

16 Exorcism
17 Apotaxis–syntaxis
18 Nicene Creed
19 Prayer of thanksgiving

The Second Service
1 *Gloria Patri*
2 Opening prayer
3 Audible/inaudible prayers
4 Signing of the forehead with oil
5 *Eqbo*
6 *Promiun Sedro*
7 *Qolo*
8 Lifting up of the veil
9 *Etro*
10 *Consecration of the water:* Audible/inaudible prayers
11 Breathing over the water
12 Epiclesis
13 Infusion of Myron
14 Audible/inaudible prayers
15 Anointing of the whole body with olive oil/hymn
16 Immersion/hymn
17 Chrismation
18 Audible/inaudible prayers
19 [Lord's Prayer: optional]
20 Crowning
21 Communion
22 *Hutomo* and Dismissal

In the case of the baptismal *ordo*, the important elements of the first part are the Scripture lessons, the signing of the forehead without oil, exorcism, apotaxis and syntaxis. Their place in the baptismal *ordo* has been attested since the fourth century. The Creed was probably added in the fifth century. The other elements were added in the following centuries. Thus the oldest elements can be seen as the 'essentials', and the remaining as the 'accessories'. The essentials constitute the core of the *ordo*. They belong to the tradition of the undivided Church, as they are found in most of the ancient liturgical texts. The essentials 'represent' the baptismal mystery and the accessories serve to illustrate the meaning of the former. The accessories were often open to additions, revisions or even selective use. Thus in an ordinary celebration, a few stanzas are selected from a hymn given in the *ordo*. In the case of a baptism administered in an emergency, the celebrant has the freedom to leave out all the accessories or the selective use of the 'essentials' of the first service.

The second service consists of the essential elements of baptism, preceded by a few 'accessories' (for example *Promiun Sedro*). The number of the 'accessories' in the second service is limited compared to the first.

The baptismal liturgy had a comparatively simple structure at least until the beginning of the second millennium. The essential elements were the signing of the forehead without oil (which was probably part of the enrolment of the catechumens), exorcism, apotaxis–syntaxis, one or two pre-baptismal anointing(s), consecration of the water with an epiclesis (similar to that of the Eucharist), followed by the infusion of Myron, immersion, Chrismation, crowning and finally the Communion. In the course of development, the essentials remained essentially unchanged, and the 'accessories' were introduced to bring out the significance of the 'essentials' and their place in the *ordo*. This principle is applicable to most West Syrian liturgical celebrations. As we have seen, the 'essentials' were fixed in the golden age of liturgical development, and in the later period, the main interest was to elaborate the original structure by adding secondary elements such as hymns or *Promiun Sedro*. The addition of the secondary elements sometimes served to give a touch of uniformity among the *ordos*.

The *ordos* of Baptism, Consecration of Myron and of new churches, and Ordination were apparently modelled on the Eucharistic celebration. In its structure, the consecration of water on the feast of Epiphany closely follows the baptismal *ordo* (which in turn was inspired by the Eucharistic *ordo*). Similarly, the consecration of palms on Palm Sunday was also inspired by the structure of the Eucharist. Thus the Eucharist served as the model for the fixation of the core of most of the celebrations. Thus, corresponding to the Institution Narrative and the epiclesis, a blessing and the epiclesis became the core of the consecration of the baptismal water and Myron or the Ordination.

The introduction of the St James Liturgy was of decisive importance for West Syrian Liturgy. The Antiochene Church adopted the anaphora of Jerusalem, probably in the first half of the fifth century, which gradually replaced the local anaphoras (attested by the *Apostolic Constitutions* and the *Testament of our Lord*). Similarly, the Syriac version of St James had probably replaced the indigenous anaphoras which once circulated among the non-Chalcedonians. Finally, the so-called 'New and Correct Recension' of St James (wrongly attributed to Jacob of Edessa) became the standard anaphora of the West Syrians. Its careful and balanced arrangement of the elements (*ordo*) became the model for the West Syrian anaphoras. The liturgies of Baptism, Consecration of Myron and Ordination owe their structure to a certain extent to the essentials of St James.

The West Syrians claimed apostolic origin for the anaphora of St James, so that the addition of accessories was almost never tolerated in the anaphora. Thus in St James, between the Trinitarian blessing and the epiclesis, no hymn, not even the censing, was added. (The only change introduced may be an expansion of the deacon's exhortation during the epiclesis.) To a certain extent, this principle has been respected in the structure of the second part of the baptismal *ordo*. The reason may be summarized as follows. In the anaphora, the central elements (sanctus, institution, anamnesis, epiclesis) formed a single liturgical unit. The introduction of secondary elements may disrupt the harmony of the Eucharistic prayer, which has been carefully and logically formulated to reflect the mystery of salvation and its Trinitarian dimension. The

Eucharistic prayer, which was originally a single unit (or prayer), was divided into different units by adding 'Amens' or the deacon's exhortation (during the epiclesis). Then parts of the Eucharistic prayer were arranged as inaudible prayers. Thus in the Syriac version of the St James Liturgy, the 'preface', 'post-sanctus' and the first part of the epiclesis were prescribed as inaudible prayers. When and why this arrangement was made is still not known. In the case of St James, the inaudible prayers have in fact distorted the sequence and logic of the Eucharistic prayer.[4]

Then, most probably, by imitating the Eucharistic *ordo*, inaudible prayers became part of the liturgies of Baptism, Consecration of Myron and Ordination. Under the influence of the Eucharistic *ordo*, the epiclesis was understood as inaudible prayer, during which the deacon exhorted the people: 'In calm and in awe should you be standing and praying.' This further led to the 'mystification' of the epiclesis and the inaudible prayers. In the Syrian Orthodox Church, in some places, the celebrant knelt down during the first part of the epiclesis and recited the prayer inaudibly. However, kneeling during the epiclesis became obsolete by the eleventh century.

The descent of the Holy Spirit in the Eucharist was often referred to as 'hovering' (*rahep*), which was eventually 'ritualized' by the waving of hands over the gifts. Thus in the Syrian Orthodox Church, the waving of hands became an essential gesture of epiclesis or a blessing. (Originally the gesture during the epiclesis was a signing of three crosses over the gifts.[5]) Gradually, the waving was extended to other inaudible prayers of the anaphora, namely the 'preface' and 'post-sanctus'. Thus certain ideas found their ritual expression in the *ordo* and were incorporated into the essentials. As we shall see, the idea of prayer as 'an incense pleasing to God' had probably led to the use of incense as an essential element of the *ordo*.

2. The Eucharist and the Sacramental Celebrations

As we have already noted, several of the sacramental and liturgical celebrations owe their basic structure to the Eucharistic *ordo*. Some of them are celebrated in a Eucharistic context. Thus at least since the fourth century, ordination was held before or after the anaphora. The Syrian Orthodox Church has placed it between the *Sancta Sanctis* and the Communion. Similarly, the consecrations of Myron and a new church are held before the anaphora. The insertion of an *ordo* into the Eucharistic *ordo* has virtually no impact upon the celebration of the Eucharist. On the contrary, the ecclesial and the Eucharistic dimension of these celebrations are thereby brought out.

Marriage, funeral and the anointing of the sick are almost always celebrated outside the Eucharistic *ordo*. Though the blessing of a marriage on Sunday morning, after the Eucharist, is common practice in modern times, the *ordo* of matrimony makes no provision for the couple to receive Communion together. This does not mean that the

---

4 See Varghese, *St James*, pp. 23–28.
5 See Jacob of Edessa's letter to the Presbyter Thomas, in Bar Salibi, *Eucharist* 3:8.

Eucharist has no place in the mystery of the marriage. The very condition to solemnize a marriage in the Syrian Orthodox tradition is the possibility for the couple to receive Communion together. In other words, the Syrian Orthodox Church does not permit a 'mixed marriage'. It blesses the marriage of two of its members. However, the *ordo* of matrimony has little in common with the Eucharist. There is no epiclesis in the proper sense of the word. This means that the Eucharistic *ordo* was not the only model for some of the celebrations. The *ordo* of the daily office seems to have been influential in determining the structure of several of the rites. Thus to a large extent, the first part of the preparation rites of the Eucharist was inspired by the daily office.

3. The *Ordo* of the Daily Office

The liturgical *ordo*, as Schmemann says, is a combination of two essential elements: 'the Eucharist (with which all other sacraments are connected in some way) and the divine office'.[6] This means that a sacramental celebration includes the celebration of the daily offices, beginning with Vespers. In the case of the consecration of churches, the celebration is incorporated into the daily office. Thus the first part is celebrated on the evening after Vespers, and the rest after the *Sapro* and the third hour. Similarly the blessing of water on the feast of Epiphany as well as the Palm Sunday services are held after the *Sapro* and the preparation rites. Similarly, the special services of Nativity and Easter are held as part of *Lilyo*. Thus even if certain liturgical celebrations are held during the daily offices, they are included in the *ordo*, of which the Eucharist is the fulfilment.

We shall give the structure of the daily offices to show how it has influenced other celebrations. The major canonical hours, namely *Ramsho* and *Sapro*, have the following structure.

Table 1

1 Introductory prayer
2 Psalms
3 *Eqbo* or *Enyono*
4 *Promiun Sedro*
5 *Qolo I* (20–24 stanzas)
6 *Etro*
7 *Qolo II* (20–24 stanzas)
8 *Quqliun*
9 *Eqbo*
10 *Promiun Sedro*
11 *Qolo III* (4 stanzas)
12 *Bo'uto*

---

6 Schmemann, *Liturgical Theology*, pp. 33–34.

The structure of each of the *qole* (I and II) needs to be noted. The themes of the *Qole* have been arranged as follows. (We shall give the structure of the *Qole* of Monday *Ramsho* and *Sapro*.)

Table 2

Monday *Ramsho* (*Qolo I*: 20 stanzas: cf. No. 5 in Table 1)	Monday *Sapro* (*Qolo I and II*) (*Qolo I*: 20 stanzas = No. 5 in Table 1)
1 Addressed to God (four stanzas)	1 Addressed to God (four stanzas)
2 Mother of God (four stanzas)	2 Mother of God (four stanzas)
3 Saints (four stanzas)	3 Saints (four stanzas)
4 Repentance (four stanzas)	4 Repentance (four stanzas)
5 Departed (four stanzas)	5 Departed (four stanzas)
Qolo II (24 stanzas = No. 7 in Table 1)	*Qolo II* (22 stanzas = No. 7 in Table 1)
1 Addressed to Christ (four stanzas)	1 God the Trinity (four stanzas)
2 Mother of God (four stanzas)	2 Mother of God (four stanzas)
3 Saints (four stanzas)	3 Saints (four stanzas)
4 The Patron Saint (two stanzas)	4 Patron Saint (two stanzas)
5 Sunday (two stanzas)	5 Repentance (four stanzas)
6 Repentance (four stanzas)	6 Departed (four stanzas)
7 Departed (four stanzas)	

The same distribution of the themes is found in the daily prayers from Monday to Saturday. However, the distribution of the themes on Sunday is slightly different. The dominant theme of Sunday is generally resurrection or the theme of the day. The offices of a feast are similar to those of Sunday, both in their arrangement and in the distribution of the themes. The Passion Week offices have yet a different arrangement, though, generally speaking, the structure is similar to that of a feast.

The minor offices (third, sixth and ninth hours) have rather a simple structure consisting of an introductory prayer, *Promiun Sedro*, *Qolo* and *Bo'uto*. The *Lilyo* consists of three nocturns or *qaume* (four in the Passion Week), preceded and concluded with introductory and concluding parts. Each nocturne follows the pattern of a minor office. The theme of each nocturne is almost always fixed. The structure of the *Lilyo* is as follows:

1 Introductory prayer (fixed)
2 Psalms 134; 119:169–79; 117
3 *Enyono* (twelve stanzas)
4 First Nocturn (*Qaumo*)

4.1   Introduction
4.2   *Eqbo*
4.3   *Promiun Sedro* (Mother of God)
4.4   *Qolo* (four stanzas: Mother of God)
4.5   *Bo'uto* of Mar Jacob
5   Second Nocturn (*Qaumo*)
5.1   Introduction
5.2   *Eqbo*
5.3   *Promiun Sedro* (Saints)
5.4   *Qolo* (four stanzas: Saints)
5.5   *Bo'uto* of Mar Ephrem
6   Third Nocturn (*Qaumo*)
6.1   Introduction
6.2   *Eqbo*
6.3   *Promiun Sedro* (Repentance or the Departed)
6.4   *Qolo* (four stanzas)
6.5   *Bo'uto* of Mar Balai (fixed)
7   Fourth Nocturn
7.1   Halleluiah (candles on the altar are lit and the curtain drawn)
7.2   *Promiun Sedro*
7.3   Magnificat (Luke 1:46–55)
7.4   *Maurbo*
7.5   Ps. 113
7.6   *Enyono* (fixed)
7.7   Pss. 148, 149, 150.
7.8   *Ququliun*
7.9   *Qolo*
7.10 *Bo'uto*
8   Concluding part
8.1   Hymn of the Angel ('Hymn of St Athanasius of Alexandria')
8.2   Concluding prayer (fixed)

The importance of the daily offices in the liturgical *ordo* is evident from the fact that some of the celebrations, including the preparation rites, follow their structure.

The constitutive elements of the daily offices are the Word of God and its exposition. The doctrinal themes presented in the daily offices are to be understood as part of the exposition of the Word of God. The central element in office is the reading of the Gospel, which is always performed with great solemnity, exactly as in the Eucharistic celebration. The reading of the Gospel is an invariable element of every canonical hour of Holy Week. (The *Lilyo* of Holy Week has four to five Gospel lessons.) In the case of Sundays or feast-days, the Gospel is read in the *Ramsho* as well as in the *Sapro* (before the *Ququliun* – No. 5 in Table 1). The special services of the Nativity, Epiphany, Easter and Pentecost include the Gospel reading, preceded by lessons from the Old Testament and the New Testament Epistles. Similarly, during the Great Lent, and Passion Week, the Gospel of *Sapro* is preceded by lessons from the Old and the New Testaments.

Originally the reading of the Scripture seems to have been limited to the celebration of the Eucharist.[7] The introduction of the lessons from the Bible might have been aimed at emphasizing the sacramental, or rather the Eucharistic character of the canonical hours. In fact, the distinction between the 'liturgy of the Word' and the 'anaphora' is artificial. Though it is convenient for the study of the structure, in reality the liturgy of the Word is an integral part of the Eucharist. From a theological point of view, the distinction is inconceivable for Easterners.

The Gospel reading announces the theme of the day or the hour. However, the ordinary weekly cycle (*Shehimo*) does not include the reading of the Gospel, for reasons unknown to us. This is a serious omission and its consequences have not yet been evaluated by the West Syrians. However, each day and hour of the weekly cycle has a dominant theme that has been expounded in the hymns and in the *Sedre*. Although the reading of the Gospel as such is absent, the Word of God serves as the soul and source of the daily office. The fixation of the structure and content of the office surely implies a hermeneutical principle shaped by doctrinal tradition. The revolving of the *ordo* has a doctrinal basis: that is, to convey the correct vision concerning the Incarnation and its implications in our life and destiny; thus to live as a community redeemed by Christ, as the Body of Christ which looks forward to the coming of the Bridegroom, and to live as the manifestation of the Kingdom of God. The themes of the days and the hours are selected and arranged to reflect this fundamental vision. The Word of God has been constantly expounded on the basis of this vision and conveyed to the faithful in and through the daily offices. The Church 'breaks the Word of God'[8] and distributes it to its members for their spiritual nourishment.

Thus the Word of God and its correct exposition is the soul of the daily office. Doctrine guides and corrects our vision, and enables us to see the meaning of everything in relation to the plan of the triune God for our salvation. Doctrine thus opens our eyes to behold the living presence of the risen Lord in our midst and thus to be 'rooted in him' and to be built up as the Body of Christ – the goal of all doctrinal discussions. This has been further underlined by the use of incense, the symbol of Christ, as well as 'the fragrance of right doctrine' (see below).

It is significant that some of the fundamental themes are repeated in the weekly cycle of prayers (God, Mother of God, Saints, Repentance and the Departed). This would imply a theological vision according to which the Church, in its glorification of God, joins the assembly of the Mother of God, the saints and the faithful departed. It is our doxological union with them that makes the liturgical assembly the

---

[7] Justin Martyr, *First Apology*, p. 67.

[8] Cf. 2 Tim. 2:15; *Ap. Const.* VIII, 10, 6: the Eucharist, the litany prays for the bishops: 'For every episcopate which is under heaven, of those who rightly divide the word of truth, let us pray.'

manifestation of the *Ekklesia* of God, the one community of the entire humanity in Christ. The unity of human beings in Christ in the Kingdom of God is thus actualized. The liturgical assembly becomes the epiphany of the Kingdom, as it exists in the eternal plan of God. Repentance – the very sign of the dynamic presence of the Kingdom (Matt. 3:1; 4:17) – is the expression of our willingness to be united to the saving will of God, which unites us with the company of the saints 'whose names have been inscribed in heaven'. Thus the Church, the mystery of the new creation, is re-enacted in each liturgical hour. The *ecclesia orans*, the living and the departed, together assemble in the hope of the 'Lord's Day', both the Sunday and the eighth day of the coming world.

Thus, in a daily office, the hymns and the prayers are theological meditations and poetic narrations of the content of the Word of God and doctrinal truths. An office is concluded with a *Bo'uto* (= supplication). This pattern of a theological meditation followed by a supplication is regularly maintained in a *sedro*. This means that doctrine as a right vision of reality provides the background and basis for right praise and supplication. In fact the Greek word *orthodox* means right doctrine as well as right doxology.[9] Right doxology implies right doctrine and the right way of expressing it. Thus the *ordo* serves as the expression of the faith of the Church and its actualization as the presence of the Kingdom of God on earth.

4. Time and the *Ordo*

In the East, time is an essential element of the *ordo*. Although the Eucharist was instituted in the evening (1 Cor. 11:23), the early Church preferred to celebrate the 'Lord's Supper' in the morning, most probably because of its early association with the resurrection of Christ. Thus 'morning' became a quasi-permanent element in the celebration of the Eucharist in the East. However, in recent years, for the 'convenience' of Christians in the urban areas, some Eastern Churches have introduced the custom of celebrating Eucharist in the evening. The theological consequences of this reform have not yet been fully understood by those who have changed an important element of the *ordo* for the 'convenience' of the people. Liturgy is not a 'service' performed for the 'convenience' of a group of people by a professionally trained clergyman, for which he is paid. This is, in my opinion, a distortion of the *lex orandi* of the Church. If we see the liturgy as the 'actualization' of the Church of God, the epiphany of its *lex credendi*, we cannot violate the *ordo* 'for convenience'.

The celebration of the Eucharist in the morning is preceded by the daily offices or the offices of the feast. The Vespers celebrated on the eve is also part of the *ordo* of the Eucharist. The offices of the night, in a sense, stand for the Vigil, an essential

---

[9] In the writings of the Greek Fathers, the meaning of the words, theology, doxology and orthodoxy interpenetrate one another and the terms are often used interchangeably. See Constantine Scouteris, 'Doxology, the language of Orthodoxy', *The Greek Orthodox Theological Review* 38 (1993), 153–62.

element of the feasts in many Eastern Churches. Fasting is a prerequisite for the celebrant as well as for the participants. Fasting and Vigil and the morning Eucharist reintegrate a Sunday or a feast into the paschal mystery. In some places in the East, even the Easter Eucharist has been celebrated on the eve 'for the convenience' of the people, which is a distortion of the significance of the day. Easter symbolizes the passage from darkness to light, from death to life, and thus is a 'sacrament' of the final resurrection of the entire creation at the 'dawn' of the Second Coming of Christ. The morning Eucharist contains this meaning as well. Baptism, Ordination, Consecration of Myron and new churches, as well as several other celebrations, are also associated with the 'time' of the Eucharist. Thus they are integrated into the paschal mystery.

The entire daily office, with its sevenfold division, is part of the *ordo* of the Eucharist. The sevenfold division of the canonical prayers makes a day a miniature week. The Eucharist on a feast or an ordinary day is being integrated into the mystery of Sunday, the weekly Easter.

5. The Meaning of the Lectionary

Scripture was the most important element that determined the content and style of the hymnody and the prayers of the West Syrians. In the case of the lectionary, it was the development of the Church year and the *ordo* which determined its content and arrangement. As in the case of the anaphoras and other liturgical celebrations, the West Syrians used different lectionaries, with considerable variations.[10] In spite of the variations in the readings of the 'saints' days', a relative uniformity is found in the readings of the major dominical festivals.[11] However, the guiding principle of the lectionary was to unfold the mystery of Christ before the eyes of the faithful. In several of the dominical festivals, typological exegesis seems to have been an important factor in the selection of the Old Testament lessons. Among the Old Testament books, Isaiah was the most used. Thus almost every Sunday and feast has a lesson from Isaiah.

One of the major aims seems to have been to illustrate the teaching of the day from every part of the Bible. In the early Syriac lectionary system, the books were arranged in what appears to be an order of merit or importance, the weightiest coming the last.[12] This has not been strictly followed in the later Syriac lectionaries. However, almost always, the Book of Isaiah comes as the last among Old Testament lessons.

---

10 F.C. Burkitt, 'The Early Syriac Lectionary System', *The Proceedings of the British Academy* 10 (1921–23), extract pp. 1–38, 301–39. A. Baumstark, *Nichtevangelishe syrsche Perikopenordnungen des ersten Jahrtausends* (Münster, 1921). L. Chidiac and G. Khouri-Sarkis, 'Tableau des péricopes bibliques dans les Eglises de langue syriaque', *OS* III (1958), 359–86; P. Vermeulen, *OS* XII (1967), 211–40, 371–88, 525–48.

11 On the diversity, see A. Vööbus, *The Lectionary System of the Monastery of Azizael in Tur Abdin, Mesopotamia*, CSCO 466 (1985), 1–49.

12 Burkitt, 'Early Syriac Lectionary System', p. 21.

The Syrian Orthodox lectionaries give up to a dozen Old Testament readings for important feasts, whereas the New Testament lessons are limited to three (one from the Acts or the General Epistles, one from St Paul and finally one from the Gospels). Following the Peshitta, the New Testament lessons have been limited to twenty-two books (2–3 John, 2 Peter, Jude and Revelation are excluded). The lectionary is a witness to the Church's position *vis-à-vis* the Bible as a whole or a particular book. Thus the Epistle to the Hebrews is reckoned as Pauline.

The Gospel readings during the daily offices or a liturgical celebration are usually preceded by a verse from the Psalms sung with Halleluiah.[13] This might be a survival of the early Syriac lectionary system, in which a whole psalm was sung (or chanted) before the Gospel.[14] In the present system, the verse from the psalm corresponds to the theme of the day or occasion.

Liturgical theology should investigate the theological principles that have guided the fixation of the lectionary and establish guidelines for the often-demanded revision of the lectionaries. In the case of the selection of liturgical hymns from a mass of poetic literature, the lectionary has obviously played a role. This could serve as a guideline for the selection and inclusion of new hymns in our liturgical services. The Syriac liturgical hymns are in no way fixed once for all. The content of the hymns needs to be critically studied in relation to the lectionary and the theme of the occasion.

In some of the liturgical services, the readings from the Old Testament have been selected according to the discretion of the reader or omitted completely. In the New Testament, the reading has sometimes been limited to St Paul and the Gospels. This selective reading is often arbitrary and done to make the service not too long. But the consequence is that we are ignoring an essential element for the sake of accessories for example hymns). The West Syrians are not always aware of the existence of different lectionaries and need to adapt the current system in a more consistent way. The possibility of alternative readings for some services should be explored.

6. The Meaning of Incense

Censing is an integral part of the present Syrian Orthodox *ordo*. We do not know when and how censing became an invariable element of the liturgical celebrations in the East.[15] The Jewish liturgical use of incense, especially its offering as part of some sacrifices, has influenced the symbolic explanations given to the incense by the Syriac writers.

First, in the Old Testament, the offering of incense was the privilege of the priests (Num. 16:36–48). When plague broke out, Aaron offered incense and made atonement

---

13 Known as *Sumoro* = song. This corresponds to the Western Gradual. Occasionally, *a sumoro* is replaced with a stanza from hymns inspired by the Psalms.

14 Burkitt, 'Early Syriac Lectionary System', p. 21.

15 See E.G. Cuthbert F. Atchley, *A History of the Use of Incense in Divine Worship* (London, 1909).

for the people (Num. 16:47). Here the incense served as a means of atonement to appease God's wrath. In the Old Testament, incense was offered as part of certain kinds of burnt offerings, and was qualified as 'a pleasing odour' to the Lord (Exod. 29:18).[16] Pauline imagery of Christ's death as a 'fragrant offering and sacrifice to God' (Eph. 5:2) was undoubtedly inspired by this type of sacrifice. Along these lines, the West Syrian prayers of incense (*Etro*) qualify Christ as the 'incense/censer of atonement', or as 'the pure incense offered as a pleasing odour' to God.

Second, in the later Jewish tradition, prayer itself was interpreted as an offering of incense (Ps. 141:2) or as a sacrifice (Ps. 51:17 etc.).[17] This also was a favourite idea of the Syrians.

Third, to the Hebrews, the smoke of incense veiled the presence of Yahweh in the Holy of Holies (Lev. 16:12–13). Here the censing by the High Priest marked the beginning of the service. But in the West Syrian liturgical texts we find no trace of the influence of this idea. However, the initial censing by the Jewish High Priest corresponds to the pre-anaphoral censing of the whole nave by the bishop (attested since the time of Pseudo-Dionysius the Areopagite). This does not mean that the Jewish ritual served as a direct model. In fact the use of incense became part of the liturgical *ordo* centuries after the destruction of the Temple of Jerusalem. However, the Old Testament symbolism of incense and sacrifice reached the Syrian Church through the Jewish exegetical traditions, known to the Syrians at least from the time of Aphrahat and St Ephrem.

Fourth, in the Rabbinic tradition, the symbolism of incense was sometimes extended so that the four ingredients of the holy incense (Exod. 31:34) had been held to signify the four elements (water, earth, fire and air). Since it was seasoned with salt, the incense was seen as a combination of the products of the sea and the earth and hence incense offering as a token of the whole creation.[18] In the Syriac tradition similar interpretations were given to the ingredients of the Eucharistic bread. Such traditions have not become common among the Syrians to explain the symbolism of incense.

Fifth, the 'incense' and 'the pure offering' of which the prophet Malachi speaks (1:11) were associated with Christian worship (or the Eucharist) as early as the end of the first century (*Didache* 14). A few decades earlier, St Paul qualified the gifts of the Philippians as 'a fragrant offering, a sacrifice acceptable and pleasing to God' (Phil. 4:18). It is striking that here St Paul uses the same terminology that he used for describing the atoning death of Christ in Ephesians ('fragrant offering and sacrifice to

---

[16] Incense burned with the sacrifices was probably an antidote to the smell of the burning meat. See 'Incense and Perfumes', *Encyclopaedia Judaica* 8 (Jerusalem, 1971), 1310–16; see also, Atchley, *History*, pp. 28–40.

[17] Nigel Groom says: 'The spreading of the smoke and fragrance and the visible movement of that smoke upwards towards the heavens has given it a symbolical relationship to prayer, making the offering synonymous with worship.' Nigel Groom, *Frankincense and Myrrh. A Study of the Arabian Incense Trade* (London and New York, 1981), p. 2.

[18] Ibid., p. 2. In Jub. 16:24, seven ingredients are named. Josephus speaks of thirteen ingredients. Josephus, *De Bello Judaica*, V.v.5. See H.H. Rowley, *Worship in Ancient Israel* (London, 1967), p. 86.

God' – 5:2). Elsewhere Paul uses similar imagery to refer to his own death ('I am being poured out as a libation' – 2 Tim. 4:6, Peshitta). Thus we can find an extension of the symbolism of incense (offering) to prayer, sacrifice, the death of Christ, a material help, martyrdom, or Christian worship, particularly the Eucharist.

Finally, the use of incense was taken for granted in the heavenly liturgy described by St John (Rev. 5:8; 8:3–4). Whether this is an allegorical reference to the prayers of the saints or not is open to discussion. However, the Syriac writers usually associated the incense with the prayer of the saints.

Incense as a Symbol of Christ

As Christian worship has its source in the person and work of Christ, its meaning is invariably explained in relation to the mystery of Christ. The best example of this approach is Theodore of Mopsuestia, who related the elements of the Eucharistic celebration to different phases in the earthly life of Christ. This type of symbolic explanation has often been extended to the liturgical objects as well. Thus the altar, cross, light and the incense offering were held to be the symbols of Christ. In the West Syrian tradition, Christ has been called 'incense (*besmo*), censer (*pirmo*), sweet odour (*riho basimo*), incense offering (*etro*), herb ('*eqoro*), atoning censer (*pirmo mhasiyono*), true censer of absolution, fragrant incense of reconciliation'.[19]

The symbolic association of incense with Christ was inspired by the biblical symbolism of incense offering on the one hand, and the West Syrian theology of Myron on the other. Since Pseudo-Dionysius the Areopagite, the Syro-Antiochene tradition has attributed great importance to the Holy Myron and its consecration, which has been compared to the Eucharist. The West Syrians had written commentaries on Myron, comparing it to Christ. In the early Church we have several examples of this association. Thus in a Coptic fragment of *Didache*, a text added to ch. 10 associates Myrrh with Christ: 'Regarding Myrrh, give thanks thus: "We thank Thee Our Father, for the Myrrh that you have made known to us by Christ your servant. Glory to you forever".'[20]

Following this, the West Syrians have developed a 'theology of fragrance' in terms of Christology, which has not yet been studied. As we shall see, this theology was inspired by the allegorical interpretation that Pseudo-Dionysius gives to the incense and the patristic exegesis of the Song of Songs 1:3 ('Your name is the Myron poured out').[21]

In his *Ecclesiastical Hierarchy* (III, 3), Dionysius compares the spreading of the smoke and fragrance of incense to our divinization that Christ has inaugurated by his 'descent and ascent':

---

[19] Jacob Thekkeparampil, 'Weihrauchsymbolik in den syrischen Gebeten des Mittelalters und bei pseudo-Dionysius', in *Typus, Symbol, Allegorie bei den östlichen Vätern und ihren Paralelen im Mittelalter*, ed. Margot Schmidt, Eichstädter Beiträge IV (Regensburg, 1982), pp. 131–45.

[20] French translation. A. Benoit, *Le baptême chrétien au second siècle* (Paris, 1953), p. 5.

[21] Following LXX and Syro-Hexapla. See the comments by S. Brock, 'Jacob of Edessa's discourse on the Myron', *OC* 63 (1979), 31, n.63.

I think we must now go inside the sacred things and reveal the meaning of the first of the images. We must look attentively upon the beauty which gives it so divine a form and we must turn a reverent glance to the double movement of the hierarch when he goes first from the divine altar to the far edges of the sacred place spreading the fragrance and then returns to the altar. For the blessed divinity, which transcends all being, while proceeding gradually outward because of goodness to commune with those who partake of him, never actually departs from his essential stability and immobility. Enlightening anyone conforming as much as possible to God, Deity nevertheless maintains utterly and unshakably its inherent identity.[22]

For the West Syrians, who had known the works of Dionysius through the Syriac translations of Sergius of Reshaina (d. 536) and Phokas of Edessa (seventh century), the content and form of his commentary was one of the models. The roots of this 'theology of fragrance', as we have seen, might very well go back to St Paul and even to the Old Testament. However, this was further developed by George, Bishop of the Arabs (d. 724) and Moses Bar Kepha (d. 903). In his commentary on the Eucharist, George faithfully follows Dionysius and comments on the censer:

The censer, which the deacon takes about the whole nave, signifies the care of God for all and the condescension and sweet savour of Christ. The return of the censer to the sanctuary signifies the fixedness and unwaveringness of the divine care, which remains as it is, without diminution: even as a lamp, which is not diminished by the taking from it of many (lights).[23]

According to George, the Myron 'portrays and shows to us Emmanuel Himself'.[24] In his metrical homily, George calls Christ 'the pure Myron hidden in the bosom of the Father'.[25] This identification is, in fact, based on the exegesis of the Song of Songs 1:4. Jacob of Edessa's homily on Myron provides the best example for the Syriac exegesis of the text:

Formerly, when the Bride saw the Bridegroom in symbol and gained knowledge of him by means of small sparks of light, she compared him to scented oil, saying: 'Your name is oil of Myron emptied out; for this reason the young girls have loved you. Let us run to the fragrance of your scent; bring me in to your chamber, O King'. Here, however, the Church sees openly and clearly, with a pure face, God the Word who became man and betrothed her to himself in a holy and spiritual betrothal. She compares him to oil because he anointed and united with his eternal

---

[22] *HE* III, 3; *PG* III, 428D–429A. Eng. tr. Colm Luibheid, *Pseudo-Dionysius. The Complete Works* (Paulist Press, New York, 1987), p. 212.

[23] George, *Commentary*, Connolly, p. 16. Here George speaks of the initial censing of the whole nave by a deacon. But in the Church of Ps.-Dionysius, the bishop did the censing. George's comments in its present form have been taken from a sixth-century anonymous commentary: Brock, *JTS* 37 (1980), D.34–35.

[24] Connolly, p. 22.

[25] V. Ryssel (ed.), *Poemi Siriaci di Giorgio vescovo degli Arabi*, in *Atti della Reale Accademia dei Lincei*, IV-9 (Rome, 1892), pp. 46–80. Here line 352.

Godhead our temporal humanity. 'Emptied out', because, being full and overflowing, he emptied himself into our human form, and made our wretched and feeble race full, and no longer deficient . . . 'His scent', again, is divine knowledge of all sorts, and the variety of glorious understanding concerning him, with which he makes fragrant all those who have shared in his glory, making them fellows and sharers in the Mysteries . . .[26]

It is interesting to note that the fragrance ('His scent') has been associated with doctrine, which eventually led commentators to see incense as the symbol of true doctrine or the Gospel.[27] In his metrical homily on Myron, Bishop George developed the theme of fragrance, and used a series of titles to qualify Christ:

Pure Myron that filled his Church with the fragrance [*line* 1]; . . . Aromatic oil, which was poured out on humanity [*l.* 3]; . . . Fine nard that filled the universe with its intense smell [*l.* 5]; . . . Beautiful rose, by whose smell the dead live [*l.* 7]; . . . Chosen perfume to which no aroma can be compared [*l.* 11]; . . . Chosen censer who reconciled his sender by its fragrance (*l.* 17: cf. Num. 16:43–48]; . . . Son of fragrance, from which flows every fragrance [*l.* 27].

These texts witness to the importance that the Syrians have attached to the symbolism of incense and fragrance. Christ is the heavenly 'perfume' poured out upon humanity for granting it the fragrance of immortality, holiness and life.[28] He is the 'incense' offered for us, whose fragrance spread in the world to perfume it with the knowledge and worship of God. Thus in the *Sedro* of the preparation rites we find:

We worship and give thanks and glorify you, O Creator of the worlds and the Framer of all creation, the Blessed Shoot that budded forth and sprang up out of dry ground, even of Mary, and who have filled all the earth with the fragrance of your glorious sweetness and have driven out the foul odour of paganism from all regions by your glorious doctrines . . .[29]

The fragrance of incense or of the Holy Myron symbolizes also the holiness of the Church,[30] and the pure doctrine that it preserves.[31]

The Syriac fascination with the symbolism of incense would perhaps explain the origin of its liturgical use. As various theological developments have found their expression in the *ordo* – in the form of gestures, objects and liturgical texts – the

---

[26] S. Brock (ed.), 'Jacob of Edessa's Discourse on the Myron', *OC* 63 (1979), p. 31 (= no.7).

[27] See George, *Myron*: 'Twelve censers go before him, for it by the twelve, that the fragrance of the Gospel spread in the whole world.' Ryssel, *Poemi*, Lines 369–70. Cf. the *Etro* of Pentecost, Lilyo, second *Qaumo*: 'Be pleased in the pure incense of our faith', Pampakuda MS 200, p. 94, Mal. tr. p. 172.

[28] It is interesting to note the same Greek verb (*keneo*) has been used in Song of Songs 1:4 and in Phil. 2:7 (the kenotic Christological text). In his commentary on Myron, Moses Bar Kepha associates these two texts in this sense. Ch.6 (ed. W. Strothmann).

[29] Second Service, Athanasius, *Anaphora*, p. 16.

[30] The association of fragrance with holiness is found in Ezek. 20:41.

[31] Bar Kepha, *Commentary on Myron*, ch.18.

allegorization of the worship as an 'incense offering' must have been one of the decisive factors in the introduction of censing as an essential element. Other factors include, perhaps, the cultic use of incense in the Old Testament and in the Mesopotamian religions.

The use of incense cannot be explained merely in terms of the 'aesthetic dimension of worship' or of a practical act to perfume the liturgical space. Its symbolism is more rich and eloquent than that of music or architecture. It is a 'quasi-sacramental act', as is evident from the liturgical commentaries. Its invariable position in the beginning part of the *ordo* should be noted. The censing in the preparation rites or in the pre-anaphora underlines the 'priestly dimension' of Christian worship. The Church, 'the royal priesthood', offers its Eucharist, its prayer *par excellence* as a 'fragrant offering' pleasing to God. The fact that this idea has been repeatedly evoked in the prayers demonstrates its centrality in Syriac liturgical theology. In the concluding prayer (*Hutomo*) of the first part of the preparation rites we find:

> O Pure and spotless Lamb, who offered Himself to the Father as acceptable offering for the expiation and redemption of the whole world, make us worthy that we may offer ourselves to you a living sacrifice well-pleasing unto you after the manner of your sacrifice for us. May we be accounted worthy to offer unto you, O Lord, sacrifices of praise and thanksgiving for a savour of spiritual sweetness. Let all our thoughts and words and actions be a whole burnt offering unto you. Grant us, O Father, Son and Holy Spirit, to appear before you without blemish all the days of our life, and ever be well-pleasing to your Godhead.[32]

According to John of Dara (ninth century), the meaning of incense is similar to that of the Holy Myron. Thus the fragrance of both Myron and incense symbolizes the Holy Spirit who sanctifies humanity with his heavenly fragrance:

> The incense symbolizes also that the bishop will introduce his flock before Christ with confidence on the day of judgment, when it will be made fragrant with the Holy Spirit that it has received by baptism, and having no filth in it; and with a voice of triumph he will cry out before God and say: 'Behold me, and the children whom thou has given me' (Heb. 2:13; Isa. 8:17–18).[33]

In his commentary on the Eucharist, Dionysius Bar Salibi has summarized various interpretations:

> The censer is the figure of John the Baptist. Again, censer is the [figure of the] upright heart, which does not alienate itself from God. The censer of Aaron, which did not alienate itself from God and held back the plague from the people, witnesses to it. Again, censer is the figure of Emmanuel, for the censer leaves the sanctuary, which symbolizes Emmanuel, and goes around the whole nave and gets the consent

---

[32] Athanasius, *Anaphora*, p. 9. In the *Sedro* of the third Sunday after Easter (*Lilyo*, First *Qaumo*): 'Today we offer you the pure incense that raises from the bottom of our hearts.' Pampakuda MS 200, p. 29, Mal. tr. p. 46.

[33] John of Dara, *Eucharist* (tr. B. Varghese), II: 21, p. 47.

and good will of the faithful towards him, and returns to the holy of holies with their consent. Again, the censer indicates the Virgin and the fire of God the Word, for she bore the fire of divinity in her womb. The perfume of the censer, which leaves the sanctuary and goes around, indicates the blessedness of the Holy Trinity. Even though that blessedness is spread by providence on all saints, its firmness is neither changed, altered nor diminished. The perfumes symbolize the offerings of our intelligence. Again, the incense indicates God the Word who came down from heaven, and became sweet odour and incense of reconciliation. He offered Himself to God the Father for us. He made atonement and perfumed the whole world. He returned to His Father, without change or without losing His divinity.[34]

Since Christ is the content and the message of the *ordo*, every element points to him. Incense symbolizes that our prayers are joined as 'incense' to the 'fragrant offering' of Christ. We are transformed, and christified with the 'heavenly gifts' and made 'spiritual censers'. This has been beautifully presented in an *etro*: 'Breathe in us the fragrance of your divine and spiritual gifts, so that we will become spiritual censers that always offer pleasant odour of the fruits of holiness.'[35]

Perfume symbolizes sweetness, joy, warmth and peace. In the liturgical context, it symbolizes the presence of Christ.

7. Liturgical Music

The purpose of singing and music is to awaken and to articulate the meaning of the text and to induce an attitude. It adds new power to a text and provides a time for contemplation, to dwell on the meaning of the text. By enlightening and highlighting the meaning, hymns and music sow the seed of the word in the human mind. This germinates and gives rise to faith, hope and trust in God, thus serving as a vehicle for the mystery of God.

Although the West Syrians have a large number of hymns in their weekly and festal breviaries, as well in almost every sacramental celebration, music and hymns have a secondary place in the celebration of the Eucharist. In the pre-anaphora, anaphora and the *ordo communis*, only a limited number of hymns are used.

In the New Testament, the characteristics of singing are twofold: it must be filled with the Holy Spirit (1 Cor. 14:13–17; 26) and it must be the expression of a common faith.[36] The Syrians have followed these principles and are particular in using the hymns of 'the Father' for preference. However, Syriac poetry has remained closer to

---

34 Bar Salibi, *Eucharist*, 6:12 (tr. B. Varghese, pp. 33–35).

35 *Revelation to Joseph, Ramsho, Etro*, Pampakuda MS 13, pp. 110–11; Mal. tr. p. 107. Cf. *Revelation to Zechariah, Lilyo*, First *Qaumo, Sedro*: 'With this sweet incense from our censer exhale in us the fragrance of your holiness . . . And make us the trees that bear sweet fruits of pleasant odour.' Pampakuda, MS 13, p. 48; Mal. tr. p. 45.

36 J. Gelineau, 'Music and Singing in the Liturgy', in Cheslyn Jones et al. (eds), *The Study of Liturgy* (London, 1979, 3rd edn), p. 445.

that of the Bible and usually prefers rhythmic prose. This underlines the priority given to the words of the text rather than to the poetic or musical aspects. The music is vocal and generally of a loud nature, a characteristic of Hebrew music. Polyphony is unknown to the Syrians.[37] Singing in unison is the purpose of the liturgical music. Thus hymns become the 'single' voice of the church. Their function is essentially unification, to enable the liturgical gathering to become one, the Church of God, the *ekklesia orans*.

8. The Meaning of the Liturgical Space

In the East, the architectural setting of the liturgical space is part of the *ordo* and hence it is an expression of the *lex orandi* of the Church. The liturgical architecture expresses the corporate character of Christian worship, which is primarily a *synaxis*. It is the coming together of the people of God around the Eucharistic table. The developments in Eucharistic theology were reflected in the setting of the liturgical space. The table was begun to be seen as the heavenly altar or the 'throne' of Christ, before which the people gather. Since the fourth century, the eastern liturgical architecture follows the 'heavenly liturgy' principle.

In the early Church, at least for the first two centuries, no special building was thought to be necessary for the liturgical gatherings. Thus the third-century Roman convert Minucius Felix said: 'We have no temples; we have no altar.'[38] However, by the fourth century, 'temples and altars' became invariable elements of the *ordo*, in both the East and the West. Secular and religious elements have been decisive in determining the style of the Christian 'temples'. However, in the mystagogical tradition, biblical architectural vocabulary was freely used, often metaphorically. Thus 'altar', 'holy of holies' or 'holy place' became part of the Christian architectural vocabulary. In the fourth century, the status of Christianity as a state religion soon found its expression in the architecture.

The earliest monument of Syriac architecture is the church of St Jacob in Nisibis, which was probably built in AD 359. The church was rebuilt in the sixth century in Byzantine style.[39] Edessa had an ancient church built in the middle of the sixth century by Bishop Amazonius and dedicated to the Holy Wisdom (*Sophia*). The church has been destroyed but we have a poem (*sugitho*) describing its architecture and

---

[37] On the history of West Syrian liturgical music, see Alfred Cody, 'The Early History of Octoechos in Syria', in Nina G. Garsoian et al. (eds), *East of Byzantium: Syria and Byzantium in the Formative Period* (Washington DC, 1982), pp. 89–113 (with bibliography).

[38] Quoted by Peter G. Cobb, 'The Architectural setting of the Liturgy', *The Study of Liturgy*, pp. 473–74.

[39] See the illustrations in: S. Brock, *The Hidden Pearl*, II, pp. 218–19. For an introduction to Syriac church architecture, see ibid., pp. 209–28. Several illustrations of the early monuments are found in Hans Hollerweger, *Living Cultural Heritage: Tur Abdin* (Linz, 1999).

decorations.[40] This is one of the earliest commentaries on liturgical space. We shall quote a few stanzas. The poem describes the domed church as the cosmos in miniature.

> Its ceiling is stretched out like the sky, arched without any column;
> it is decorated with golden mosaics with shining stars, like the firmament.
> Its lofty dome resembles the highest heavens . . .
> The splendour of its broad arches portrays the four ends of the earth . . .

According to the poem, each side of the church had an identical façade, as a type of the Holy Trinity. Its altar (*madbeho*) was illuminated by 'a light' coming through the three principal windows 'announcing the mystery of the Holy Trinity'. Numerous (additional) windows 'represent the Apostles, Our Lord, the Prophets, the martyrs and the confessors'.

Then in the nave, there was a *Bema* or raised platform for readings and sermon:

> The bema placed in the middle of the church represents in type the Upper Room
>   on mount Sion;
> under it are eleven columns, Like the eleven apostles who were hidden there.
> And the column in the bema symbolizes Golgotha by its form.
> Above it is fixed a cross of light like our Lord between the two robbers.

There were nine steps in the sanctuary (*madbeho*) and for the altar (*thronos*) symbolizing the nine angelic choirs. The poem concludes with the following lines:

> Exalted are the mysteries (*roze*) of the church
> in which the heaven and the earth are represented,
> the sublime Trinity and the earthly life of our Saviour.
> The Apostles had founded it in the Spirit and the prophets and the Martyrs are
>   represented in it.
> By the prayer of the blessed mother, may they have memory in the highest.

The poem gives a summary of the West Syriac theology of liturgical space. As in the case of a liturgical celebration, the church has a mystery (*rozo*), a meaning that needs to be explained. The poet expounds the meaning in relation to the worship and the fundamental Christian doctrines of the Trinity and the communion of saints. The function of liturgical space is precisely to place us before the Holy Trinity and the throne of Christ. Everything stands in a harmony, for which the church has been called out. The church bears the whole cosmos and presents it to God and it becomes a 'type' of God's glorious presence. The great 'cloud of witnesses' participates in the cosmic liturgy. The church portrays the whole earthly life of Christ and proclaims its

---

[40] Syriac text and French translation: Basile Aggoula, 'Une description de la cathédrale justinienne d'Edesse dans un poème syriaque', in Ayoub Chehwan and Antoine Kassis (eds), *Etudes Bibliques et Proche-Orient ancien. Mélanges offerts au Père Paul Feghali* (Beyrouth and Jounieh, 2001), pp. 309–22. For an English translation: A.N. Palmer, 'The inauguration anthem of Hagia Sophia in Edessa', *Byzantine and Modern Greek Studies* 12 (1988), 117–67.

cosmic significance. The Incarnation was not merely for the salvation of man, but on the contrary for the restoration of the whole cosmos as a 'liturgical symbol', capable of sharing in the glory of God, for which everything has been created.

The architecture reveals that, in the liturgy, heaven and the earth stand face to face, and the Incarnation has provided 'the space' for this encounter. This fundamental idea has found its visible expression in the setting of liturgical space, even in its simplest form. Thus the sanctuary and the nave are the basic components of liturgical space in the Syriac tradition. This is in no way a separation between the sacred and the profane, between the clergy and the laity, but a gathering together before the throne of God. It is the manifestation of our recapitulation in and around the person of Christ. This fundamental vision is reflected in the liturgical texts.

The *bema*, or raised platform, in the middle of the church is attested in the poem on the Cathedral of Edessa as well as in several archeological findings. In the East and West Syriac traditions, the *bema* was an important element in the celebration of the Word. Among the West Syrians, the *bema* had disappeared or simply lost its significance at an earlier date. Obviously financial constraints led to the construction of rather small churches, which have not enough space to accommodate a *bema* in the middle of the nave. The *qestromo*, or the space between the nave and the sanctuary, or the sanctuary itself, served for the celebrations once held on the *bema*. The *bema* had practical as well as symbolic functions. The Word of God was read or expounded in the midst of the people. (Usually men occupied the space between the *bema* and the nave and the women and children behind the *bema*.) Some of the solemn celebrations were held on the *bema*. Thus in the consecration of Myron, the bishop/patriarch ascended the *bema* and the Myron was exalted toward the four sides. Similarly, the exaltation of the cross at Easter or at another dominical feast was done on the *bema*. Thus the *bema* assured that the liturgy, at least in part, is celebrated in the midst of the people, with their close participation and before their reverential gaze. The *bema* brought the liturgy close to their experience and presence. The West Syrians have not fully evaluated the consequences of the disappearance of the *bema*. The sanctuary became the sole centre of almost every celebration.

As the Syrian Orthodox churches are generally constructed in the east–west direction, the sanctuary is naturally located in the eastern end. This architectural setting emphasizes the eschatological orientation of the liturgy. This has also led commentators to see the sanctuary as the symbol of Paradise, our former home. Thus turning to the east or to the sanctuary symbolizes a 'nostalgia' for our former home.

The central object in the sanctuary is the altar (*madbeho* or *thronos*). The altar has been seen as the symbol of Christ's tomb or of Christ himself. Pseudo-Dionysius the Areopagite called Christ 'our most divine altar'.[41] Following this tradition, the sixth-century commentary on the Eucharist qualifies the altar as the Tree of Life: 'The altar indicates to us Emmanuel, who is the Tree of Life; and the bread and wine on it the body of God in which blood was also present, they being the fruits of the Tree of

---

41 *EH* IV-iii, *PG* III, 484D.

Life'.[42] This interpretation seems to have enabled the Syrians to call the altar 'the Table of Life', especially in the liturgical texts. This symbolism was meaningful to the West Syrians, as the altar was usually made of wood.

In the first part of the sixth-century commentary (attributed to St John Chrysostom), the altar has been seen as a symbol of Christ's tomb ('The altar is the place of Christ's sepulchre').[43]

Moses Bar Kepha discusses these interpretations and concludes that for him, the altar 'stands for' (*bdukat . . . itaw*) 'the cross or the tomb of Christ':

> What the altar signifies: – Saint Dionysius says that the altar signifies Emmanuel, who is the tree of life. But others say that the altar represents (*bdukat . . . itaw*) the cross, upon which the Lord was sacrificed and offered as an oblation. The holy Mar Johannes[44] says that the altar represents (*bdukat . . . itaw*) the tomb of Christ. But we say that we know that the altar is called Christ, and is called the tree of life, and is called the cross, and other similar (names); but here the altar signifies the tomb of Christ, and is in the place (*bdukat . . . itaw*) of His tomb, in which he was laid when he had been fastened to the cross. And hence it is right that when we build an altar we should make it long from north to south, in the likeness of the tomb. Again if the altar signifies Emmanuel, and the body and blood are Emmanuel Himself, there are found to be two Emmanuels here.[45] And if the altar signifies the cross, as others say, and we offer upon it the body and blood of Christ, it follows that we make a commemoration of His crucifixion and He being sacrificed; and [so] we become as it were crucifiers. But Paul says: 'He was sacrificed once' (Heb. 9:28). It remains that the altar be instead of (*bdukat . . . itaw*) the tomb of Christ; and it is evident from that: 'Thus be ye making a commemoration of My death' etc.; now His death and His resurrection were in the tomb and from the tomb.[46]

What is important for liturgical theology is the theological approach of the West Syrians. The meaning of the church architecture and the liturgical space integrates perfectly with the meaning of the liturgy, especially that of the Eucharist as a whole. Architecture is part of the *ordo*, and it serves as a means to manifest the meaning of the liturgy. The Church as an eschatological gathering re-enters Paradise and approaches the Tree of Life. The Church gathers together before the tomb of Christ to see Him and to announce his resurrection in and through the anamnesis.

The West Syrian commentators like Bar Kepha saw the altar as the essential part of the liturgical space. Bar Kepha's commentary seems to have exercised a decisive influence in the setting of liturgical space. Thus the West Syrians of the second millennium have shown a preference for the 'tomb' symbolism, which was eventually reflected in the construction of the altar. Thus Dionysius Bar Salibi, who is largely dependent on Bar Kepha's commentary, gives the following direction:

---

42 D.38–39; S. Brock, p. 393; George, Bishop of the Arabs, quotes this text. Connolly, p. 17.

43 R.23, Brock, p. 391.

44 Anonymous Commentary, R.23, Brock, p. 391.

45 Apparently Bar Kepha fears that it would suggest the 'diophysite' and 'two hypostases' Christologies.

46 Bar Kepha, *Commentary on the Eucharist*, Connolly, pp. 34–35.

Then the altar stands for the tomb in which our Lord was placed when He was entombed, as says Saint Ivanios and Moses Bar Kepha. Therefore, when we construct an altar we should make it long in a north–south direction, like the tomb in which our Lord was placed, according to the custom of the Hebrews.[47]

However, Bar Salibi adds that 'spiritually' the altar symbolizes the 'invisible altar', that is, the heavenly altar, the throne of God:

Again, spiritually, by the visible altar we understand that which is invisible; by the priest who stands [before it], the Great High Priest, and the *qurobo* which is offered, He who became *qurobo* for us.[48]

Although the tomb symbolism was the most favoured one among the commentators (such as Bar Kepha, Bar Salibi and Yahya ibn Garir), the liturgical texts show a preference for 'the throne of God' or 'heavenly altar' symbolism. The reason is evident. The tomb symbolism cannot fully bring out the meaning of the Eucharist as participation in the eternal sacrifice of Christ that takes place in the heavenly sanctuary. One of the earliest prayers of the preparation rites (attested by several of the tenth-century manuscripts, now placed as the opening prayer of the second part of the Preparation rites) evokes this idea:

Account us worthy, O Lord God, that having our hearts sprinkled and cleansed from all things evil, we may enter into Thy great and exalted Holy of Holies. May we be enabled to stand in purity and holiness before Thy sacred altar, and in true faith offer reasonable and spiritual sacrifices unto Thee, O Father, Son, and Holy Spirit, Amen.[49]

The symbolism of the heavenly altar is further emphasized by the construction of the sanctuary, two or three feet above the *Qestromo*. This arrangement was probably introduced for practical reasons. However, the celebrants' movements between the *Qestromo* and the sanctuary were interpreted as 'ascension' or 'descent'. This has eventually led to allegorical interpretations of certain movements, especially the processions in terms of 'Christ's descent' from and 'ascension' to heaven. Thus Moses Bar Kepha comments on the entrance procession (which disappeared after the thirteenth century):

Concerning the going forth of the mysteries from the altar and their going about the nave and their return to the altar: – That the mysteries go forth from the altar, and go about the nave in seemly order, and return to the altar, makes known that

---

47 Bar Salibi, *Eucharist*, 6:6; p. 31. The altars in Syria were normally rectangular. See Jean Lassus, *Les sanctuaires chrétiens de Syrie*, p. 199. However, there were semi-circular altars (p. 200). On the altars of Syria, ibid., pp. 198–203.

48 Bar Salibi, *Eucharist*, 6:7, p. 31.

49 Athanasius, *Anaphora*, p. 9 As the celebrant enters the sanctuary he recites Ps. 43:4 ('I will go unto the altar of God...') and Ps. 118:27–28. Here the references to the altar seems to have been taken in the sense of 'heavenly altar'.

God the Word came down and was made man, and went about in the world and fulfilled the dispensation for us, and then ascended the cross, and afterwards ascended to His father.[50]

In his commentary on the Myron, Bar Kepha had elaborated the theme:

Why does the Myron leave from the sanctuary and go around the nave and return to the same sanctuary? We say: Because, by this, it indicates God the Word who became incarnate. The sanctuary represents the heaven and the nave the world. In the same way as the Myron leaves the sanctuary and goes around the nave and returns to the sanctuary, God the Word left heaven, came to the world, became incarnate and [became] man, and fulfilled the economy and returned and ascended to heaven to the place from where He descended.[51]

As an articulation of a vision, *ordo* assures the continuity and stability in the life of the Church. It serves as a link with the Church's living past. To a large extent, the *ordo* assures identity among the worshipping communities in space and time. But its essential function is to relate the worshipping community with the People of God in the Old Testament ('all those who have pleased God since Adam'), with the People of God in the New Dispensation, and with the eschatological community ('those who have been inscribed in heaven'). Thus the *ordo* assures the unity of the worshipping communities and makes them the manifestations of the 'One, Holy, Catholic and Apostolic Church'.

In a sense, *ordo* is a 'language', an 'ordered way' of manifesting the mysteries of faith. Thus the *ordo* represents the mind of the Church in relation to Scripture and tradition. In the *ordo*, the Church articulates its vision of God, man and the world. In this task, it makes use of the elements drawn from the society and culture in which it lives, especially language, literary forms, music, art, architecture and symbols. They are integrated into the *ordo*, and are offered to God in Christ for their 'pneumatization'.

---

[50] Bar Kepha, *Eucharist*, p. 34. Pseudo-Dionysius the Areopagite expounds the meaning of the censing of the whole nave by the celebrant in similar terms. *EH* III-iii, 428D–429B.

[51] Commentary on Myron, ch.13 (Syr. text W. Strothmann).

Conclusion

In the East, liturgy is the source and the expression of the entire spiritual experience. In prayers, the Church articulates its vision of God and the destiny of humanity and the entire creation. The liturgy is rooted in the eternal plan of the triune God regarding the destiny of man and the universe. Christianity is founded on the conviction that the world was created and is sustained by the eternal will of the triune God. Incarnation is the integral part of the eternal plan of the Holy Trinity and the mission of the Holy Spirit has confirmed it. The world was created to be a sanctuary, a dwelling place of God. Man was created to dwell in this sanctuary, in the presence of God. His life and destiny (also that of creation) depend on his openness towards God, the source of life. The whole Bible speaks of God's desire that man should live in communion with him, in a relationship of love and adoration. Revelation is God's initiative to restore the relationship often broken by man. In the Old Dispensation, the covenant, Law, *ekklesia*, worship and the temple were part of God's desire to maintain the relationship. The New Dispensation marks a new stage in the divine initiative. The *ekklesia* of the New Testament, the Gospels and the liturgy are also the means of living in a relationship of love and adoration, that is, a life in the presence of God, in communion with him. Faith means a dynamic relationship with the living God. Doctrine is the articulation of the new community's vision of God, and therefore it serves as a basis for the relationship. Doxology is an act that binds many with God and therefore the very condition for their oneness as a community, as the *ekklesia* of God. Therefore *leitourgia* is primarily an act by which humanity is constituted as a community. In Christ we have been constituted as the *ekklesia*, the first fruits of the final recapitulation of the whole of humanity in the Kingdom of God. The liturgical assembly is the manifestation of this final eschatological gathering, called to be present in the world as the community of the eighth day, to witness to the reality, and the ontological significance of the Incarnation, 'until Christ comes'. Liturgical theology is concerned with bringing out the relationship between the liturgy, the Church and eschatology.

There are two ways of approaching liturgical theology. One is to reflect on the Church's act of worship, seeking to draw out the theological meaning of the liturgy as the actualization of the paschal mystery, through the proclamation of the word and the celebration of the rites. The other way is to believe that there is only one mystery, the mystery of the Holy Trinity, of which the mystery of Christ is an integral part, in which the entire mystery of our salvation is rooted. In the first, every particularity of the liturgy is seen in the light of the salvific death of Christ and its consequences, in the context of the communication of the word of God, the implanting of the faith of the Church. In the second, the *leitourgia* is understood within the context of the wider horizon of the *oikonomia* of the triune God, whose mysterious plan leads the world from creation to consummation. In spite of the apparently different emphases, both these ways attempt to explain the meaning of the *leitourgia* in relation to the mystery of Christ. The West Syrians, as the other Eastern Christians, follow the second approach.

One of the main concerns of liturgical theology is the place of worship in the Christian experience. The Christian West takes the Church in its empirical sense. Thus the proclamation of the word, celebration of the cult, hierarchy, teaching function and the mission are some of the priorities. In the West, as I understand it, there is a tendency to list the priorities in the life and mission of the Church. One of the main concerns of the Western liturgists, both Catholic and Protestant, is the place of worship in the 'list of priorities'. Western liturgical theology is to a large extent preoccupied with this problem.

But in the East, the Church is understood in relation to the mystery of Christ, to the economy of salvation from creation to redemption. The Church is the integral part of God's plan for the renewal and redemption of creation. In its mission in the world, the Church manifests itself liturgically and its mission consists of proclaiming the meaning of each and every thing in relation to the Kingdom of God, the restored state, the destiny of the entire creation. The nature and task of the Church, especially the liturgy, is understood in the light of this meta-historical meaning of creation.

Both approaches have their own merits and limitations. The West takes social reality more seriously and the ethical implications of the Christian revelation are duly emphasized. However, the 'exhortative' aspect of the content of the revelation has been given priority at the expense of the doxological dimension of the Christian experience. For the East, divine life has been offered to man to be participated in, to live in union with God, and doxology is the very means to appropriate this free gift offered to man in Christ. The dynamic vision of the Trinitarian relationship, especially the role of the Holy Spirit in the economy of salvation, enables the East to understand redemption as the restoration of communion, that is, to live as one community in Christ. The West has often been tempted to be 'individualistic' in its approach to spiritual reality, and this has found its expression in the medieval mysticism and the modern revival groups. The West seems to be more interested in the place of worship in man's experience of God, whereas in the East, the concern was to understand its place in God's plan for man. In the West, at least for some, redemption is a *fait accompli*. We adhere to it by free response. Sacraments and liturgical rites are channels of grace, a means that helps man to respond to God. This seems to be the result of giving undue emphasis to Christology at the expense of pneumatology. In this theological framework, the Church has a subordinate place, often taken in its empirical reality, as an institution exterior to one's own personal relationship with Christ. In the Eastern understanding, creation looks for liberation and the coming of the Kingdom. The sacraments and the liturgical rites are the means of man's growth from glory to glory. In this process of renewal of creation, man cooperates with God, for he bears the image of God, and has been created as the priest of creation to offer it to God, that is, to bring everything into a doxological union with God. This understanding of the *leitourgia* has far-reaching implications for liturgical theology.

Liturgy is not merely 'prayers' or a set of rituals. It is primarily an act, an assembly, a gathering in Christ, by the Spirit, in which the meaning of Christian 'togetherness' is continually revealed and sealed. The liturgical celebrations constitute the Church.[1] Christ is 'a constituent component of the liturgy'.[2] A liturgical celebration is the icon of the presence of Christ in us, in the world. The Eucharist is primarily the presence of Christ, and consequently that of the triune God, in the world. It is his presence in us that determines Christian life, and all our 'mission' in this world and our salvation. Faith is the awareness of his presence in us and with us. Liturgy is the expression of the Church's faith, its certainty about the presence of Christ in it and with it. The New Testament images of the Church as the Body of Christ and Bride of Christ express the depth of its unique relationship with the triune God. The doctrines are the expressions of its experiences and convictions, which it reiterates in its gatherings as part of its vocation to build up the human community. The meaning of the doctrine of the Trinity – the Fatherhood of God, the sonship and the oneness of humanity in Christ and the indwelling of the Holy Spirit for the renewal of humanity as one community – becomes a concrete reality in the Church's *leitourgia*. The consubstantiality of the three divine hypostases serves as the basis and model for fellowship.

Everything that the Church does – its proclamation of the Word of God, its mission, doctrinal formulations, sacramental celebrations and its *leitourgia* – has been aimed at restoring the communion between Creator and creation. That is why the East always says that the liturgy continuously manifests the unity of the Church, as a community, an *organism* that dwells in Christ, a community that looks beyond history for the meaning of its existence. The unity of the local assembly springs from the Eucharist. A canonical hour is an extension of the Eucharistic gathering, for it is rooted in and it anticipates the assembly on Sunday and prepares for it. It is the members of the Eucharistic assembly that gather together to pray in a canonical hour. The link between the two is implied in the fact that the canonical regulation for the presidency of both is the same. An excommunicated bishop or priest cannot preside over any sacramental celebration, including the daily office.

In a liturgical gathering, each individual transcends his 'religious narcissism' and is organically united with others. Liturgy is 'celebrated' or 'gathered together' in view of communion, which means a life in union with God and with others and with the entire creation. Everything has been created as a potential means of establishing relationships, communion, and the building up of humanity as a community. Liturgy is a relationship, liberation from individualism and egoism and therefore it is a means of salvation. In fact *ekklesia* is primarily a relationship, a communion, a fellowship in Christ (Acts 2:44–45), and is constantly revealed in the Church's *leitourgia*. Therefore, *ekklesia* and *leitourgia* are synonymous.

---

1 Georges Florovsky, 'The Church: her Nature and Task', in *The Universal Church in God's Design* (SCM, London, 1948), p. 47.

2 R. Taft, 'What does Liturgy do? Toward a Soteriology of Liturgical celebration', *Worship* 66 (1992), 199.

Church is a sacramental society. '*Sacramental* means no less than *eschatological*.'[3] In the words of Fr Florovsky, '*eschaton* does not mean primarily *final*, in the temporal series of events; it means rather *ultimate* (decisive); and the ultimate is being realized within the stress of historical happenings and events'.[4] Liturgy is an eschatological act, for the ultimate unity of all in Christ has been manifested in it. Christian eschatology is not future-oriented. It implies that something has been 'restored' in Christ and that it bears the presence of the Spirit. Church and its liturgy are eschatological, because they imply a new relationship in Christ, sealed with the permanent presence of the Spirit. It is the presence of the Spirit – a unique characteristic of the Christian liturgy, according to the New Testament – that makes liturgy an eschatological act. It is an act in Christ, in the Spirit – an act of the new humanity. Liturgical assembly manifests the Church as the community that incorporates the entire creation, the entire culture and brings them back to God. It manifests the ultimate destiny of each and every thing in relation to the Kingdom of God. Material objects, gestures, movements, music, art, architecture, poetry and literature serve as 'symbols' that reveal the Creator and his infinite wisdom.

Liturgy expresses a whole network of relationships. It celebrates the interdependence and interrelatedness of God, man and the world. The task of liturgical theology is precisely to bring out the implications of these relationships in man's search for the meaning of life.

---

[3] Florovsky, 'The Church', p. 54.
[4] Ibid.

Bibliography

1. Manuscripts

Jacob of Edessa: *Commentary on the Eucharist addressed to George, the Stylite of Serugh*, Berlin, Sachau 218, fol. 178–86.

Moses Bar Kepha, *Festal Homilies*, OTS MS 5861, Orthodox Theological Seminary, Kottayam.

Pampakuda Manuscript 13 = *Promiun Sedro (from Qudosh 'Edto to Sunday of the departed)* (= Malayalam tr. Mar Augen, Vol.I).

Pampakuda Manuscript 200 = *Promiun Sedro (from Easter to Pentecost)* (Malayalam tr. Mar Augen, Vol.III).

Anon., *Penkito* (= Festal Breviary), 3 vols; Pampakuda, 1963. [A different version: Mosul, 7 vols; 1886–96] (*see Crown*).

Anon., *Le Génie de la messe syriaque. Patrimoine syriaque. Actes du Colloque II*, Centre d'Etudes et de Recherches Pastorales, Antelias, 1994.

Abhishiktananda, *Prayer*, SPCK, New Delhi, 1993.

Afanassief, Nicholas, *L'Eglise du Saint Esprit*, Paris, 1975.

Aggoula, Basile (tr.), 'Une description de la cathédrale justinienne d'Edesse dans un poème syriaque', in Ayoub Chehwan and Antoine Kassis (eds), *Etudes Bibliques et Proche-Orient ancien. Mélanges offerts au Père Paul Feghali* (Beyrouth and Jounieh, 2001), pp. 309–22.

Allchin, A.M., *The Encounter between Orthodoxy and the West*, London, 1979.

Allmen, Jean Jacques von, *Célébrer le salut. Doctrines et Pratiques du culte chrétien*, Collections Rites et symboles 15, Paris, 1984.

Annapuro (1932) = Ktobo d-tekso d-annapuro (The Book of the Order of the Anaphora), Pampakuda, 1932.

Annapuro (1986) = Ktobo d-tekso d-annapuro, Pampakuda, 1986.

Aphrahat, *Demonstrations* = Valavanolickal, Kuriakose (tr.), *Aphrahat. Demonstrations I*, Changanassery, 1999.

Aron, Robert, 'Réflexions sur la notion de temps dans la liturgie juive', *LMD* 65 (1961), 12–20.

Arranz, M., 'L'économie du salut dans la prière du Post-Sanctus des anaphores de type antiochiens', *LMD* 106 (1971), 46–75.

Arseniev, N., *Mysticism and the Eastern Church*, SVSP, New York, 1979.

Assemani, J.S., *Bibliotheca Orientalis*, 2 vols, Rome, 1719–21.

Atchley, E.G.C.F., *A History of the Use of Incense in Divine Worship*, Alcuin Club Collections XIII, London, 1909.

Athanasius, *Anaphora* = Mar Athanasius Yeshu Samuel (ed.), *Anaphora. The Divine Liturgy of Saint James the First Bishop of Jerusalem*, 1967.

––––––– *Baptism* = idem (ed.), *The Sacrament of Holy Baptism according to the Ancient Rite of the Syrian Orthodox Church of Antioch*, 1974.

––––––– *Letter to Serapion* = *Athanase d'Alexandrie: Lettres à Serapion*, SC 15, Paris, 1947.

Augen I (Mar), Baselius (tr.), *Promiun (and Sedra) for the Festal offices*, 3 vols, Kottayam 1948–51 (2nd edn. 1969–70).

Baggley, John, *Festival Icons for the Christian Year*, London, 2000.

Bar Hebraeus, *Nomocanon* = P. Bedjan (ed.), *Nomocanon. Gregori Barhebraei*, Paris, 1898.

––––––– *Ethicon* = Herman G.B. Teule (tr.), *Gregory Barhebraeus. Ethicon: Memra I*, CSCO 535, Louvain, 1993.

Bar Kepha (Moses), 'Exposition of the feast of Resurrection' (unpublished manuscript), OTS 5861, fol.122–40.

––––––– *Commentary on Baptism* = R.A. Aytoun (tr.), 'The Mysteries of Baptism by Moses Bar Kepha compared with the Odes of Solomon', *The Expositor*, Ser.VIII-ii (1911), 338–58. Reprinted in J. Vellian (ed.), *Studies on Syrian Baptismal Rites*, Syrian Churches' Series VI, (Kottayam, 1973), 1–15.

––––––– *Commentary on Eucharist*, see Connolly and Codrington.

––––––– *Commentary on Myron* = W. Strothmann (ed.), *Moses Bar Kepha, Myron Weihe*, GOFS 7, Wiesbaden, 1973.

Barnabas, Mathews Mar, *A Devotional Study of the Holy Qurbana*, New York, 1999.

Bar Salibi, *Against the Melchites* = A. Mingana (tr.), *A Treatise of Bar Salibi against the Melchites*, Woodbrooke Studies I, Cambridge, 1927.

––––––– *Against the Armenians* = A. Mingana (tr.), *The Work of Dionysius Bar Salibi against the Armenians*, Woodbrooke Studies IV, Cambridge, 1931.

––––––– *Commentary on the Eucharist* = B. Varghese (tr.), *Dionysius Bar Salibi. Commentary on the Eucharist*, Moran 'Etho 10, Kottayam, 1998.

Barsoum, Patriarch Ignatius Aphram I, *The History of Syriac Literature and Sciences*, Pueblo, 2000.

Bauckham, R.J., 'Sabbath and Sunday in the Post-Apostolic Church', in D.A. Carson (ed.), *From Sabbath to Lord's Day. A Biblical, Historical and Theological Investigation* (Michigan, 1982), pp. 251–98.

Baumstark, A., *Festbrevier und Kirchenjahr der syrischen Jabobiten*, Paderborn, 1910.

––––––– *Nichtevangelische syrische Perikopenordnungen des ersten Jahrtausends*, Münster, 1921.

––––––– *Liturgie comparée*, 3e edn (révue par B. Botte), Chevetogne, 1953.

––––––– 'Die armenische Rezension der Jacobusliturgie', OC 7–8 (1918), 1–32.

Beck, E., 'Symbolum-Mysterium bei Aphrahat und Ephraem', OC 42 (1958), 19–40.

Bedjan, P. (ed.), *Homiliae selectae Mar Jacobi Sarugensis*, 5 vols, Paris and Leipzig, 1905–10.

Benoît, A., *Le baptême chrétien au second siècle*, Paris, 1953.

Beuley, Robert, 'La prière continuelle chez les spirituels syro-orientaux', *Notre Vie Liturgique. Etudes Inter-Religieuses* 3 (2000, CERO, Lebanon), 87–111.

Bobrinskoy, Boris, 'Réflexions d'un théologien orthodoxe', *LMD* 121 (1975), 70–75.

——— 'Liturgie et ecclésiologie trinitaire de Saint Basile', in B. Botte et al. (eds), *Eucharistie d'Orient et d'Occident*, Lex Orandi 47 (Paris, 1970), 197–240.

Bolgiani, Franco, 'La théologie de l'Esprit de la fin du 1ᵉʳ siècle après Jésus Christ au Concile de Constantinople (381)', *Les Quatre fleuves* (1979), 33–72.

Bornet, Réné, *Les commentaires byzantines de la divine liturgie du VIIe au X siècle*, Archives de l'Orient chrétien 9, Paris, 1966.

Botte, B., 'Les Dimanches de la dédicace dans les Eglises syriennes', *OS* 2 (1957), 65–70.

Bouyer, Louis, *Eucharist*, Notre Dame and London, 1968.

——— 'L'office divin ferment de la prière personnelle', *LMD* 64 (1960), 135–42.

Bradshaw, Paul F., *Daily Prayer in the Early Church*, Alcuin Club/SPCK, London, 1981.

Breck, John, 'The Two Hands of God. Christ and the Spirit in Orthodox Theology', *SVTQ* 40/4 (1996), 231–46.

Brightman, F.E., *Liturgies Eastern and Western: I Eastern*, Oxford, 1896.

Brock, S., *Holy Spirit in the Syrian Baptismal Tradition*, The Syrian Churches Series 9, Kottayam, 1979.

——— *The Liturgical Portions of the Didascalia*, GLS 29, 1982.

——— *The Luminous Eye. The Spiritual World Vision of Saint Ephrem*, Rome, 1985.

——— A *Brief Outline of Syriac Literature, Moran 'Etho* 9, Kottayam, 1997.

——— *Syriac Studies. A Classified Bibliography (1960–1990)*, Kaslik, 1996.

——— *The Hidden Pearl. The Syrian Orthodox Church and its Ancient Aramaic Heritage*, Vol.I–III, Rome, 2001.

——— 'The Epiklesis in the Antiochene Baptismal ordines', in *Symposium Syriacum, 1972*, OCA 197 (Rome, 1974), 183–215.

——— 'Poet as Theologian', *Sobornost* 7–4 (1977), 243–50.

——— 'Baptismal Themes in the Writings of Jacob of Serugh', *Symposium Syriacum 1976*, OCA 205 (Rome, 1978), 325–47.

——— 'Some Early Syriac Baptismal Commentaries', *OCP* 46 (1980), 20–61.

——— 'An Early Syriac Commentary on the Liturgy', *JTS*, n.s. 37 (1986), 387–403.

——— 'The Thrice-holy Hymn in the Liturgy', *Sobornost/ECQ* (1986), 24–34.

——— 'Two recent editions of Syrian Orthodox Anaphoras', *EL* 102 (1988), 436–45.

——— 'Les poèmes dialogues dans la tradition liturgique syriaque', in *La Génie de la messe syriaque* (1994), pp. 11–24.

——— 'Syriac Studies. A Classified Bibliography', *Pd'O* 23 (1998), 241–350.

——— 'The Background to some terms in the Syriac Eucharistic Epiklesis', *The Harp* XI–XII (1998–99), 1–12.

Brown, Raymond E., *The Semitic Background of the term 'Mystery' in the New Testament*, Facet Book Biblical Studies 2, Philadelphia, 1968.

Burkitt, F.C., 'The Early Syriac Lectionary System', *Proceedings of the British Academy* 10 (1921–23), extract, pp. 9–38.

Cappelle, B., 'L'introduction du symbole à la messe', *Travaux liturgiques* III (1967), 60–63.

Carlton, Clark, *The Faith. Understanding Orthodox Christianity. An Orthodox Catechism*, Salisbury, MA, 1997.

Chidiac, L. and G. Khouri-Sarkis, 'Tableaux des péricopes bibliques dans les Eglises de langue syriaque', *OS* 3 (1958), 359–86.

Clément, Olivier, *Le chant des larmes. Essai sur le Repentir*, Paris, 1982.

–––––– 'The Eucharist in the Thought of Paul Evdokimov', *Eastern Church's Review* (1975), 113–24.

Cody, A., 'L'office divin chez les syriens jacobites. Leur eucharistie épiscopale et leur rite de pénitence', *POC* 19 (1969), 293–319.

–––––– 'The early history of Octoechos in Syria', in N. Garsoian et al., *East of Byzantium, Syria and Armenia in the Formative Period* (Washington, DC, 1982), pp. 89–114.

Congar, Yves M., *Je crois en l'Esprit saint*, 3 vols, Paris, 1979–80.

Connolly, R.H. (tr.), *The Liturgical Homilies of Narsai*, Cambridge, 1909.

–––––– (tr.), 'A Homily of Mar Jacob of Serugh on the Reception of the Holy Mysteries', *Downside Review* 28 (n.s. 8, 1908), 278–87.

–––––– 'The Book of Life', *JTS* 13 (1912), 580–94.

Connolly, R.H. and H.W. Codrington (eds), *Two Commentaries on the Jacobite Liturgy By George Bishop of the Arab Tribes and Moses Bar Kepha: Together with The Syriac Anaphora of St James and a Document entitled 'The Book of Life'*, London, 1913 (= Connolly and Codrington).

Conybeare, F.C. and Oliver Wardrop, 'The Georgian Version of the Liturgy of St James', *ROC* 18 (1913), 396–410.

Coquin, R.G., 'La consécration des églises dans le rite copte; ses relations avec les rites syrien et byzantin', *OS* 9 (1964), 149–87.

Crown I–III = Acharya Francis, *Prayer with the Harp of the Spirit*, Vols II–IV: *Crown of the Year*, Parts I–III, Vagamon, 1982, 1985, 1986. [Adapted translation of Mosul Penkito (1886–96).]

Cullmann, O., *Prayer in the New Testament*, SCM, London, 1995.

Cunningham, Agnes, *Prayer. Personal and Liturgical*. Message of the Fathers of the Church, Vol.16, Washington, 1985.

Dalmais, I.H., *Eastern Liturgies*, New York, 1960.

–––––– 'Une relique de l'antique liturgie de Jérusalem: L'office de l'ensevelissement du Christ', *OS* 6 (1961), 441–54.

–––––– 'L'hymnographie syrienne', *LMD* 92 (1967), 63–72.

–––––– 'La thème de la lumière dans l'office du matin des Eglises syriennes orientales', in *Noël, Epiphanie, retour du Christ*, Lex Orandi 40, (Paris, 1967), 257–76.

–––––– 'Source baptismale et le mystères pascales d'après les homélies de Sévère d'Antioche sur la préparation quadragésimale et l'entrée au baptême'; *Pd'O* 6–7 (1975–76), 349–56.

―――― 'L'Esprit Saint et le mystère de salut dans les épiclèses eucharistiques syriennes ', *EL* 90 (1976), 262–71.

―――― 'Quelques traits caractéristiques des liturgies syriennes', in A.M. Triacca and A. Pistoia (eds), *La Liturgie: son sens, son esprit, sa méthode, Conférences S. Serge, EL* Subsidia 20 (Rome, 1982), 57–70.

―――― 'Time in the Liturgy', ibid., Vol.IV (1986), pp. 1–7.

―――― 'Mémoire et vénération des saints dans les églises de traditions syriennes', in A.M. Triacca and A. Pistoia (eds), *Saints et sainteté dans la liturgie: Conférences S. Serge, EL* Subsidia 40 (Rome, 1987), 79–91.

―――― 'The Eastern Liturgical Families', in A.G. Martimort (ed.), *The Church at Prayer,* Vol.I (new edn, Collegeville, 1987), pp. 27–43.

―――― 'La mystagogie dans les églises d'expression syriaque', in A.M. Triacca and A. Pistoia (eds), *Mystagogie: Pensée liturgique d'aujourd'hui et liturgie ancienne. Conférence S. Serge, EL* Subsidia 70 (Rome, 1993), 3–14.

Daniélou, Jean, *Bible et Liturgie*, Lex Orandi 11, Paris, 1958.

Dewailly, Louis M., 'Le temps et la fin du temps selon Saint Paul', *LMD* 65 (1961), 133–43.

Dix, Gregory, *The Shape of the Liturgy*, London, 1982.

Doresse, J. and E. Lanne, *Un témoin archaique de la liturgie copte de Saint Basile*, Bibliothèque du Muséon 47, Louvain, 1960.

Emperor, James, *Models of Liturgical Theology*, GLS 52.

Ephrem (Saint), *An Exposition of the Gospel* (tr. George A. Egan), *CSCO* 292, Scriptores Armeniaci 6, Louvain, 1968.

Euringer, S., 'Die Anaphora des hl. Jacobus des Bruders des Herrn', *OC* 4 (1915), 1–23.

Evdokimov, Paul, *La nouveauté de l'Esprit. Etude de spiritualité*, Spiritualité orientale 20, Abbayé de Bellefontaine, 1975.

―――― *Présence de l'Esprit Saint dans la tradition orthodoxe*, Paris, 1977.

Fagerberg, David W., *What is Liturgical Theology? A Study in Methodology*, The Liturgical Press, Collegeville, 1992.

Feuillet, André, 'Le temps de l'Eglise d'après le quatrième évangile et l'Apocalypse', *LMD* 65 (1961), 60–79.

Feulner, H.J., E. Velskova and R.F. Taft (eds), *Crossroad of Cultures: Studies in Liturgy and Patristics in Honour of Gabriele Winkler*, OCA 260, Rome, 2000.

Fisch, Thomas (ed.), *Liturgy and Tradition. Theological Reflections of Alexander Schmemann*, SVSP, New York, 1990.

Florovsky, G., *Bible, Church, Tradition. An Eastern Orthodox View*, Vol.I, Massachusetts, 1972.

―――― '(The elements of Liturgy): Orthodox', in Pehr Edwall et al. (eds), *Ways of Worship: Report of a Theological Commission of Faith and Order* (SCM, London, 1951), 53–65.

―――― 'Worship and Everyday Life: An Eastern Orthodox View', *SL* 2 (1963), 266–72.

Florovsky, G., ' The worshipping Church', in Mother Mary and Archmandrite Kallistos Ware (tr.), *The Festal Menaion* (London, 1969), pp. 21–37.

Fuchs, H. (ed.), *Die Anaphora des monophysitischen Patriarchen Johanan I*, Münster and Westfalen, 1926.

Galeriu, Constantin, 'The Structure of Sacrifice', *SVTQ* 30 (1986), 43–66.

Gamayel, P.E., *Avant-Messe Maronite*, *OCA* 174, Rome, 1965.

Gauthier, L., 'Le présence du Père et du Fils par l'Esprit', *Verbum Caro* 79 (1966), 41–50.

George, Bishop of the Arabs, *Homily on Myron* = V. Ryssel (ed.), *Poemi Syriaci di Giorgio vescovo degli Arabi*, in Atti della Reale Accademia dei Lincei, IV-9 (Rome, 1892), 46–80.

——— *Commentary on Eucharist* = 'An Exposition of the Mysteries of the Church made by a certain bishop named George', in R.H. Connolly and H.W. Codrington (eds), *Two Commentaries on Jacobite Liturgy*, pp. 11–23.

——— *On Mar Severus* = K.E. Mcvey (ed.), *George Bishop of the Arabs. A Homily on Blessed Mar Severus, Patriarch of Antioch*, *CSCO* 531, Louvain, 1993.

George, K.M., 'Why turn to East for Prayer?', *Sahayatra* (Nagpore, June 2002), 26–28.

Gerhards, A., *Die Gregor von Nazianz (329/30–c.390) zugeschriebene Anaphora und ihre Stellung inder Geschichte des Eucharistiegebets*, *LQF*, Münster and Westfalen, 1982.

——— 'Prière adressée à Dieu ou au Christ? Relecture d'une thèse importante de J.A. Jungmann a la lumière de recherche actuelle ', in A.M. Triacca and A.Pistoia (eds), *Liturgie, Spiritualité, Cultures. Conférences Saint Serge* (Rome, 1983), pp. 101–14.

Graffin, F., 'Les catéchèses de Sévère d'Antioche', *OS* 5 (1960), 47–54.

Gregorios, Paulose (= Paul Verghese), *The Joy of Freedom. Eastern Worship and Modern Man*, London, 1967 (reprint, *CLS*, Madras, 1986).

Grelot, Pierre, 'Liturgie et vie spirituelle', *Dictionnaire de Spiritualité* 9 (1975), 873–84.

Gribomont, J., 'Les catéchèses de Sévère d'Antioche et le Credo', *Pd'O* 6–7 (1975–76), 125–58.

Groom, Nagel, *Frankincense and Myrrh. A Study of the Arabian Incense Trade*, London and New York, 1981.

Grumel, V., 'L'auteur et la date de composition du Tropaire Ho Monogenis', *EO* 22 (1923), 398–418.

Hollerweger, Hans, *Living Cultural Heritage: Tur Abdin*, Linz, 2000.

De Halleux, A., 'Hellénisme et Syrianité de Romanos le Mélode', *Revue d'Histoire Ecclésiastique* 73 (1978), 632–41.

Heiming, O. (ed.), *Anaphora Syriaca sancti Jacobi fratis Domini*, *AS* II-2 (Rome, 1953), 109–79.

Herbert, A.H., *Worship in Ancient Israel*, Ecumenical Studies in Worship 5, London, 3rd edn, 1963.

Imbs, Paul, 'Du langage humain à la parole de Dieu', *LMD* 53 (1958), 9–22.

Incense and Perfumes, Encyclopaedia Judaica 8 (Jerusalem, 1971), pp. 1310–16.

Irwin, Kewin W., *Liturgical Theology. A Primer*, American Essays in Liturgy, The Liturgical Press, Collegeville, 1990.

—— 'Liturgical Theology', in Peter E. Fink (ed.), *The New Dictionary of Sacramental Worship* (The Liturgical Press, Collegeville, 1990), pp. 721–32.

Jacob of Edessa, *On Myron* = S. Brock (ed.), 'Jacob of Edessa's discourse on the Myron', *OC* 63 (1979), 20–36.

—— 'Epistles to the Presbyter Thomas', in Bar Salibi, *Commentary on the Eucharist* (tr. B. Varghese), 3:4, pp. 9–10 (also in Brightman, *LEW*, pp. 490–94).

Janeras, V.S., 'Les byzantins et le Trisagion christologique', in *Miscellanea Liturgica in onore de Cardinale Giacomo Lercaro*, t.II (Rome, 1967), pp. 469–99.

Jedlicka, J., 'Das Präger Fragment der altgeorgischen Jacobusliturgue', *Archiv Orientalini* 29 (1961), 183–96.

John of Dara, *Commentary on the Eucharist* = B. Varghese (tr.), *John of Dara. Commentary on the Eucharist*, Moran 'Etho 12, Kottayam, 1999.

Jungmann, J., *The Place of Christ in Liturgical Prayer*, London, 1989.

Kakanatt, A., *Christological Catechesis of the Liturgy. A Study of the Great Feasts of Our Lord in the Malankara Church*, Mar Thoma Yogam, Rome, 1996.

Kesich, Vaselin, *The First Day of the New Creation. The Resurrection and the Christian Faith*, SVSP, New York, 1982.

Konat, Abraham (ed.), *Ktobo d-sluto d-saumo*, 5th edn, 1967.

—— *Ktobo d-ma'de'dono d-hudro sha(n)tonoyo*, Pampakuda, 1984 (Syriac and Malayalam) (first edn, 1920: Syriac text only).

Krivocheine, Archbishop Basil, *In the Light of Christ. St Simeon the New Theologian Life, Spirituality, Doctrine*, SVSP, New York, 1986.

Lanchon, R., 'Le temps pascale dans la liturgie syrienne', *OS* 7 (1962), 332–56.

Lassus, Jean, *Sanctuaires chrétiens de Syrie: Essai sur la genèse, la forme et l'usage liturgique des édifices du culte chrétien en Syrie du IVe siècle à la conquête musulmane*, Paris, 1944.

Leaney, R., 'The Lucan Text of the Lord's Prayer (in Gregory of Nyssa)', *Novum Testamentum* 1 (1956), 103–11.

Lecuyer, J., 'Théologie de l'anaphore chez les Pères de l'Eglise d'Antioche', *OS* 6 (1961), 385–412.

Lincoln, A.T., 'Sabbath Rest and Eschatology in the New Testament', in D.A. Carson (ed.), *From Sabbath to Lord's Day. A Biblical, Historical and Theological Investigation* (Michigan, 1982), pp. 197–220.

Lossky, Nicholas, 'Liturgy and liturgical art from an Ecumenical Perspective', *Sourozh* 36 (May 1989), 36–41.

Lossky, Vladimir, *The Mystical Theology of the Eastern Church*, London, 1957.

Louth, Andrew, *Denys the Areopagite*, London, 1989.

Lubac, Henri de, *Histoire et esprit. L'intelligence de l'Ecriture d'après Origène*, Théologie 16, Paris, 1950.

——— *Exégèse médiévale. Les quatre sens de l'Ecriture*. Pt. I; Vol.1–2; Pt. II, Vol.1–2, Théologie 41, 42, 59, Paris, 1959–64.

Macomber, W., 'A History of the Chaldean Mass', *Worship* 51 (1977), 107–20.

Ma'de'dono = Mar Athanasius Yeshu Samuel (ed.), *Ma'de'dono. The Book of the Church Festivals according to the Ancient rite of the Syrian Orthodox Church of Antioch*, 1984 (Syriac and English).

Ma'de'dono (Pampakuda) = *see* Konat.

Madey, J. (ed.), *The Eucharistic Liturgy in The Christian East*, Paderborn, 1984.

Mary (Mother) and Kallistos Timothy Ware (tr.), *The Lenten Triodion*, London, 1978.

Mateos, J., 'Les matins chaldéenes, maronites et syriennes', *OCP* 26 (1960), 51–73.

——— 'Sedre et prières connexes dans quelques anciennes collections', *OCP* 28 (1962), 239–87.

——— 'Une collections syrienne de "prières entre les marmyata"', *OCP* 31 (1965), 53–75; 305–35.

——— 'L'invitatoire du nocturne chez les Syriens et chez les Maronites', *OS* 11 (1966), 353–56.

——— 'Prières initiales fixes des offices syrien, maronite et byzantin', *OS* 11 (1966), 489–98.

——— 'Trois recueils anciens de Prooemia syriens', *OCP* 33 (1967), 457–82.

——— 'Prières syriennes d'absolution du VIIe–IXe siècle', *OCP* 34 (1968), 252–80.

——— 'Les strophes de la nuit dans l'invitatoire du nocturne syrien', in F. Graffin (ed.), *Mémorial Mgr. Gabriel Khouri-Sarkis* (Louvain, 1969), pp. 71–81.

Matons, Grosdidier de, *Romanos le Mélode et les origines de la poésie religieuse à Byzance*, Paris, 1977.

Mazza, Enrico, *Mystagogy. A Theology of Liturgy in the Patristic Age*, New York, 1989.

Mckenna, John H., *Eucharist and the Holy Spirit. The Eucharistic Epiklesis in 20th Century Theology*, Alcuin Club Collections 57, London, 1957.

McPartlan, Paul, *The Eucharist makes the Church*, Edinburgh, 1993.

Mercer, S.A.B., 'The Epiklesis in the Ethiopic Liturgy', in *Oriental Studies to Paul Haupt* (Baltimore and Leipzig, 1926), pp. 446–53.

Mercier, B.C. (ed.), *La liturgie de S. Jacques*, *PO* 26/2 (Paris, 1946), 121–249.

Meyendorff, J., *Byzantine Theology*, New York, 1974.

Meyendorff, P., *St Germanus of Constantinople on the Divine Liturgy*, SVSP, New York, 1984.

(A Monk of the Eastern Church), *The Year of the Grace of the Lord. By a Monk of the Eastern Church*, SVSP, New York, 1980.

Narsai, *Homilies* (Mingana) = A. Mingana (ed.), *Narsai Doctoris Syri, Homiliae et Carmina*, Mosul, 1905.

——— *Homilies* (Connolly) = R.H. Connolly (tr.), *The Liturgical Homilies of Narsai*, Cambridge, 1909.

Nissiotis, Nikos A., 'The Importance of the Doctrine of the Trinity for Church Life and Theology', in A.J. Philippou (ed.), *The Orthodox Ethos. Studies in Orthodoxy*, Vol.I (Oxford, 1964), pp. 32–69.

Palmer, A.N., 'The inauguration anthem of Hagia Sophia in Edessa', *Byzantine and Modern Greek Studies* 12 (1988), 117–67.

Paulin, A., *Saint Cyrille de Jérusalem. Catéchète*, Lex Orandi 29, Paris, 1954.

Van der Ploeg, J., 'Une homélie de Jacques de Saroug sur la réception de la sainte communion', in *Mélanges Eugène Tisserant, Vol.III, Orient Chrétien, IIe partie*, Studi e Testi 233 (Vatican, 1964), pp. 395–418.

Pseudo-Dionysius (the Areopagite), *The Ecclesiastical Hierarchy (= EH)*, in Colm Luibheid (tr.), *Pseudo-Dionysius. The Complete Works*, New York, 1987.

Puyade, Julien D., 'Le tropaire *ho Monogenis*', *ROC* 2nd s. VII (= XVII, 1912), 253–58.

Rahmani, I.E., *I Fasti della Chiesa Patriarcale Antiochena*, Rome, 1920.

—— *Les liturgies orientales et occidentales*, Beyrouth, 1929.

Renhart, E., *Das syrische Bema. Liturgisch–archäologische Untersuchungen*, Grazer Theologische Studien 20, 1995.

Riley, H.M., *The Christian Initiation. A Comparative Study of the Interpretation of the Baptismal Liturgy in the Mystagogical Writings of Cyril of Jerusalem, Theodore of Mopsuestia and Ambrose of Milan*, Studies in Christian Antiquity 17, Washington, 1974.

Roques, R., *L'univers dionysien*, Théologie 29, Paris, 1954.

Rordorff, W., *Sunday*, London, 1968.

—— 'Sunday. The Fullness of Christian Liturgical Time', *SL* 14 (1982), 90–96.

Rorem, Paul, *Pseudo-Dionysius*, Oxford, 1993.

Rowley, H.H., *Worship in Ancient Israel*, London, 1967.

Rücker, A. (ed.), *Die syrische Jakobusanaphoa nach der Rezension des Jaquob(h) von Edessa*, LF 4, Münster and Westfalen, 1913.

—— *Anaphora syriaca Timothei Alexandrini*, AS I-1, (Rome, 1939), 3–47.

Sader, Jean, *Le lieu de culte et la messe syro-occidentale selon le 'De Oblatione' de Jean de Dara. Etude d'archéologie et de liturgie*, OCA 223, Rome, 1983.

Sahdona, *Perfection* = A. de Halleux (ed.), *Martyrius (Sahdona). Œuvres spirituelles I, Livre de la Perfection*, 1ʳᵉ Partie, *CSCO* 200, Louvain, 1960.

Salavile, S., 'Epiclèse eucharistique', *DTC* 5, 194–300.

Sauget, J.M., *Bibliographe des liturgies orientales* (1900–1960), Rome, 1962.

Schmemann, Alexander, *Introduction to Liturgical Theology*, New York, 1975 (2nd edn).

—— *The Eucharist, Sacrament of the Kingdom*, SVSP, New York, 1988.

—— 'Debate on the Liturgy: Liturgical Theology, Theology of Liturgy and Liturgical Reforms', *SVTQ* 13/4 (1969), 217–21.

—— 'Liturgical Theology: remarks on Method', in Thomas Fisch (ed.), *Liturgy and Tradition* (New York, 1990), pp. 137–43.

—— 'Liturgy and Eschatology', ibid., pp. 89–99.

Scouteris, Constantine, ' Doxology, the language of Orthodoxy', *The Greek Orthodox Theological Review* 38 (1993), 153–62.

Severus of Antioch, *Select Letters* = E.W. Brooks (ed.), *The Sixth Book of the Select Letters of Severus*, 2 vols, London and Oxford, 1904.

────── *Hymns* = idem, *Hymns of Severus of Antioch*, *PO* 6-1, 1910.

────── *Homilies* = M. Brière and F. Graffin (eds), *Les Homélies Cathédrales de Sévère d'Antioche*, Hom. 1–17, *PO* 38, pp. 1–100; Hom. 32–39, *PO* 36, pp. 391–533.

Shehimo = Bede Griffiths (tr.), *The Book of Common Prayer of the Syrian Church*, Vagamon, n.d. (translation of *Ktobo d-sluto shehimto*, 3rd edn, Pampakuda, 1968, 5th edn, 1988. Different pagination from 4th edn, 1977).

Sherwood, P. (ed.), 'Mimro de Serge Reshayna sur la vie spirituelle', *OS* 5 (1960), 433–57; *OS* 6 (1961), 91–115, 121–56.

Siman, E.P., *L'Expérience de l'Esprit par l'Eglise d'après la tradition syrienne d'Antioche*, Théologie Historique 15, Paris, 1971.

────── 'La dimension pneumatique de l'Eucharistie d'après la tradition syrienne d'Antioche', in *L'Expérience de l'Esprit: Mélanges Schilleebeeckx, Le Point théologique* 18 (1976), pp. 97–114.

Soloviev, Vladimir, *God, Man and the Church*, Greenwood, 1974.

Sony, B., 'La méthode exégétique de Jacques de Saroug', *Pd'O* 9 (1979), 67–103.

Sperry-White, Grant (ed.), *The Testamentum Domini*, *GLS* 66, Nottingham, 1991.

Spinks, Brian D., *The Sanctus in the Eucharistic Prayer*, Cambridge, 2002.

────── 'The Consecratory Epiklesis of the Anaphora of Saint James', *SL* 11 (1976), 19–38.

────── 'The Original form of the Anaphora of the Apostles: A Suggestion in the light of Maronite Sharar', *EL* 91 (1977), 146–61.

Staniloe, D., *Theology and the Church*, SVSP, New York, 1980.

St James, Greek: *see* B.C. Mercier.

St James, Syriac: *see* O. Heiming.

Styliniapoulos, Theodore, *The Good News of Christ*, Holy Cross Press, Brookline, MA, 1991.

Taft, Robert, *The Great Entrance*, OCA 200 (Rome, 1978, 2nd edn).

────── 'Some notions on the Bema in the East and West Syrian Tradition', *OCP* 34 (1968), 326–59.

────── 'The Liturgy of the Great Church: An Initial Synthesis of Structure and Interpretation on the Eve of Iconoclasm', *Dumbarton Oak Papers* 34–35 (1980–81), 45–75.

────── *The Diptychs*, OCA 238, Rome, 1991.

Tarby, A., *La prière eucharistique de l'Eglise de Jérusalem*, Théologie Historique 17, Paris, 1972.

Thekkeparampil, Jacob, 'Weihrauchsymbolik in den syrischen Gebeten des Mittelalters und bei Pseudo-Dionysius', in Margot Schmidt (ed.), *Typus, Symbol, Allegorie bei den östlichen Vätern und ihren Parralen im Mittelalter*, Eichastädter Beiträge IV (Regensburg, 1982), pp. 131–45.

Theodore, *Homily on the Eucharist* = A. Mingana (tr.), *Commentary of Theodore of Mopsuestia on the Lord's Prayer and the Eucharist*, Woodbrooke Studies VI, Cambridge, 1933.

Tomajean, Jean, 'Les Dimanches du carême dans le rite syro-antiochien', *OS* 7 (1962), 357–64.

―――― 'La semaine liturgique dans le rite syrien', *Melto* 2 (1966), 95–114.

Urumpackal, Alex Paul, *The Juridical Status of the Catholicos of Malabar*, Rome, 1977.

Valuparampil, K., 'An Investigation into the theology of the "Resurrection Service" in The Syro-Malankara Church', *Christian Orient* 6 (1985), 137–41; 175–80.

Varghese, Baby, *Les onctions baptismales dans la tradition syrienne*, *CSCO* 512, Subsidia 82, Louvain, 1989.

―――― *The Syriac Version of the Liturgy of St James. A Brief History for Students*, *GLS* 49, Cambridge, 2001.

―――― 'West Syrian Anaphora as an Expression of the Trinitarian Doctrine', *The Harp* 4 (1991), 215–23.

―――― 'Canonical Fasts in the West Syrian Tradition', *The Harp* 7 (1994), 89–108.

―――― 'East Syrian Liturgy as an Expression of Christology', in Alfred Stirnemann and Gerhard Wilflinger (eds), *Syriac Dialogue. Second Non-Official Consultation within the Syriac Tradition* (Vienna, 1996), pp. 153–61.

―――― 'Holy Week Celebrations in the West Syrian Church', in A.G. Kollamparampil (ed.), *Hebdomadae Sanctae Celebratio* (Rome, 1997), pp. 165–86.

―――― 'Early History of the Preparation Rites in the Syrian Tradition', *Symposium Syriacum VII*, *OCA* 256 (Rome, 1998), 127–38.

―――― 'Some Common Elements in the East and the West Syrian Liturgies', *The Harp* 13 (2000), 65–76.

―――― 'Some aspects of West Syrian Liturgical Theology', *SL* 31 (2001), 171–78.

Vavanikunnel, G., *Theodore of Mopsuestia, Narsai, Gabriel Qatraya Bar Lipah: Homilies and Interpretation of the Holy Qurbana*, Changanachery, 1977.

Verghese, Paul, 'Relation between Baptism, Confirmation and the Eucharist in the Syrian Orthodox Tradition', *SL* 4 (1965), 81-93. (*See also* Gregorios, Paulose).

Vermeulen, P., 'Tableau des péricopes bibliques dans les Eglises de langues syriaque', *OS* 12 (1967), 211–40, 371–88, 525–48.

Vööbus, A. (ed.), *The Synodicon in the West Syrian Tradition*, Vol.I & II, *CSCO* 368–69, Louvain, 1975–76.

―――― *The Lectionary System of the Monastery of Azizael in Tur Abdin, Mesopotamia*, *CSCO* 466, Louvain, 1985.

Voste, J.M. (tr.), *Pontificale iuxta ritum Ecclesiae Syrorum Occidentalium id est Antiochiae, Pars.I, continens consecrationem Myri et Ecclesiae*, Versio Latina, S. Congregazione Pro Ecclesia Orientali, Vatican, 1941.

Wagner, G., *Der Ursprung der Chrysostomosliturgie*, LQF 59, Münster, 1973.

Ware, Kallistos (Timothy), *The Orthodox Church*, Penguin Books, 1975.

―――― 'One Body in Christ: Death and the Communion of Saints', *Sobornost* 3-2 (1981).

Ware, Kallistos (Timothy), *The Orthodox Way*, rev. edn, New York, 1995.

Whitaker, E.C., *Documents of the Baptismal Liturgy*, London, 1977.

Winkler, Gabriele, 'Nochmals zu den Anfängen der Epiklese und des Sanctus im Eucharistischen Hochgebet', *Theologische Quaretlschrift* 174 (1994), 214–31.

Witvliet, J.D., 'The Anaphora of Saint James', in P.F. Bradshaw (ed.), *Essays on Early Eastern Eucharistic Prayers* (Collegeville, 1997), pp. 153–72.

Wright, William, *The Apocryphal Acts of the Apostles*, Vol.I (Syriac); II (Tr.), London, 1871 (reprint: Amsterdam, 1968).

Wybrew, Hugh, *The Orthodox Liturgy*, SVSP, New York, 1990.

Yarnold, E.J., *The Awe-Inspiring Rites of Initiation: Baptismal Homilies of the Fourth Century*, Slogh, 1971.

Yousif, P., *L'Eucharistie chez Saint Ephrem de Nisibise*, OCA 224, Rome, 1984.

—— *A Classified Bibliography on the East Syrian Liturgy*, Rome, 1990.

Zankov, Stefan, *The Eastern Orthodox Church*, London, 1929.

Zernov, Nicholas, *The Church of the Eastern Christians*, London, 1947.

—— 'The Worship of the Orthodox Church and its message', in A.J. Philippou (ed.), *The Orthodox Ethos. Studies in Orthodoxy*, Vol.I (Oxford, 1964), pp. 115–21.

Zizioulas, John D. (of Pergamon), *Being as Communion*, SVSP, New York, 1985.

—— *L'Eucharistie, l'évêque et l'église durant les trios premiers siècles*, Paris, 1994.

—— 'The Eucharist and the Kingdom of God', *Sourozh* 58 (Nov. 1994), 1–12, 59 (Feb. 1995), 22–38, 60 (May, 1995), 32–46.

—— 'Symbolism and Realism in Orthodox Worship', *Sourozh* 79 (2000), 3–17.

Glossary

Annapuro	The Eucharistic prayer or canon
Bema	Raised platform in the middle of the nave
Bo'uto	Supplication; a hymn sung at the end of an office
Enyono	Antiphon; anthem
Eqbo	A variable termination or a prayer
Etro	Prayer of incense
Hutomo	Concluding prayer
Lilyo	Night prayer
Madbeho	Altar; sanctuary
Ma'de'dono	Book of the special services of the festivals
Madrosho	A doctrinal hymn; ode or hymn
Memro	Metrical homily; a hymn (plural: *memre*)
Penkitho	Festal Breviary
Petgomo	Verse from the Psalms sung before a *qolo*
Presto	Eucharistic bread
Promiun	From *Prooimion* (Gk): an introduction to a prayer called *Sedro*
Qaumo	Nocturn; one of the four stations of *Lilyo*
Qolo	A hymn
Qudosh 'Edto	Consecration of the Church: first Sunday of the Liturgical Year

Quqliun	A cycle of hymns beginning with verses from the Psalms
Qurbono	Oblation; offering; the Eucharistic liturgy: the consecrated bread
Qurobo	The anaphora; oblation
Rozo	Mystery; sacrament; symbol; Eucharist
Ramsho	Vespers
Sapro	Morning prayer
Sedro	A long prayer in the form of expositions or meditations preceded by *Promiun* (plural: *Sedre* plural)
Shehimo	Breviary for the weekly cycle
Sluto	A prayer
Sugito	A song; canticle
Sutoro	Compline
Tablito	A wooden tablet on which paten and chalice are placed on the altar
Teshmeshto	Service; part of an office

Indices

Old Testament

New Testament

Patristic Authors

Index of Anaphorae

Quotations from West Syrian Anaphorae

Index of Modern Authors

Index of Syriac Words

barek 46
'bd 85
bdukat itaw 166
bema 12, 164, 165
besmo 158
bukro 123

dehlo/dehalto 46

enyono 128
eqbo 97
'eqoro 158
ethkashap 43
etro 157, 158

gmiruth gmirutho 44

had bshabo 123
hawi 85
hudosh 'edto 136
hutomo 52, 161

Ihidoyo 5, 69

kad magen 83, 84
knushyo 44, 92

madbeho 25, 164–5
madrosho 6
memro/memre 6, 10, 20, 22, 32
mkahnin 39
mkaprono 32

oto/otwoto 33, 41

paino 25
penkito 7
petgomo 8
pirmo (*hasiyono*) 158
pristo 70

promiun 69
pulhono 46

qareb 44
qaumo 96, 133
qestromo 165, 167
qolo 8
qudosh 'edto 93, 136
quqliun 96
qurobo 14, 25, 26, 44–5, 53, 90
qurbono 44–5, 92
qymto 123, 135

rahef 83, 84
ramrem 46
raz 35
riho basimo 158
rozo 14, 16, 33, 35–42

sedro/sedre 10, 16–17, 33, 58, 60, 69
sged 46
shabah 46
shamesh 43
shawtoputo 44
shro 83, 84
slo/sali 45
sluto 45
sugito 6

tablito 25, 31
taudito 45
teshmeshto 14, 42–4, 137
tho 81
thronos 164
tupso 33, 39
turgome 33
tuyobo 52

yabeb 46

General Index